THE NEW UNHAPPY LORDS

THE NEW UNHAPPY LORDS

AN EXPOSURE OF POWER POLITICS

by

A. K. CHESTERTON

The A.K. Chesterton Trust

2013

© **The A.K. Chesterton Trust**, BM Candour, London, WC1N 3XX, UK.

Website: www.candour.org.uk

ISBN: 978-0-9575403-2-3 (Paperback)

Cover Design: E.G. Molesworth

First published, July 1965

First paper-back Edition, August 1965

Second Edition, April 1967

Third Edition (Revised & Enlarged) August 1969

Fourth Revised Edition, October 1972

Fourth Revised Edition, Second Printing, September 1975

Fifth Edition, August 2013

This book is dedicated to my colleagues and to the true patriots of every land.

A.K.C.

They have given us into the hand of new unhappy lords,

Lords without anger and honour, who dare not carry their swords.

They fight by shuffling papers; they have bright dead alien eyes;

They look at our labour and laughter as a tired man looks at flies.

And the load of their loveless pity is worse than the ancient wrongs,

Their doors are shut in the evening; and they know no songs.

G. K. CHESTERTON,

"The Secret People".

A.K. Chesterton

CONTENTS

FOREWORD TO THE FIRST EDITION, 1965

ALTHOUGH this book is written from a British point of view, my hope is that it will prove useful to the patriots of other lands, not least those of the United States and South Africa. In recent years several excellent American books, devoted to an exposure of traitors on that side of the Atlantic, and of their powerful protectors, have been published, and if their authors care to study the facts here made available, and the deductions drawn from them, they may conclude, as I have done, that the conspiracy in their midst, so far from having a purely American significance, is global and aims at securing as far as possible control over the whole world. They will certainly perceive that the techniques employed to bring about the subjugation of mankind are very much the same as, and sometimes identical with, the techniques used for the furtherance of traitorous policies in the United States.

As a conspiracy by its very nature is secret, it is not often possible to bring against it a direct case, as distinct from a case based on circumstantial evidence. When a conspiracy has been active for many years, however, there are bound to be occasions when it reveals its existence, and these self-exposures have to be used as pointers to its overall plan. What provides the main proof is that, the policy objective having become known, there has been continuity of the policy pursued to achieve it in one country after another, with no turning aside during the course of several decades. Whether or not one takes a deterministic view of human life, multitudinous events have the appearance of being accidental. Even so, where policies all over the world are shaped to the attainment of one end, the explanation that they can be traced to a large number of accidents or coincidences places a greater strain on credulity than does the belief that they have been deliberately contrived, especially when the mass of circumstantial evidence is examined. Any belief that the present drive for political monopoly derives from a universal fear of further wars can scarcely survive the evidence produced in this book of the actual use for which the various internationalist agencies have been employed. The fear undoubtedly exists, but my thesis is intended to make clear beyond doubt that it has been and is being shamelessly exploited for the setting up of a world tyranny.

It is exasperating to the author, and so it may be to the reader, that the makers of the conspiracy have to be given some general name, such as the Money Power, or the Power Elite, or the manipulators of international policy. As they do not name themselves, and as they work sometimes in one combination, sometimes in another, and as — like the rest of humanity — they are often rent by internal dissension and by rival bids for power, I do not know of any way of avoiding this difficulty. One can but vary the message contained in Holy Writ and say : "By their policy objectives shall ye know them". Several of the agents and agencies are not thus hidden, and these I have duly named.

Readers accustomed to take happenings in the world at their face value may find it hard, if not impossible, to accept this conspiratorial interpretation of contemporary history, which at first sight may appear to them far-fetched.

Yet many minds, working upon widely differing data, have reached the same broad conclusions, and I can but request patience from readers new to the theme — and a fair hearing. They are asked to study such facts as have been ascertained, and to judge whether, on a weighing of probabilities, the deductions based upon the facts are logical and make good sense.

The strength and the weakness of this book is that it is not annotated. Its weakness is that the author, having checked his facts to the best of his ability, does not cite his authorities, partly because some of the information has come to him under confidential cover from highly placed persons in different parts of the world who would face ruin if their identity were divulged, and partly because, the facts having been checked as far as that was possible, the sources have not been filed and listed. Its strength, on the other hand, is that the reader is presented with a continuous narrative which enables him to follow the workings of the conspiracy without having his attention distracted by the abundance of foot-notes which otherwise would have been necessary.

A bibliography is given, not because the works cited have necessarily provided the author with his authorities — few indeed have done so — and not because the author necessarily endorses their contents, but to show that his view of the forces operating in the modern world is far from being held in isolation.

This foreword ends with the reiterated plea for a fair and patient hearing, especially from those readers who may find some of their popular heroes treated with less respect than is habitually accorded to them. In the search for underlying truths it nearly always happens that inflated reputations are among the first casualties.

A.K.C.

FOREWORD TO THE FIFTH EDITION, 2013

If you mention the word *conspiracy* to those who would see themselves as 'political scientists', you will elicit a Pavlovian response. You will, at best, be treated with benign condescension or, at worst cynical disregard. You will not have to wait for long before the word *paranoia* emerges.

It is for this reason, if for no other, that AK was ill-advised to use it so frequently and to use it in the singular. His book is informative and well worth reading and it would be better if prospective readers were not put off from the outset.

However, in Chapter XXV, he used the word in the plural and wrote of: "a continuing policy enforced by a series of conspiracies that may often differ about methods but which direct their thoughts and actions to the attainment of the same broad objective". Furthermore, he acknowledged in Chapter XXVI the role played by the impersonal forces fuelled by *laissez-faire* economics that facilitated the formation of international trusts, combines and cartels – what we would call multinational and global companies. Indeed modern students of 'business' are told to think of legislative sovereignty and indeed the existence of nation states as impediments to the efficiency of global business.

The question is the extent to which we are seeing overlapping conspiracies and the extent to which we are simply seeing overlapping consensuses. Of one thing we can be certain: many apparently distinct ideological doctrines are driving quite consciously towards the process of political and economic globalisation and have woven into their ideologies, an identical strand of globalism.

Even those who do not share all or many of his conclusions must explain to themselves the existence of organisations that include financiers, global business personnel and mainstream politicians who meet in the utmost secrecy with elaborate – dare I say paranoid – security.

Chapter XXIII details the membership, secrecy and enormous influence of the Council on Foreign Relations in the United States and The Royal Institute of International Affairs (Chatham House) in the United Kingdom – organisations AK called 'the conspiratorial bureaucracy'. Chapter XXIV covers what he called Prince Bernhard's secret society – the shadowy Bilderberg Group.

AK did not deny that well-meaning people, innocent of power addiction were to be found among the membership of both the Council and the Royal Institute. Curiously, I do not recall his saying the same of the Bilderberg Group. Perhaps that was an oversight or perhaps it was not.

The remarkably frank book by Dr. Carroll Quigley, *Tragedy and Hope*, claimed noble motives for the globalist project of which he was a key player. We must not assume that conspirators are all self-conscious villains. Whilst some undoubtedly are, others are, in my view at least, misguided idealists

Organisations that discuss political matters in secrecy because they know that the general public would disapprove of their conclusions can hardly be offended if they are described as conspiratorial. When those bodies comprise the most senior politicians in the world, the most powerful international financiers and representatives of global business, they cannot be written off as insignificant eccentrics. When their ideology of Globalism is embraced by virtually all governments in the developed world, they cannot be said to lack influence.

Even those of us who are sceptical of much theorising about conspiracies must take account of extremely incongruous facts that AK brought to our attention.

These would include: the role of Kuhn, Loeb and Co in the financing of the Bolshevik coup in Russia; its lobbying in favour of the Federal Reserve Board; its partner, Paul Warburg, accompanying President Wilson to the Versailles peace conference, while his brother Max Warburg, was an adviser to the German delegation; and the presence of both Paul Warburg and Otto Kahn of Kuhn Loeb on the first board of the Council on Foreign Relations.

They would also include the incongruity of the former Communist Denis Healey rubbing shoulders with some of the richest men in the world at Bilderberg meetings

AK revealed the telling quotation from the arch internationalist, Arnold Toynbee, Director of Studies at Chatham House. He said that (he and they were) "engaged in removing the instrument of sovereignty from the hands of local national states" and that they were doing with their hands what they were denying with their lips.

Much of the material is dated and many of the people referred to are dead and buried. However, the earlier perpetrators have their successors and in the case of Toynbee, descendants, eager to pursue his project.

There is today a greater frankness about 'post-national' aims. One has only to listen to debates in the European Parliament to witness everybody from the 'former' Communists in GUE, through the Socialists, Liberals and Greens to the Christian Democrats of the European People's Party singing from the same cosmopolitan sheet. Even those in the Conservative group and UKIP who pretend to different degrees of Euro-scepticism, embrace Globalism enthusiastically.

I ask you to read *The New Unhappy Lords* carefully and critically, just as I hope you have read my foreword carefully and critically. Then make up your own mind.

Andrew Brons M.E.P.

PREFACE TO THE FIFTH EDITION (2013)

The New Unhappy Lords was first published in 1965, and from the first was a great success. The initial run of a cloth bound hard cover books was sold out within three months, and more had to be created by adapting the paperback books to meet demand. This first edition had been funded by a wealthy supporter.

The paperback edition was also in heavy demand, and a second edition was required by October 1966. This was impossible due to the state of the finances which were full engaged in the long running R.K. Jeffery will battle.

Happily *Candour* readers, then as now a supportive group, stepped into the breach and funded a second edition in 1967.

A revised and enlarged third edition proved necessary in 1969 which was funded by a young American Anglophile. This was followed by a revised and updated fourth edition in 1972, and a reprint after the author's death.

This fifth edition has been made possible by the advances in printing, such as print-on-demand. It is based on the second printing of the fourth revised edition from 1975, and the preface for the fourth edition is included for the sake of completeness.

A.K. Chesterton died in 1973 and obviously his narrative stops then.

To the discerning reader it must be obvious that subsequent events have proved The New Unhappy Lords in so many ways to be prophetic. AK is giving us an old-fashioned lesson here. Take heed! We must relearn how to 'read between the lines' when anti-British propaganda is daily force fed.

Almost forty years since we printed the last edition of this classic work, it is nice to be able to say welcome to this one.

Colin Todd

The A.K. Chesterton Trust
August 2013

PREFACE TO THE FOURTH EDITION (1972)

Where needed, events related in earlier editions have been brought up-to-date at the end of chapters.

The final chapter, after the first paragraph, consists of new material dealing with the dishonest methods used to secure Great Britain's adherence to the European Economic Community and the national awakening which has taken place consequent upon the Government's acceptance of Uganda's rejected Asians.

It also points to the menace of the new agreements between the United States and Russia on the one hand and between the United States and China on the other.

Note

This book is a second printing of the Fourth Edition. Due to the death of the author in 1973 it does not comment on recent events which were envisaged by him when the book was first written in 1965.

It will, however, be obvious to the discerning reader that subsequent events have underlined the truth of this classic analysis.

Chapter I

THE ASSAULT ON PATRIOTISM

THE history of civilized man for a thousand years and more has been the history of nations. Whatever the nations may owe to antiquity — and in Europe the debt is a heavy one — they owe at least as much to their own distinctive national genius, which is both the animating spirit and the product of centuries of common effort, of living together, striving together, rejoicing together, being bound together in times of hardship and adversity. The amazing richness and fertility of European culture are conceivable only in terms of national diversity within the unifying context of Christendom.

Until our own day this diversity was cherished. Pride in one's own nation, which never precluded recognition of the achievements of other nations, was a value not to be questioned, let alone derided and spurned. Patriotism made all men taller. Then came the First World War and with it one of the supreme historical ironies — in that holocaust, patriotism, which made its greatest demands on the men of all the warring nations to meet the needs of the time and which brought forth from them the most superb qualities of their manhood, nevertheless encountered in the aftermath its first serious questioning.

There were several reasons. One no doubt was a general revulsion against the appalling slaughter, combined with an assessment of the gains, if any, in relation to the cost in human life and misery. But such calculations alone were unlikely to have cast more than a temporary slur on the concept of patriotism : criticism would have concentrated more on its abuse than on its values. It was necessary to look elsewhere for the real motive-power. As we now know, other forces were released to play a most sinister part in the shaping of the post-war world. One was the Bolshevist Revolution, with its allegedly anti-nationalist bias expressed in the slogan "Workers of the World Unite!" Another, perhaps much more important event, was the shift of financial power from London to New York, a cosmopolitan city strangely remote from the European tradition.

Nor were the two events unrelated. The partners of the New York international lending house of Kuhn, Loeb and Co., despite vigorous denials for many years afterwards, were the instigators and financiers of the Bolshevik regime. They and their European affiliates were Trotsky's paymasters and in addition met the expense of transporting to Russia for the role of the "men of Marseilles" (who had been the mob-leaders in the French Revolution) a gang of "American" thugs who had been trained in New York for the job of creating riots in the streets of Moscow and otherwise producing a climate of revolutionary fervour.

Nor were these the only services for the Revolution performed by the master-usurers of New York. The Germans had a clear-cut motive in allowing the repatriation of Lenin and his followers from Switzerland to Russia : the Communists, once established, could be relied on to sue for peace. The British, on the other hand, had a no less indisputable interest in keeping the Russian armies in the field. How, then, does one explain the action of the British War Cabinet in granting Trotsky safe-conduct for his return home from Newfoundland? The only possible explanation of that action is that Great Britain was financially at the end of her tether and seeking a £1,000,000,000 loan from the United States, a factor which made her amenable to the will of the New York Money Power, so that travel facilities extended to a revolutionary in exile seemed a small price to pay for such support. It was the same expediency that led to the drawing-up of the Balfour Declaration promising a national home for the Jews in Palestine — a document written by Herbert Samuel, then Home Secretary, as he himself was to admit thirty years later.

As the result of the establishment in 1913 of the Federal Reserve Board system, the United States itself had come under the control of the great financial houses, with some startling consequences. One was that President Wilson, who had been used as a puppet to sponsor the Federal Reserve scheme, found his auspices extended willy-nilly to embrace the Russian Revolution, with all its murderous horrors and atrocities. The sixth of his "Fourteen Points", on which the subsequent peace was supposed to be founded, read :

"The evacuation of all Russian territory, and such a settlement of all questions affecting Russia as will secure the best and freest co-operation of the other nations of the world in obtaining for her an unhampered and unembarrassed opportunity for the independent determination of her own political development and national policy, and assure her of a sincere welcome into the society of free nations under institutions of her own choosing, and more than a welcome, assistance also of every kind that she may need and may herself desire. The treatment accorded Russia by her sister nations in the months to come will be the acid test of their good will, of their own comprehension of her needs as distinguished from their own interests, and of their intelligent and unselfish sympathy."

Was ever such fervent special pleading made in so vile a cause?

No less indicative of the new power which aspired to take charge of the governance of mankind was the curious circumstance that Paul Warburg, partner in the firm of Kuhn, Loeb and Co., part financier of the Russian Revolution and agent-in-chief for the founding of the U.S. Federal Reserve system, accompanied President Wilson to the Versailles Peace Conference, where he acted as financial adviser to the American delegation, while the German delegation employed as financial adviser a partner in the Hamburg lending house run by Paul Warburg's brother, Max. Although Versailles has often been described as the scene of a welter of national interests contending one against the other, in truth the dominating interest to be served was infra-national, or what we should today describe as internationalist.

Powerful though it was, the internationalist cause embracing both Wall St. and the Kremlin still had a long way to go in its bid for a world monopoly of power. When President Wilson fell from popular favour in 1919 the would-be power monopolists suffered their first major defeat. The Congress of the United States then made known its will by a resolute refusal to countenance recognition of Soviet Russia and by its decree forbidding the supply of loans to Moscow. This state of affairs continued for twelve years, when the election to the Presidency of Franklin D. Roosevelt restored the *status quo ante*, ensuring recognition of the Soviet Union and Moscow's free access to the New York money market.

It is not to be supposed, however, that in the interregnum the Money Power lacked all means of sustaining life in its Bolshevist child. Although direct loans from New York were forbidden, there was nothing to prevent finance being fed to Russia through banking houses in London, Paris, and Hamburg. The huge bucket-shop known as the Weimar Republic was particularly useful for this and other services of inestimable value to the Kremlin.

The British Government was soon to become aware of the disadvantage of being entangled in a web of unpayable debt. Lord Reading in 1917 contracted on behalf of the United Kingdom a huge dollar loan which was to be repayable on call and in gold in quantity such as the nation had never possessed. It is small wonder, therefore, that although the British Government was fully aware of the source, and inspiration of Communism— Winston Churchill laid bare the facts in a newspaper article in 1920 — no serious attempt was ever made to support the U.S. Congressional action to outlaw the Soviet Union and by the middle twenties Russian oil and other products indirectly financed by Wall St. were being boosted on the British market.

Churchill had written, *inter alia*, of the birth of Communism :

"... this world-wide conspiracy for the overthrow of civilization and for the reconstitution of society on the basis of arrested development, of envious malevolence and impossible equality, has been steadily growing . . . . . . There is no need to exaggerate the part played in the creation of Bolshevism and in the actual bringing about of the Russian Revolution by these international and for the most part atheistical Jews. It is certainly a very great one; it probably outweighs all others. With the notable exception of Lenin, the majority of the leading figures are Jews. Moreover, the principal inspiration and driving power comes from the Jewish leaders."

Great Britain also experienced for the first time a successful attempt to limit her national sovereignty. Her policy of maintaining a two-power naval strength was jettisoned under pressure from the United States and she was thereby forced to abdicate the supremacy at sea under cover of which her daughter nations, including the United States, had been enabled to grow to maturity. The Washington Naval Agreement fixed the ratio of 3, 3, 2 as between Great Britain, the United States and Japan, but as America dishonoured her signature by embarking upon an intensive naval programme Great Britain was cheated even of the agreed parity.

Another assault on Britain's national sovereignty was the demand that the Anglo-Japanese Alliance should be dropped. This alliance had served Britain and her allies well, ensuring the maintenance of the *status quo* in the Far East. Had it been renewed and kept in good working order Germany would have been denied a most formidable ally in the Second World War and, in all probability, the calculated destruction of the British, French and Dutch Empires in Asia, with its attendant chaos, averted. It was a palpable British interest to maintain the Alliance and even more palpably was it an Australian interest and no less a Canadian interest. Yet, strangely enough, the pressure on Great Britain from the United States was reinforced by pressures from Australia and Canada, which shows that even in the twenties the Wall St. Money Power was able to exercise a decisive, and most malignant, influence on Australian and Canadian policies.

Grievous as were these body-blows upon the British nations, even more grievous was the assault upon the British spirit. Allowing for the revulsion against war caused by the slaughter of the 1914-1918 conflict, it was still true to say at the end of it that most Britons retained the instinct and the self-respect to play for their own side, to uphold their own national independence and to cherish the values of true manhood and true womanhood which had enabled them to meet the stern demands of their greatest ordeal. These were the attributes which next came under attack. Not all the attack was conspiratorial. It is not to be supposed that the Western Brothers, who derided the public school

22

values with their drawling "Play the game, you cads", were prompted by any motive other than to arouse laughter and to pocket the cash that went therewith. But can anybody doubt that derision of the phrase went a long way towards deriding the concept? Indeed, the spirit of subversion became entrenched in the public schools and universities — that is, in institutions of what should have been the nation's elite, charged especially with the task of preserving the national tradition and heritage. This explains something of the notorious Oxford Union resolution of the early 'thirties : "Under no circumstances will this House fight for King and Country". The same motion, introduced again in1965, was defeated because Reginald Maudling stressed Britain's obligation to meet her Nato commitments!

The *Zeitgeist*, however, does not furnish the full explanation of the attack on the British spirit. Every year it spent in opposition the Labour Party voted with monotonous regularity against the Service Estimates. The Independent Labour Party, the Communist Party and the Fabian Society could always be relied upon to support the pacifist cause everywhere on earth — except, of course, in Soviet Russia. Pacifism among the young was carried to almost unbelievable limits. Many educational authorities, for instance, holding that the word "drill" had undesirable military connotations, decreed that the school period hitherto known as "physical drill" should be renamed "physical exercise". Not long afterwards schools were told to abandon marching, presumably on the ground that if children went from one place to another as a disciplined body rather than as an unruly rabble, they would grow up with the ambition to march to war. The final absurdity was reached when the educational authorities insisted that physical exercises should consist only of games of the children's own choice, without words of command issued by the teacher in charge. This would eliminate all suggestion of a parade-ground atmosphere.

In other words, as a long-term policy the British peoples were being softened-up. Disarmed physically and, through the deliberate denigration of patriotism and a proper pride, spiritually, they were made ready for a takeover bid. By whom? Some would say "by the Communists". My own reply would be : by the new world power which saw — and sees— the possibility of using both Communism and Loan- Capitalism as twin instruments with which to subdue and govern, not the British nations alone, but all mankind.

Chapter II

REBELLION AND WAR

BEFORE the take-over bid was to reach its present titanic proportions it had to overcome immense obstacles, including the waging of the Second World War.

Mention has been made of the formation in 1913 of the United States Federal Reserve system. Its purpose, as set down in the original Bill, was to secure stability in the price level, but by the time the Bill emerged as an Act the sentence embodying this *raison d'etre* had mysteriously been lost. The general belief was still that, should there be depression in any part of the United States, the Federal Reserve Board would rush credits to the stricken area in the same way that a man overboard is thrown a life-belt. Precisely the opposite procedure was in fact followed. During the "recession" of 1922, when certain farming districts were badly hit, the Federal Reserve, so far from furnishing credits, pursued a policy of financial stringency, perhaps as a rehearsal for the great debacle of 1929.

On looking through some copies of the *New Age* which appeared in the early 'thirties I find that Professor Cassel was quoted as having "traced the restrictive action of the Federal Reserve Bank — which was the initial cause of this unexampled 1929 depression in the United States — to Puritanism, which regarded the fat years of American prosperity as sinful . . . His (Professor Cassel's) keen insight detected the preponderating Judaic element in determining U.S. history." Such naivete is almost unbelievable. What Professor Cassel and the *New Age* commentator left out of account was the fact that, other things being equal, the last thing in the world desired by the money-lender is the straightforward repayment of his debt. He prefers to negotiate a new bond carrying a higher rate of interest or often the complete inability of the debtor to repay, thus enabling him to foreclose and become possessed of the debtor's assets. In 1928 the Federal Reserve Banks and the New York wolf-packs associated with them had encouraged an orgy of short-term borrowing : a few months later they peremptorily called in the loans and many thousands of business-men, caught on the hop, went bankrupt and were placed at the mercy, if that be the word, of their creditors. The nation-wide depression soon spread to Europe, with the result that millions upon millions of men spent a wasted and embittered youth on the street-corners, eating their hearts out for the opportunity of working upon the raw materials, which existed in abundance, to turn out the goods which would meet human needs throughout the world. Yet the raw materials were left unexploited while men and women rotted through enforced idleness and human needs remained unsatisfied.

Does any sensible person believe that this misery and devastation was caused by some alleged Puritanical streak in the Jewish money-lenders which made them regard prosperity as sinful ? The idea is ludicrous. No less ludicrous was the explanation given to a gullible world that the "catastrophe" was the result of the failure of the Credit Anstalt in Vienna to meet its obligations. The simple truth is that what has become known as the "Great Depression" was a wickedness deliberately plotted by the lending-houses of the United States and Europe with the idea of furthering their drive for a monopoly of economic (and therefore of political) power. The proof of this statement was surely that, as soon as the "recovery" began, these mighty institutions (which had remained intact throughout the slump by virtue of the privilege given them by venal governments to issue national credit as a debt against the general community) were seen to emerge with illimitably increased assets, the former property of businesses which had gone bankrupt or which had sold out at ruinous prices to the all-conquering bankers and their affiliated industrial and commercial interests. The financial houses had bought up or otherwise acquired a huge variety of enterprises, ranging from Woolworths to speculative land values.

However, as has happened time and again throughout history, the moneylenders had tended to overplay their hand. The six million German unemployed who were the victims of the "Great Depression" resulted in a formidable revolt against the Money Power — the revolt of Adolf Hitler. There was also a rebellion, although of a much milder kind, in Great Britain and the British nations overseas, whose representatives met in Ottawa in 1932 to hammer out a system of Imperial Preferences calculated to insulate the British world against Wall St. amok-runs. These Preferences, as we shall see, incurred the unrelenting hostility of the New York Money Power and the only reason why a show-down was not forced was the far more serious threat to the international financial system implicit in the economic doctrines of the Third Reich.

From the point of view of New York and of other centres engaged in international lending the Third Reich held two main dangers. One was that it had been built up on an anti-Communist basis. Although in *Mein Kampf*, written many years before, Hitler had visualised a war of revenge against the West as well as the East, in fact the propaganda drive — certainly until the end of 1937 — was concentrated on the *Drang nach Osten* and the German people were conditioned to regard the Communists as their only potential foe. This was understandable in view of the presence in Germany during the Weimar regime of upwards of a million Communists whose salutation was "Heil Moskow".

After 1937 the Germans began to take more note of the warlike noises being made in the West but their chief preoccupation was still with the Soviet Union, with the result that its original Transatlantic backers became very concerned for the safety of their Bolshevik babe, now grown into a savage and violent young manhood.

The other danger inherent in the policy of the Third Reich concerned its firmly held belief that if goods were available for exchange between nations there was no need for either party to resort to international lending houses to finance the deal. Instead, the exchange should take place on a "swap" basis. No great insight is needed to perceive that the success of this system of barter, if employed on a world scale, would mean for most practical purposes the end of international finance and of the immense power which it confers on its operators. As though this were not offence enough in the eyes of the international lending houses, the Third Reich set to work sedulously to repay its external debt and thereby regain control over its own economic destiny. One thing alone could quench rebellion of such magnitude — war.

Had Hitler continued to develop Germany on an autarchical basis, bartering surplus production for needed imports, he might conceivably have conferred on mankind the greatest gift since Prometheus stole the fire from Heaven. It would have been no easy task to marshal the nations against his powerful Third Reich. The British Government of Neville Chamberlain did not want war, even after the flagrant breach of faith implicit in the German march on Prague. Gallup and other polls in the United States as late as the autumn of 1941 were so strongly isolationist (the interventionist vote averaged little more than ten percent) that Roosevelt was impelled to assure American mothers that their sons would not be sent overseas to take part in foreign wars. The Soviet Government so little wanted war that it formed a Berlin-Moscow axis to try to avoid involvement. Still less did the French Government want war. As so many governments and people wanted to maintain the peace it is pertinent to ask who wanted war.

The answer is :

(a) Hitler wanted war, but only in the East.

(b) International Finance wanted war, but not in the East.

It is surely of the greatest significance that, so far as immediate objectives were concerned, International Finance won the day. After striking down Poland and partitioning that country with the Soviet Union, Hitler turned about and deployed his full strength against the West, rolling up the French Armies, driving the British forces back to their own shores, and forcing France to sue for peace. How was the diversion of Hitler contrived? Most curiously. The British Labour Party had been howling for blood ever since the Japanese invaded Manchuria in the early 'thirties! It again howled for blood when the Italians attacked Abyssinia and yet again for Spanish right-wing blood when Franco rescued Spain from the abomination of desolation created by left-wing misrule. It howled for German blood almost on the instant that Hitler came into power and during the spring and summer of 1939 the howl became a sustained and mounting screech. But because the Labour Party in Parliament was in a minority it lacked the power to precipitate war. There was one way only of forcing the issue — the creation within the Conservative Party of a war party and that war party was duly created at a series of secret meetings at the Savoy Hotel. Its leaders were Winston Churchill, Duff Cooper, Anthony Eden and, representing the interests of International Finance, Israel Moses Sieff. The choice confronting Chamberlain in September 1939 was therefore to declare war on Germany or to fragment the Conservative Party. He chose war. That is how Hitler's *Drang nach Osten* was for a time arrested, to the ruinous hurt of Western Europe and at the cost of the British Empire.

There is a widespread belief that Great Britain was committed by treaty to the defence of Poland. That is not the fact. It is true that on August 25, 1939 Lord Halifax as Foreign Secretary (with the Polish Foreign Secretary) signed an agreement pledging mutual support should either nation be attacked by a European Power, but this did not constitute a treaty, which according to constitutional practice has to be ratified by Parliament and can only be made by Heads of State. The Halifax document was published in 1943 as a White Paper, and again in 1945, but the first White Paper omitted a curious protocol which expressly stated that by a European Power was meant Germany. It is difficult to understand the purpose of such a clause if the intention were not to indicate that the British Government declined to intervene if Poland should be attacked by the Soviet Union alone. Why the limitation? The British commitment was to the French in the event of France being involved in a European conflict and it was France which had undertaken to defend Poland —an undertaking the French Government was extremely reluctant to discharge. The British Government therefore acted in its default and declared war. Not until some hours later were the French persuaded to follow suit. It will be seen that the declaration of war by Great Britain was thus gratuitous. James Forrestal, U.S. Secretary of the Navy, states in his Diaries that the American Ambassador in London told him that Neville Chamberlain had complained of Jewish pressures to force Britain into war. Those pressures were obviously exerted with decisive effect through the Churchill-Israel Moses Sieff group.

Chapter III

BETRAYAL OF ALLIES

THE most remarkable facts about the Second World War were among the least publicized.

One is that Financial Jewry, despite its enormous power in the United States, did not bring pressure to bear on the American Government, as pressure was brought to bear on the British Government, until two years after the start of hostilities. Why such tardiness? There were three reasons for it. The first was the revelation of the public opinion polls, although in truth there has rarely been any difficulty in stampeding or circumventing public opinion. This gives added weight to the other two reasons. While America was building up her strength Great Britain was fast dissipating hers, which made her increasingly dependent on the United States and decreasingly mistress in her own domains — a state of affairs not displeasing to the Dollar Emperors. Much more important, however, was the fact that the Berlin-Moscow axis was still rotating and as long as New York's pampered pet, the Soviet Union, was preserved from the shock of invasion it was certain that the international lending houses would be content to reap the harvest of the conflict between Germany and the British nations. (Note the plural. How inexcusably smug was it to boast that "we went it alone"!)

As soon as Hitler denounced his pact with Russia, and reverted to what from the first had been his real objective, the smashing of the Soviet Union, there was an instant change of heart (if it can be said to possess a heart) in the "American" Power Elite. Hitherto its tool in the White House, Franklin Delano Roosevelt, had been murmuring his reassurances to American mothers and unofficially giving Britain sporadic and always marginal support at sea. There was now an urgent call to action, although very few understood that the call was made primarily to rescue the sorely beset Soviet Union, and secondly, to deal death to the Nazi system of barter. It was first considered expedient to change the public opinion polls by changing public opinion, for which purpose a threat to the United States more immediate than any presented by Hitler's Germany was needed. The problem was solved with diabolical cleverness. Washington set to work with cold deliberation to pick a quarrel with Tokyo. While it went through the motions of negotiating for a settlement, it ensured that no settlement would be reached by drawing up an ultimatum which no Japanese Government could accept and remain in being.

Once the ultimatum was delivered there could be little doubt about Japan's reaction. She would seek a target at which to strike what she hoped would be a shattering blow, and — from the point of view of the secret policy-makers in the United States — the bigger and more dramatic that blow the more certain was it that isolationism would be blown sky-high and American opinion galvanised and made ready for war. The prediction proved correct. Was it pure chance that at this time of gravest peril America's main Pacific Fleet, instead of being alerted and dispersed, or otherwise deployed for immediate action, was concentrated in Pearl Harbour? The question is not academic. It so happens that some months earlier the British had broken the Japanese naval code and given Washington full particulars, so that the President of the United States and the U.S. Chief-of-Staff were made aware by their own Intelligence Service that a very strong Japanese force, in answer to the ultimatum, was converging on Pearl Harbour. Is it not exceedingly strange — indeed, suspicious and something more than suspicious — that all American bases were informed of the fact with the solitary exception of Pearl Harbour, where the officers in command were left in ignorance of what portended until it was too late to disperse the Fleet? The Japanese assault had all the desired results. Isolationist opinion withered on the instant and the United States of America was at war. The loss of American lives at Pearl Harbour brought forth no tears except from the relatives. They represented only a small expenditure in relation to the object to be achieved — the mobilisation of the economic and military might of the United States in defence of the Soviet Union. In a very short time American propagandists, with President Roosevelt in the lead, began to clamour for the immediate opening of a Second Front — an agitation to which every Communist Party in the world contributed — and the clamour was sustained long after Britain's leaders had patiently explained to Washington that there were not enough military landing craft in existence to land more than a solitary division on French soil.

The war imposed upon the New York policy-makers the task of ensuring the defeat of the declared enemies in the field. But they were cool-headed enough, and cold-blooded enough, to perceive that in the process of overthrowing the Germans, Japanese and Italians, the opportunity would be presented for them, in ways more subtle, also to overthrow their allies.

I have mentioned that from the first Wall St. had shown hostility to the Imperial Preference system agreed by the British nations at Ottawa in 1932. It is not surprising, therefore, that Lend-Lease, introduced to Congress as a measure for "the defence of the American people", should have contained a clause directed against Imperial Preferences. What is at first sight surprising is that Winston Churchill should have rhetorically described it as "the most unsordid act in history". This seems even stranger when we remember that at the Atlantic

Charter meeting Roosevelt hinted at the post-war elimination of "those little old Preferences of yours" and was indignantly rounded on by Churchill, who said : "Mr. President, I believe that you are trying to do away with the British Empire. Every idea you entertain of the structure of the post-war world demonstrates it". However, as a few weeks later Churchill was proclaiming himself Roosevelt's "ardent lieutenant" the student of the back-room history of our times begins to feel inured to surprise.

As far as is known "America's" anti-British policy was first given concrete expression in the brief that General Marshall took with him to the Quebec Conference in 1943. This was to the effect that the greatest single obstacle to the expansion of America's export-capitalism after the war would be not the Soviet Union but the British Empire. What this meant, in practical terms, was that as soon as the enemies in the field had been disposed of would come the turn of the British Empire to be progressively destroyed and that means to this end would be shaped even while hostilities raged. The moment they were over the campaign could begin in real earnest, the signal for which was to be Truman's abrupt dropping of Lend-Lease to an ally whose economy had been so closely geared to war production that many markets for her goods had been systematically transferred to U.S producers.

The British Empire was not the only ally marked down for liquidation. The Dutch Empire in the East Indies and the French Empire in Indo-China and Africa were also high on the list, but of these grave matters we shall learn more in later chapters.

Nor were these the only betrayals to be carried out under the cloak of alliance. General Mihailovich of Jugoslavia was the first in the field with his partisans to begin the work of harassing the enemy. Then the Soviet Union decided to enter the lists with a rival, a man who had assumed the name of Tito, and because the main Wall St. objective was the defence of the Soviet Union and the extension of its powers, every allied nation was required to drop aid for Mihailovich and to back Tito, who was far more concerned in fighting Mihailovich than in engaging the common enemy. Indeed, within the Yugoslav context the General was made to appear the common enemy — a task which was facilitated by the action of the U.S. Office of Strategic Services and red-orientated members of British Intelligence sending home as their own reports the completely unscrupulous propaganda communiques of "Marshal Tito". To show that he understood the required form, Winston Churchill summoned King Peter and demanded that he should broadcast to Jugoslavia a denunciation of his faithful Mihailovich. When the young King demurred Churchill thumped the table angrily and said that he knew better than King Peter what was in the best interest of Jugoslavia. The broadcast duly took place. Listening to it in his mountain-fastness, Mihailovich made only one comment before switching off the set : "Et tu, Brute". At the war's end he and his fellow-patriots were handed over to Tito and put to death.

Mikolajczyk, Prime Minister of the Polish Government in exile, was another ally to be double-crossed and betrayed. Hearing rumours of a projected carving-up of his country, he hastily crossed the Atlantic to seek reassurances from the American President. These Roosevelt had no compunction in furnishing. The Poles, he said, need have no fear. At the end of the war their pre-war frontiers would be restored. He gave his personal guarantee. Soon afterwards Mikolajczyk attended the Moscow Conference and was amazed to find the partitioning of Poland taken for granted, with the Russians confirmed in their possession of the half they had already occupied. He protested. Stalin came straight to the point. "All this," he said, "was settled at Teheran". Unwilling to believe that Roosevelt could have told him a bare-faced lie, Mikolajczyk turned to Averell Harriman, the President's representative. Harriman looked away. He then turned to Churchill who said gravely : "That is so". Passionately the Polish Premier declared that he could not be a party to the betrayal of his country, whereupon Stalin brought the session to an abrupt end. Back in the ante-room reserved for the Western Allies, Churchill turned a furious eye on Mikolajczyk, told him that he was endangering allied relationships and that he ought to be in a criminal lunatic asylum. There would be no difficulty about the Polish frontiers, he asserted. He would himself give orders to the British Ambassador in Warsaw to see that the pre-war frontiers were restored. Unimpressed, the Polish Prime Minister asked to be parachuted into Warsaw so that he could die fighting the enemy instead of being shot by the Russians in front of the British Ambassador. At this point, he records in his autobiography, Churchill turned unhappily away.

That was a revealing glimpse of Winston Churchill. His turning unhappily away shows that he must have been aware of what really impended. On the other hand, his remark about instructing the British Ambassador provides more than a hint of perhaps still latent *folie de grandeur*. His making over to Roosevelt a document giving the United States sole use of atomic power for industrial purposes after the war and his initialling, together with Roosevelt, of the diabolical Morgenthau plan for the "pastoralisation" of Germany, shows the tremendous duress placed upon him. Despite his statement that he had not become the King's First Minister to preside over the liquidation of the British Empire he must have known that such in fact was now his role. So intelligent a man could not have been blind to the malignant and utterly ruthless forces which not only double-crossed him but which required him to join in the double-crossing of other allies. It is no wonder that he should have drowned his miseries in a *folie de grandeur* which eventually made him a complete convert to the legend of his own incomparable greatness. How otherwise could he have lived with himself as the dupe and victim of the Lords of Misrule who were determined to destroy all the things for which he once had stood?

Chapter IV

THE POWER OF BARUCHISTAN

THE ambivalence of post-war American policy, created by the conflicting objectives of "containing Communism" to satisfy the American Congress and American opinion, and at the same time to help to promote it, in obedience to the great financial interests which had played so large a part in establishing and maintaining the Soviet Union, was only superficially a part of Roosevelt's wartime policy. As we now know, his golden rule throughout that time was to deny the Communists nothing and in every conflict of view between Russia and the Western allies to take the Russian side. To that extent it was a simple policy and of multitudinous instances two or three, for present purposes, must suffice. Mention has been made of Roosevelt's lying assurance to Premier Mikolajczyk that after the war Poland's pre-war frontiers would be restored. At the same interview Mikolajczyk informed the American President that broadcasts to Poland and other Eastern European countries by the Voice of America consisted of blatant Communist propaganda. Roosevelt gave a solemn promise that the propaganda would be stopped at once, whereas it was not only maintained until the end of the war but continued long afterwards. Either Roosevelt was a brazen humbug or he was the dupe of the New York Power Elite which had riddled his Administration with Communist agents who disobeyed his instructions and fed him with false information. History must resolve the problem as to what extent he was a conscious and to what extent an unconscious tool of the Money Power.

Another instance was the over-running of Malaya and Singapore by the Japanese. The defence of these countries was entrusted to an R.A.F. Command which had only a few hundred obsolete planes at its disposal. By the time the Japanese struck the British aircraft industry was turning out fighters and bombers in spate. Why were these modern planes not sent to defend British possessions in Malaya? The answer is that most of them were being flown to Russia to reinforce the Red Army. The United States had now assumed the dominant role in the planning of allied war production and distribution, and it was the U.S. order of priorities which had to be observed. As a consequence, when Churchill sent H.M.S. *Repulse* and H.M.S. *Prince of Wales* to Malayan waters there were no fighter planes to provide adequate air cover, with the result that these two mighty men-o'-war were sunk — and with them, for all practical purposes, was sunk our Empire in the East. It is improbable that either Stalin or Bernard Baruch, the effective head of the Money Power, had tears to shed over the event.

A third instance concerns the development of the atom-bomb. Great Britain, through the researches of the great Rutherford, Soddy and other scientists, led the world in knowledge of how to split the atom. The results of these researches were placed at the disposal of the United States subject only to one condition — that when the know-how of the construction of the actual bombs was discovered it should be communicated to the British Government. This agreement the United States dishonoured. In later years, when the McMahon Act was passed forbidding the communication to other powers of U.S. atomic secrets, Congress had no idea of the secret agreement with the British. Prime Minister Attlee made no attempt to enlighten Congress and Winston Churchill told the House of Commons that he would have acted in Attlee's default but that President

Truman had asked him not to. How completely had the senescent British Lion been mesmerised by the American Eagle, or if not by the Eagle, then by the glint in the Baruchian glasses, which amounted to much the same thing! Yet while the British were thus abominably betrayed, the Americans were sending case-loads of secret atomic formulae to Moscow, together with quantities of processed uranium. Major Jordan, of the U.S.A.A.F., who had the task of despatching these materials, protested, but was given personal orders by Harry Hopkins to forward the consignments. Readers new to the subject may ask : "Who was this man Hopkins?" He had been an obscure charity-organiser when Roosevelt summoned him and gave him complete charge of all the millions of dollars distributed as part of the New Deal. Clearly, therefore, he was a key-man in somebody's service. During the war Hopkins moved into the White House, without official position or salary, and access to the President could only be had through him. Who was paying this master-agent? In all likelihood he was being paid, directly or indirectly, by Bernard Baruch. At all events, one day when he said something not too flattering about Baruch, Roosevelt rebuked him."Harry," said the President, "remember all that Bernie has done for you".

But by far the most important dispositions favouring Russia were those which received the seal of official approval at Yalta. As a result of decisions reached at that conference, at which Roosevelt's chief expert assistant was Alger Hiss, in after years sent for a long term of imprisonment for perjury relating to the fact that he was a Communist agent, Eisenhower later held back troops of the Western Allies from taking Berlin and Prague, which they were poised to do, so that the Red Army might be the first to enter these capitals. What happened to the women of Berlin is unspeakable, and it did not happen by accident. Eisenhower then withdrew his forces, in some sectors as much as 150 miles, and thus allowed the Mongolian hordes to occupy the European heartlands. Never has there been a betrayal of Christendom on so monumental a scale. History will record that Roosevelt contrived it, with poor old Churchill tagging helplessly along, but it does not do to forget that behind Roosevelt was the cold, calculating brain of Bernard Mannes Baruch.

During Eisenhower's Presidency of the United States he cut short one of his vacations to open a park in New York which Baruch had founded in honour of his own father. In his speech Eisenhower made a remarkable admission. "Twenty-five years ago," he said, "as a young and unknown Major, I took the wisest step in my life — I consulted Mr. Baruch." Wise step, indeed! When war broke out Eisenhower was jumped over the heads of at least 150 of his seniors to be placed in supreme command of the Allied Forces in Europe — certainly remarkable promotion for an officer without battle experience or the experience of handling large masses of men in the field. What interpretation can be put upon it other than that Eisenhower was Baruch's man, not only in exercising the supreme command but later as President of the United States?

It may be instructive at this stage to cast a glance back to the First World War and its immediate aftermath. I have earlier mentioned the sixth of President Wilson's Fourteen Points with its fantastic special pleading for help to be extended to Russia's revolutionary regime. Now Americans believe, and they are not alone in their belief, that the most powerful man in the United States is the President. Bernard Baruch, giving evidence before a Congressional Committee, disposed of that polite fiction. In answer to a question he affirmed that during the war he, Baruch, had been the most powerful man in America. The claim cut President Wilson down to size, revealing him for what he was — a mere figurehead. Was it probable, or even possible, that the Fourteen Points could have been drawn up and declared to the world without the sanction of the most powerful man in the United States? What is more, would Lenin have conveyed to Baruch that he could name his own price if he would take in hand the reorganization of the Soviet economy if there had not been, at the very least, some considerable Baruchian sympathy for the regime — a sympathy none the less real because he thought it not politic to accept Lenin's offer?

Although in the Second World War Bernard Baruch had no official position, there is every reason to think that unofficially he exercised even more power than in the first war. Certainly at the end of it, in the autumn of 1945, he conducted himself with the arrogance of a man wielding world power. There were gathered in London at the time the Foreign Ministers of the Allied nations, met to discuss the way ahead. Baruch also arrived. Asked by the famous American journalist, Victor A. Lasky, the purpose of his visit, he replied : "I've come to hold the big stick over the big boys, to make damn sure they don't foul up the peace." What "big stick" would that have been? Quite obviously, the formidable sanctions at the disposal of the New York Money Power.

On a later occasion Baruch told a newspaper correspondent : "If the British want to keep their Imperial Preferences, we'll let them — for four years." He was asked what would happen if the British wanted to retain them longer. "Why," said Baruch, "we'll extend the period by another four years." He did not explain who were the "we" who would decide the economic pattern of great nations. There was no need.

Until the middle of the Second World War the financial complex of which Bernard Baruch was the leading political figure, and in a sense the symbol, showed its greatest interest in the cornering and manipulation of gold, the manipulation of credit and gambling in foodstuffs and other commodities vital to the existence of civilized communities. After 1943, however, there was placed at man's disposal that which promised to be more potent than gold — uranium and its derivatives, such as plutonium. Nobody need have been surprised to discover, therefore, that when the mushroom blanket over Hiroshima had cleared away Bernard Baruch was to be found presiding over the U.S. Atomic Energy Commission and endeavouring to stampede mankind into an atomic energy monopoly. This, as Baruch conceived it, was to involve the entire process, from mining of uranium to the manufacture of atomic bombs and nuclear power stations. No doubt it was an attempt to implement this plan which led to the pressure on Churchill to relinquish to the United States all Britain's rights to the post-war exploitation of atomic energy for industrial purposes. *Hansard* is my authority for this statement. The reach of the plan, as so often, exceeded its grasp, and in the end Britain's surrender of atomic energy proved impractical. However, Baruchistan's power extends to governments no less than to any given material, so that it would be optimistic to suppose that Bernard simply accepted the situation, without doing anything about it. The British Government, indeed, did a very queer thing. It decided to enter the watch-making business in opposition to the Swiss. That, at least, was the cover story. But instead of approaching a British watch-making or precision-instrument-making firm it went to — of all people — a group of Jews engaged in the furrier trade and offered it public money to make watches in return for a measure of Government control. Newmarks jumped at the offer and established a watch-making industry. It is perhaps significant that the Government representative on the Board was a Colonel Rothschild. After a few years all pretence of competing with the Swiss was dropped and the announcement made that, instead of making watches, Newmarks would concentrate on manufacturing accessories for the atomic energy industry. Perhaps it was all part of the, Baruchistan monopoly. At any rate, nearly twenty years after its inception, President Kennedy publicly stated that the signing in Moscow of the Test-Ban Treaty was a further stage in the fulfilment of the Baruch Plan!

Unless there is a counter-revolution of world-shaking proportions we may be sure that atomic energy and all the associated processes will be subject to international control, which means the control of Baruchistan, its heirs and successors, forever.

Is Baruchistan a benevolent force in the world? Let every reader answer for himself. My own belief is that it is, beneath velvet gloves, an insupportable tyranny and that it aims at exercising supreme power over the human race through World Government — a power which, in the ultimate analysis, could only be enforced by atomic sanctions, and which, on a day-to-day basis, could only be upheld by internationalist police with the "right" to over-ride the national police and make its own arrests in every country by a midnight knock on the door in the now time-dishonoured Communist fashion.

Bernard Baruch is now dead, but his spirit goes marching on.

The succession so far has been kept a secret. It will be revealed when the discovery is made as to who contrived to place a certain Henry Kissinger in the citadel of power at the White House and invested him with responsibilities even more wide-ranging than those possessed by Harry Hopkins or Colonel House.

Chapter V

PREPARING THE POST-WAR PARADISE

ALTHOUGH the Money Power has taken the fullest possible advantage of the development which followed the splitting of the atom it would be a mistake to suppose that it has done so to the exclusion of perfecting its own financial techniques for the control of national economies. As early as 1943, when all decent men and women in the combatant countries were doing their utmost to help their own nations to surmount the crises of war, members of the international financial clique — "the inner steering group", as Senator Jenner of the U.S. called them — assembled their stooge experts at a place not so sylvan as its name implies to lay the foundations of the post-war system of international monetary control. While the issue of the war to most people still seemed undecided, there was no doubt in the minds of those who assembled at Bretton Woods that international finance would emerge triumphant and that suitable mechanisms for the extension and consolidation of loan-making and debt-repaying processes should therefore be available for post-war use.

Two main plans were discussed — the Keynes Plan and the White Plan — and eventually they were "married" to produce the Final Act of Bretton Woods. Many economists of the West, while not going so far as to approve Hitler's barter scheme, had been insisting that money, instead of determining production, should be based on production. The big financiers, reluctant that their money weapon should be subjected to restriction, were anxious to ensure that it should remain sovereign, in the sense that all else should be subordinated to the will of those who wielded it. Bretton Woods gave them substantially what they wanted. It produced two main instruments. One was the World Bank. The other was the International Monetary Fund. Both were, in embryo at least, projections of the U.S. Federal Reserve Board system.

The power invested in the Federal Reserve Board represented an astonishing abdication of sovereignty by the U.S. Government in that, contrary to constitutional provisions, the Board was given power to issue money as a debt against the American people. What happens is that the American Government creates bonds — which are no more than a governmental promise to repay — and hands them over to the Federal Reserve Board (an institution privately owned by the master usurers) which in turn gives orders to the Mint to produce whatever money bills and coinage may be required. In return for this purely intermediary service the Board is entitled to collect interest on the bonds, amounting to billions of dollars a year. In other words, the American people are required to pay a private concern for the issue to them of their own credit. Not even highway robbery is as blatant a method of becoming possessed of what rightly belongs to other people. It is probable that the ultimate purpose of the I.M.F. is to act as an International Reserve Board system, with sole sovereign sway and masterdom over note issues and credit control throughout the world. Indeed, over twenty years later when Prime Minister Harold Wilson was negotiating for a $3,000,000,000 loan from the I.M.F., he went so far as to fly a kite for International Finance by proposing the establishment of an international unit of currency to replace the dollar and the pound!

Although the provisions of Bretton Woods did not go as far as that, they went far enough. All national currencies were to be related to the U.S. dollar, and therefore indirectly to gold. If a nation devalued its currency above 15 per cent without permission the International Monetary Fund had power to call on its members to impose swingeing penalties upon the "offender", including full economic sanctions. In this way, to take a hypothetical case, the British could be ordered to cut off all trade with, say, Australia. As Great Britain herself had to devalue nearly double the allowed percentage to get clear of the debacle of the "Great Slump" it will be seen that such clauses were by no means academic. The capital held in reserve or loaned by the International Monetary Fund was to be furnished by member states, upon which they could draw by statute or agreement, and the I.M.F. was also to be given authority to fix the price of gold. Most of the nations of the world having found it expedient to subscribe to the Final Act of Bretton Woods, the International Monetary Fund has long been an established institution. That it represents the buyers of gold may be deduced from the fact that of all the commodities on earth gold is the only one which has not been allowed to rise in price throughout the post-war years.

The other child of Bretton Woods, the World Bank, has played, as we shall see in later chapters, a much more overtly political role. It lends, under its own auspices, monies to Governments subscribed by member states— which means that it assumes their power of patronage — and it enjoys the double blessedness of having its loans officially guaranteed at both the lender's and borrower's ends. We shall subsequently have cause to examine the part played by the World Bank in the theft of the Anglo-Persian oil industry and in the chain of events which led to the Suez crisis in 1956. Here it is necessary only to glance at a typical transaction. The major finances for the Kariba dam in the now defunct Central African Federation were found in part by the World Bank, which used for the purpose sterling deposits contributed by the British Government, and in part by the Colonial Development Corporation. It was thus almost entirely a British-financed enterprise. But the auspices were those of the World Bank and therefore it was the World Bank which appeared as the selfless benefactor, with the result that the contract for the work was not placed in the United Kingdom but given to an Italian firm which had somehow found a way into the magic circle of patronage despite the fact, soon to be established, that it lacked the equipment needed for so large a project. That one glimpse is enough to enable us to discern something of the purpose, and something of the working, of the World Bank as inspired by international finance. It should also be stressed that in many flotations in which the World Bank participates the financial wolf packs of Wall St., sometimes in one combination, sometimes in another, are also to be found operating under the Bank's umbrella, their loans officially secured. Not for nothing did the financial boys take time off from the war to make arrangements for their post-war international lending.

At this stage only one more point need be made about the Final Act of Bretton Woods — perhaps a small point. Harry Dexter White, Assistant Secretary of the U.S. Treasury, whose plan was married to the Keynes plan to form it, was a man of Russian origin and later named by Whittaker Chambers as a Communist agent. On the morrow of his exposure he was reported to have succumbed to a heart attack, but it is said that no identifiable body was produced for burial. I have been unable to check the accuracy of this statement and record it for what it is worth. Certain it is that White was seen no more — at any rate, in the United States.

Those whose concern about the conduct of the war took second place to arranging for themselves an idyllic post-war world evidently relished conference sites which had a sylvan savour. From Bretton Woods to Dumbarton Oaks was but a short spiritual journey. Leaving the conduct of the world-wide conflict to look after itself, or at any rate in the care of competent colleagues, the post-war architects gathered to create an institution which would be the complement, and something more than the complement, to the mechanisms established at Bretton Woods.

It was at once apparent that if the World Bank could be accurately described as an international debt-making agency the United Nations, born at Dumbarton Oaks, could with equal accuracy be described as an international debt collecting agency. But the United Nations, while not repudiating the role, aspired to be something very much more — indeed, to be the embryonic World Government which has been planned for the enslavement of mankind. In the meantime it busies itself with regulating the relationship between nations, while attempting to lay the foundations of the superstructure which will enable it in the not distant future to exercise supreme power. One such interim effort was to undertake nominal responsibility for the waging of the Korean War — a war carefully designed not to result in a victory for either side but to partition the country. It was the United Nations, too, which mobilized a force with astonishing rapidity to go through the motions of frog-marching the British and French troops out of Suez. Its latest triumph was to intervene in the Congo, long before the move for Katanga's secession— to ensure that the Belgian forces which had been keeping order there were booted out and replaced by a rabble array, mustered by the U.N., consisting of Ethiopians, Ghanaians and Heaven knows whom, in direct contravention of its Charter, which expressly forbids it to intervene in the domestic affairs of member states. As the Congo reveals the unscrupulous use made of the United Nations I shall reserve for a later chapter a more detailed analysis of what went on there.

As Harry Dexter White was the organizer of Bretton Woods, so was Alger Hiss, another key Communist agent, the organizer of the Dumbarton Oaks Conference. Curious, is it not, that the building of a post-war world nearer to the heart's desire of the Money Barons should have been entrusted to two traitors in the Kremlin's service? Well, perhaps in the light of what has already been recounted it is not so curious.

The abrupt haste with which the United States dropped Lend-Lease to Great Britain— it was done almost before the mushroom cloud over Hiroshima had time to clear — had a distinct purpose. More accurately, it had several distinct purposes. One was to force the British Government to borrow over £1,000,000,000 from the Transatlantic money lenders. The strings attached to the loan were that Britain should accept the authority of the institutions created at Bretton Woods and Dumbarton Oaks. Another string, about which we can be morally certain, was that British acceptance in principle be pledged in advance to what was about to be cooked up at the Havana conference, which gave birth to the General Agreement on Tariffs and Trade. This Agreement, which consists of a long and complicated series of multilateral arrangements, had for the British nations one enactment of supreme importance, being calculated to destroy the cohesion of the British world. Reference has been made to Wall St.'s strong opposition to the British Imperial Preference system agreed at Ottawa in the 'thirties. The preferences were, and still remain, based on values effective at the time of their origin well over thirty years ago. To make them truly effective today it would be necessary to upgrade them in terms of modern values. But were that to happen, the General Agreement on Tariffs and Trade would nullify the effect by forcing us to pass on the same economic benefits to every other signatory of the Havana pact, and as there are now well over a hundred signatories entitled to this most favoured nation treatment the result, so far as the British world is concerned, would be derisory. Such was the intention.

The Money Power intends that no nation shall be sovereign, that it alone shall exercise sovereign power on earth. The distance it has already travelled towards the fulfilment of its aims is terrifying.

This intention is no mere conjecture. Appearing in 1950 before a sub-committee of the Senate Committee on Foreign Relations in hearings entitled Revision of United Nations Charter, James Paul Warburg of the powerful banking family said : "The past fifteen years of my life (thus including the war years!) have been devoted almost exclusively to studying the problem of world peace and especially the relation of the United States to those problems. These studies led me, 10 years ago, to the conclusion that the great question of our time is not whether or not One World can be achieved, but whether or not One World can be achieved by peaceful means. We shall have World Government whether or not we like it. The question is only whether World Government will be achieved by consent or conquest.

So, reader, there you are—"Whether you like it or not."

The same sentiment may be attributed to Edward Heath. There is no doubt that the British people did not want to enter Europe, but political ideologues and careerists nevertheless secured their entry. The process is given the complimentary title of "democracy" but in truth it represented the biggest single step since the war towards the prison of internationalism propounded with so authoritative a voice by James Paul Warburg.

CHAPTER VI

DEAD SEA FRUITS OF VICTORY

REFERENCES have been made to plans incubated during the war for the liquidation of the British and other Western European Empires, together with some of the means for carrying them out. As soon as the war was over, the policy began of encompassing the betrayal of loyal allies. While the war was still being waged, strong United States pressure was put on the British Government to effect a settlement in India, where there had been continuous Transatlantic support for dissident elements to undermine British rule, and of course Gandhi, Nehru and their colleagues took full advantage of Great Britain's conflict with Germany to preach and practise subversion. Such was the danger that these Congress leaders had to be placed under lock and key for much of the time. As soon as "peace" came the agitation was greatly stepped up and things were made easier by the advent to office in Britain of a Labour Government which prided itself upon "giving freedom to dependent people".

What this meant, in practical terms, was handing over the Indian peasantry to the ruthless will of unscrupulous Indian landlords and money-lenders, without any benevolent and impartial British District Commissioner to see fair play. Corruption, which is endemic in the East, would triumph without let or hindrance, and all that the British had built in India would be allowed to run down and finally disappear. If the Labour Party understood these implications it took good care not to apprise the rank and file of the dark realities inherent in its policy. Instead, it gave Field-Marshal Lord Wavell a deadline for the partitioning of the sub-continent into India and Pakistan, both to enjoy sovereign independence. Because he knew that any such abrupt termination of the British Raj would lead to appalling bloodshed, Wavell to his eternal honour refused to be associated with it. He was therefore replaced by Admiral Lord Mountbatten, whose insouciance in the hauling down of the Union Jack he has evidently imparted to his nephew, now Her Majesty's Consort.

Mountbatten rushed through all the necessary measures with almost incredible light-heartedness, which amounted at times to irresponsible facetiousness. Because honour was to count for nothing in the politics of the post-war world, our solemn undertakings to the Indian Princes were brushed aside while Mountbatten justified the soundness of his appointment to his Labour Masters. Partition was duly agreed and power transferred. As Hindu fell upon Muslim and Muslim upon Hindu nobody knows how many lives were lost in the immediate aftermath. A conservative estimate places the number at 1,000,000

43

but other observers, well placed to judge, believe that over 3,000,000 innocent people lost their lives. This was in addition to innumerable rapings and maimings. The carnage would have been even worse had it not been for the presence of British military formations retained in the country during the process of handing over power.

There was one ironic consequence of the surrender of India to its babus and their Transatlantic sponsors. The British Raj had kept alive Gandhi the "saintly" apostle of Indian freedom, for nearly eighty years. The Indian Government was able to keep him alive for only a few months before he was assassinated by one of his own countrymen.

A few months later Nehru proclaimed India an independent republic which recognized the Queen as Head of the Commonwealth. This was a relationship which, implicitly rejecting allegiance, meant absolutely nothing. It was an empty formula. However, the British Conservatives seem to have found some vague satisfaction in the meaningless title "Head of the Commonwealth", and of all the public men in the British world only Jan Smuts had the nous and boldness to perceive that the formula made absolute nonsense of the whole Commonwealth concept.

Burma, which also had independence bestowed upon it, soon resolved itself into an even ghastlier shambles. The British transferred power to one Aung San, who had served during the war as a Major-General in the Japanese Army. Kingsley Martin, editor of the British left-wing *New Statesman*, attended the "freedom" celebrations for the purpose of handing Aung San a special message of honour from George Bernard Shaw, playwright and Fabian Socialist. Soon afterwards Aung San must have incurred Kingsley Martin's displeasure, because his paper began to refer to the man as "a typical Eastern thug". Displeasure seems also to have been incurred nearer home, for soon assassination put an end to Aung San and almost his entire cabinet. Thereafter civil war broke out between "White-band Communists" and "Red-band Communists" and between various other groups of bandits, some in uniform and some not, and warfare has continued sporadically until the present day. Some years after "independence" an American journalist visited Burma and wrote an article describing how carrion fought carrion for the garbage in the Rangoon streets. That was a perfect comment on what happens to a territory when the British (or other European) presence is withdrawn.

Nor was it the British Empire alone which came under immediate post-war attack.

When the Japanese evacuated the Dutch East Indies they left behind a puppet called Sukarno, who at once formed a "government" which laid claim to rule over the whole vast area. It was in essence a rebellion against Holland. The Dutch authorities in the Indies refused to have any dealings with the rebels and the Dutch in Holland, who had contributed to the allied shipping pool the second largest number of merchant ships of any Western European nation, asked for the immediate release of sufficient vessels to enable an expeditionary force to be sent out east to deal with Sukarno. The release was held up for months — indeed, until it was too late for Holland to take adequate countermeasures. In the meantime Admiral Lord Mountbatten, soon to become Viceroy of India and at this stage Supreme Commander of Allied Forces in South-East Asia, used his authority to compel the local Dutch officials to confer with Sukarno's puppet government. This was the beginning of the end. Before long Holland was dispossessed of her East Indies Empire, where she had maintained peace and prosperity for upwards of three centuries. Eventually life was made so intolerable for the Europeans living there that 600,000 people of Dutch extraction, who had no other homeland, uprooted themselves and were scattered over the world in an endeavour to find countries which would welcome their industry and skill.

Huge mobs of disparate peoples were herded together to form a synthetic nation to which the name Indonesia was given. The U.S. State Department, on the orders of Wall St., ensured that the rabble State should receive American blessings as it received the Kremlin's instant acknowledgement. Both the Americans and the Russians constructed military, naval and air force bases for the Indonesians, both supplied them with arms and the United States taxpayers have also been called upon to find billions of dollars in the way of economic aid. President Kennedy, who had mastered the art of double-speak at least as well as any of his predecessors, prevailed upon Congress greatly to step up annual subsidies on the laughable plea that Indonesia was an anti-Communist bastion. The subsidies have since been reduced to a mere $10,000,000 a year.

France was another victim. The British commander of the troops which landed in Indo-China after Japan's surrender had strict instructions not to do more than establish an Allied "presence". On no account was he to engage Viet-Minh, a Communist puppet outfit which later became an "army of liberation" and finally showed itself in its true colours as a Communist military organization. The result of this initial inactivity on the part of the Allies was to enable Viet-Minh to become firmly established, thereby adding vastly to the difficulty of the French when they reoccupied the territory and, like the Dutch, found a full-scale rebellion on their hands. For years France fought the battle alone. Wall St., which was frantically looking for countries, possible or impossible, upon which to offload American aid, steadfastly refused to allow any supplies to reach the French in Indo-China. That is, until the time of the conflict in Korea. After that time any such discrimination would have been ridiculous.

It is perhaps unfortunate for the French that the discrimination did not continue. As soon as the American aid began to arrive the Americans regarded themselves as the masters of the situation. They insisted upon the three component States — Viet-Nam, Laos and Cambodia — appointing their own ambassadors to Washington and it became the amiable custom of the State Department, when wishing to discuss matters concerning Indo-China, to summon the three ambassadors without reference to the French Ambassador. This was far more than a display of revoltingly bad manners — it was a calculated move to undermine the authority of France in Indo-China.

When the French were fighting the battle of Dien-Bien-Phu, the most critical in the whole war, President Eisenhower said a strange thing: "Viet-Nam," he asserted, "is essential as a market for Japanese products." Such a pronouncement is understandable only when one remembers that Japan had now become a financial colony of Wall St. It is natural that Baruchistan should seek to look after its own! Soon afterwards, at a "Summit" meeting in Europe, the decision was made to partition Indo-China, the northern areas going to the Communists and the southern, nominally, to France. That was the alleged theory of the settlement. The reality was different. Within a very short time South Viet-Nam had gone off the franc and joined the dollar area.

In the final analysis, events in Indo-China can be described as constituting a model in miniature of almost every post-war internationalist policy. Large areas — indeed the world itself — have been partitioned between Communists and nominal anti-Communists, and, where the anti-Communists have acted under Western European influence, that influence has been supplanted by the influence of the United States acting in the interests of the big financial, industrial and commercial combines. That the U.S., through its later policies, found itself landed with a tremendous military problem, involving the employment of an army of upwards of 400,000 strong, cannot have been displeasing to the armament industry or innumerable other contractors, least of all to the makers of hundreds of thousands of bombs dropped with an open-handed largesse on large tracts of impenetrable jungle.

By this time there can scarcely be any doubt about who won the Second World War. It was won by the international lending houses of New York. The Western European nations were all among the losers, although perhaps the greatest losers of all are those millions of former "subject" peoples to whom Western civilization extended protection and the rule of law.

Chapter VII

BOGUS ALARUMS AND EXCURSIONS

AT this point the ambivalence of United States policy should be noted. The great majority of Americans are anti-Communist, so that any Washington Government feels obliged to make anti-Communist noises and even, in a small way, to undertake anti-Communist actions. When on the other hand these actions are at the expense of the Western European nations the secret government in New York will support them, as in the business of getting the Belgians out of the Congo. Thereafter in all likelihood the support will be switched over to rebellious elements calculated to advance the cause of Communism. Thus two main purposes are served— the elimination of Western European influences in overseas territories (in pursuance of Lenin's dictum that the European nations could best be destroyed by attacking them at their peripheries) and the advancement of the general Communist cause. There are also important subsidiary purposes. The more unrest that can be created in the world the greater the benefit to the armaments industry, with which international finance is intimately interwoven, and the greater the impetus towards integrated economies. When the war in Korea was being fought Bernard Baruch went so far as to advocate that the entire United States economy should be brought under centralized control! Nor is this all. The driving of mankind into two nominally antagonistic sheep-pens, as a prelude to merging the pens to form the all-embracing empire over which World
Government intends to rule, requires in all but the final stage an unending series of alarums and excursions.

If the alarums and excursions do not occur naturally they have to be created, even though there may be no specific Western European interests to be destroyed in the process. One such instance was the conflict in Korea. Dean
Acheson, then U.S. Secretary of State (and an avowed friend of Alger Hiss), went out of his way gratuitously to announce that Korea lay outside the bounds of the United States defence system, which was a pretty clear invitation to Northern Koreans to invade South Korea. They did what was expected of them, whereupon the United States Government entered, and stampeded the so-called United Nations into entering, a "cosy" little war which would serve, and did serve, all the subsidiary purposes I have mentioned, besides enabling the United States to play a flamboyant role as the vaunted champion of the anti-Communist cause. Nevertheless the New York Money Power, while willing to cash in on the benefits, was determined that the end result should be a draw and not the crushing defeat of the Communists. American commanders in the field, headed

by the redoubtable General MacArthur, later testified to a Congressional committee that they were not allowed to win the war. Hostilities ended with the virtual restoration of the *status quo*. For what good purpose had so many men died?

Another instance of the duality of American political attitudes was the insurrection against Castro. The anti-Communist force which was to invade Cuba had been organized on American soil with the connivance of the United States Government. Yet that Government was (and remains) so white-anted, with known Communists holding key posts at every level of the administration, that it was possible for a fantastic miscellany of arms to be supplied to members of the force, all with ammunition of a different calibre — which of course rendered them useless. The final betrayal was the withholding of promised air support at a critical stage of the invasion, with the result that it ended in fiasco. Every anti-Communist Cuban was betrayed as every anti-Communist American was betrayed, but such is the general apathy in that country as well as our own, that when details of the infamy were told to Congressional committees few indeed were the Americans moved to make any kind of protest. The final stage of the farce was reached when the late President Kennedy was hailed as a conquering hero for compelling Kruschev to withdraw the nuclear weapons sent to Cuba. As Kruschev had responded with alacrity, the chances are perhaps a million to one that the withdrawal was completely bogus. There is no evidence which would establish Kruschev's good faith, a commodity in which that gentleman did not happen to deal. It is quite certain that if the Soviet Union sent nuclear weapons to Cuba, in Cuba they are still to be found.

A third instance concerns the Congo, about which I shall write at greater length in a subsequent chapter. At the beginning of 1965, by which time the United States at one remove had taken over from Belgium responsibility for that vast territory, action was directed against allegedly pro-Communist rebels in the eastern areas and America was also accused, rightly or wrongly, of bombing a couple of villages said to have been on the Uganda side of the frontier. Vigorous protests were made, not only about the latter incidents (if they ever occurred) but also about arms having been brought to bear, under United States auspices, against the rebels operating in and around Stanleyville. Yet protests were made to Washington not only by the Uganda Government but also by the Governments of Kenya, Tanzania and Zambia, all of which had achieved "independence" with the aid of finances provided by the New York Money Power during long years of local subversion. The pro-Communist lending houses in America had gladly acquiesced in the acceptance by the United States of responsibility for the Congo, for that meant the elimination of Western European influence, but once the United States was installed the lending houses still felt free to sustain the pro-Communist elements waging war against the central authority.

For the most glaring example of Wall St.'s subterranean nexus with the Kremlin we must go back to the war and its immediate aftermath. When Germany was about to be over-run, Henry Morgenthau, Secretary of the Treasury, ordered that American plates for the printing of occupation marks should be sent to the Soviet Union so that the Russians could make what use they liked of them, but of course these notes printed for the Red Army had all to be redeemed by the American taxpayers. Is there any explanation of that act other than that the United States Government was in league with Moscow at the expense of its own citizens? In this instance the overt Government in Washington showed itself to be at one with the secret government in New York, no doubt because at that time the Red Army was in general favour and the American reaction against Communism was still confined to the small group of informed patriots who could conveniently be dismissed from the mind as "cranks". What was the *quid pro quo*? It was even stranger, suggesting that the plot had long ago been incubated.

The dominant elements in Wall St., as might have been expected, had a very special interest in clearing the British out of Palestine and securing as large a part of the country as possible in which to set up a Jewish State. The British Government, on the other hand, felt itself bound to keep some kind of ring for the Palestinian Arabs, who had already been badly betrayed, and with Ernest Bevin, one of the few courageous politicians produced during this century, as Secretary of State for Foreign Affairs, it set a limit to the numbers of Jews to be allowed into the country. There was a howl of protest from World Jewry and a secret organization was set up to take Jews from every part of Europe to ports in Italy and France, where they were embarked for Palestine. The Soviet Union had always sternly discouraged Zionism inside Russia, and when in 1942 General Sikorski, a leader of the Poles in exile, flew to Moscow to negotiate for the Polish forces raised on Russian soil to join the Allies in the West, Stalin gave permission for these forces to be evacuated through Teheran, after which they would come under British auspices, but he made a proviso, inexplicable at the time, that no Polish Jews were to be included among them. At the war's end, however, when the illegal trek to Palestine from all over Europe was in progress, train-load after train-load of Jews, all well fed and dressed, with their pockets bulging with occupation marks, arrived in central Europe from the Soviet Union to join the throng making its way to Palestine. On arrival the trains were met by U.S. Army rabbis, who conducted their occupants to the embarkation ports. Was this the *quid pro quo* for the American plates sent to the Soviet Union? If so, then it is obvious that the secret agreement must have been made at least four years earlier and Stalin must have kept back the Polish Jews for this specific purpose. It is difficult to think of any other reason.

Information about the train-loads of Jews arriving from Russia was made public by General Sir Frederick Morgan, the British architect of the D-Day invasion and at this time head of the European section of the United Nations Relief and Rehabilitation Administration (U.N.R.R.A.) There was a widespread campaign of vilification against the General by the Jewish Press, which did not stop short of branding him a liar. Sir Frederick, probably to conform to the wishes of the British Government, crossed the Atlantic to express regret to Herbert Lehmann, the Jewish head of U.N.R.R.A., who graciously forgave him and allowed him to return to his post. Some months later Sir Frederick Morgan made another revelation. U.N.R.R.A., he said, was being used as a network of Communist espionage and intrigue. There was another roar of protest throughout the world. Lehmann had been succeeded as U.N.R.R.A. chief by the half- Jew, La Guardia, former Mayor of New York. La Guardia without hesitation gave Sir Frederick Morgan the sack. Although these incidents formed no part of the ambivalence of American policy, and although there was certainly nothing bogus about the alarums and excursions they caused, they showed not only the strength of the bonds between New York and Moscow but also the terrifying extent to which Communist H.Q. in the United States had penetrated the U.S. Administration and taken virtual charge of internationalist organisations which the unsuspecting peoples of the West had accepted in all good faith.

For further evidence of the bogus we must cast a glance at the cold war, which from beginning to end was almost entirely fraudulent. The Soviet Union's field of safe manoeuvre was confined to Berlin, where periodically "incidents" were arranged which caused an international pother. These demonstrations, from every practical point of view, were so utterly senseless that they can be explained only on the hypothesis that the intention behind them was to maintain international tensions while the sheep were being shepherded into their pens through such media as the North Atlantic Treaty Organization, the South-East Asia Treaty Organization, the Warsaw Pact and the Baghdad Pact, and while earlier schemes for breaking down national sovereignty such as the Schumann Plan for wedding German and French steel and coal industries were being consolidated. Incidentally, the *Jewish Chronicle* of London is my authority for recording that the Schumann Plan was in fact devised by Lilienthal of Tennessee Valley and Atomic Energy "fame". Lilienthal it was who expressed the belief that the sacred mission of the Jews was to lead mankind into universal brotherhood under World Government, into which the intention of the internationalist policy makers was, and is, to transform the United Nations.

Communist China, possessing a much wider field of safe manoeuvre than Communist Russia, has played a full part in creating the alarums and excursions of the cold war. The occupation of Tibet, it is true, was all too real, but not so the sporadic mock attacks on the off-shore islands occupied by Chiang Kai-shek's troops. There have been, periodically, local struggles for power in Viet-Nam, Laos and Cambodia, but their chief use to Communism was to keep the pot of internationalist agitation on the boil. This may also be said of the incursion of Red China's troops into the remotest fastnesses of the Indian Himalayas.

The most spectacular recent instance of cold war strategy was provided by the late President Kennedy, who, in conjunction with Prime Minister Macmillan, issued in England a communique expressing full confidence in the West's ability to work in harmony with the Communist countries. Three days before, President Kennedy had delighted the Western Berliners by exclaiming "He who thinks it is possible to work with Communist Russia, let him come to Berlin!"

Who was fooled? Alas, pretty well the entire human race.

President Kennedy has not lacked successors. It is the "right-wing" denouncer of Alger Hiss, Richard Nixon, who has done a gigantic deal with the Soviet Union and pioneered the way for the great complexes of the industrial West to build up the power of Mao's China.

Finance capitalism has no conscience and only one final objective – the control of the human race in its entirety.

Chapter VIII

CAMPAIGN AGAINST "ANGLO-PERSIAN"

WE now resume our account of the internationalist attack on British overseas interests. These were not directed solely against our territorial possessions but no less against our spheres of influence, trading posts, and military bases. To show the techniques employed we cannot do better than relate in some detail the events which led up to the theft of our Anglo-Persian oil interests. Oil, of course, is one of the key raw materials of the modern age: without it most industries and all the transport systems would come to a full stop and almost universal starvation would follow. That is why the control of oil is considered an essential weapon in the armoury of those who would control mankind.

In Persia British business and technological brains, British initiative and British capital had built up a prosperous oil industry, with a gigantic refinery at Abadan. Jealous eyes were fixed on the Anglo-Persian enterprise and plans incubated for taking it over. These plans were stepped-up when the pro-British Prime Minister of Persia, General Razmara, extended our oil concessions into the nineteen- nineties.

Soon afterwards, the World Bank sent a mission to the country and brought with it members of a private firm called Overseas Consultants Inc. The Overseas Consultants soon became exceedingly active, prospecting, discovering the terms on which businesses could be taken over, establishing contacts with newspapers in Teheran and enlisting the support of Persian politicians. It is not known whether the politicians were bought, but East is East and it is fair to base one's assumptions on age-old practices.

"Anglo-Persian" almost certainly regarded Overseas Consultants Inc. and the World Bank Mission with deep suspicion and General Razmara, with all the facts at his disposal, was more than suspicious. So assured was he of the subversive nature of the intrusion that he cancelled the licence of Overseas Consultants, perhaps unaware that by offering an affront to the World Bank he was challenging the most formidable power-complex on earth.

I make no charge of cause and effect because I have no evidence to support it. I merely record that almost immediately afterwards General Razmara was dead — assassinated.

A temporary incumbent was found for the Premiership and then little Moussadek took over. The U.S. State Department's Middle East expert, a man called McGhee, arrived in Teheran, where he was closeted for many hours a day with the new Prime Minister. No sooner had he left than Moussadek dishonoured Persia's contractual obligation to Great Britain by nationalizing the Anglo-Persian industry and, in effect, closing down the great refinery at Abadan. U.S. Ambassador Grady was on hand to make a public declaration that although there would be a temporary loss of royalties the Persian Government need have no fear: financially the United States would tide Persia over the crisis.

This was too much even for the timorous British Government and a protest was made to Washington. In response President Truman delivered himself of some conventional claptrap to the effect that he hoped the dispute would be amicably settled. As the Persian move was a *fait accompli* it might seem to have ruled out all possibility of an "amicable settlement", but Moussadek, being a very foolish fellow, took Truman's meaningless statement as a personal reproach. "But," he blurted out, "we approached President Truman before we nationalized the oil-fields and were given the promise of America's neutrality".

"America's neutrality" — what was that if not an injunction for Persia to go ahead with the plans which no doubt had been drawn up by McGhee? The statement made by Ambassador Grady about U.S. financial help during the crisis, and the fact that the Soviet Union was putting on one of its stage growls about "British Imperialism", gave Moussadek all the encouragement he needed. He then went further, uprooting British Consulates all over the country and expelling them. Finally even the British Embassy in Teheran had to pack up and clear out.

It is fashionable these days to sneer at "gun-boat diplomacy", but in all likelihood the despatch of a single British warship to Abadan would have put an end to the persecution of the British in Persia and given Moussadek grave second thoughts about the nationalization of Anglo-Persian oil. There were no orchids to be had by any American President who ordered the bombing of London, and the Soviet Union was much too unsure of itself to risk a war with Great Britain. But the British Government was too frightened to act in defence of British interests and when a warship was sent to Abadan — on the orders of the heroic Herbert Morrison, then Foreign Secretary — its role was confined to evacuating British citizens. Heavily indebted to the New York Money-Lenders, the only policy which Britain pursued was the habitual post-war policy of scuttle. In former times, whenever there had been trouble with Persia, a brigade from what is now known as Pakistan always restored the balance and kept the peace. But of course the modern Pakistan, greedily absorbing "American aid", merely added its voice to the general clamour against the evils of "Imperialism".

The dispute between Great Britain and Persia dragged on, and in an effort to avoid stale-mate the two Governments accepted the offer of the good offices of Averell Harriman, a highly placed stooge of the Money Power to whom Washington had given many delicate assignments, including the post of U.S. Ambassador in Moscow during the war. Harriman was to act as "an honest broker", but so little does honesty matter in the post-war world that the "honest broker" had no compunction, as soon as he arrived at Teheran airport, in telling a press-conference that, come what may, the United States would continue to stand financially behind the Persian Government. The Harriman mission achieved nothing.

Then what the present writer had expected duly happened. The suggestion was made that the World Bank should take over the control of what had been the Anglo- Persian oilfields, as the Persians were palpably unable to get the oil flowing again on their own. A kite to this effect was flown by Henry Morgenthau Junior, former Secretary to the U.S. Treasury whom we have briefly met earlier in this narrative. World Bank control would be an admirable means of demonstrating that the Bank could not be flouted as it had been flouted by General Razmara's treatment of its protégé, Overseas Consultants Inc. Accordingly, a World Bank mission consisting of two "experts" arrived in Teheran to consult with the British and Persian Governments.

I have mentioned the tendency of the internationalist policy-makers to overplay their hand. This was one such occasion. The move to give the affronted World Bank control over Persian oil was just a little too blatant and more than a little too far removed from its acknowledged role. The discussions came to nothing. What is remarkable, however, is that the two World Bank "experts", after the negotiations had broken down, stayed on as financial advisers to the Persian Government, which they represented at the wider conference that finally disposed of the matter. This fact alone shows the extent to which international affairs are "cooked" by the controlling cabal.

The final settlement was shameful to Britain. Persian oil was to remain nationalized and its exploitation was to be entrusted to a consortium in which the British were to have only a 40% interest — in an industry which they alone had created. American oil companies, reaping where they had not sown, were also to have a 40% interest and the remaining 20% interest was to go to European oil companies affiliated to the American companies. No Briton was to be allowed to take any part in the management of the enterprise and no British technician was to be allowed back into Abadan. British acquiescence represented at the time a scuttle on a truly grand scale. Yet Harold Macmillan declared, in the hearing of the present writer, that the Persian oil dispute settlement was "most satisfactory". Some of us thought, on the contrary, that it represents the depth of Great Britain's humiliation, but we have since learned to our sorrow that there were still greater depths awaiting us.

The theft of our oil industry had of course been plotted long before — while the war still raged. Roosevelt said to his son: "I want you to do something for me, Elliott. Go find Pat Hurley, and tell him to get to work drawing up a draft memorandum guaranteeing Iran's independence and her self-determination of her economic interests." The occasion was the Teheran conference, called, as most people believed, to discuss means of defeating the German enemy, not of robbing the loyal British ally of her Anglo-Persian oil industry.

One interesting by-product of the dispute should perhaps be mentioned. Percipient observers of the international scene must be aware that after both world wars a crop of crowned heads rolled in the sand. As such happenings are never accidental, the assumption must be that the Money Power has a rooted objection to the principle of Monarchy.

The reason, no doubt, is that historically the role of the Monarch has been to protect the people against those who were their oppressors, sometimes "wicked barons", at other times the great vested interests, and at yet other times the usurers — particularly the usurers. That is why Edward I of England, a great King, should be honoured by every Englishman. To historically informed minions of the Money Power, however, his name is accursed. After endeavouring to secure fair dealing for his subjects against the extortions of money, by means of a notable piece of legislation called the Statute of Jewry, and after his discovery that the Statute was being circumvented in every possible way, he decided to expel the Jews from England. This and many other endeavours by the Monarchies in other lands to save their subjects from persecution have built up a strong bias against Kingship in those who today aspire to rule the world, with the result that almost all the crowned heads have disappeared from off the face of the earth.

Cock-a-hoop over the victory scored against the British in the final settlement of the Anglo-Persian oil dispute, the international policy-makers thought that advantage should be taken of the occasion to get rid of the Shah of Persia. A "revolt" was thereupon stage-managed which resulted in the Shah's having to take refuge in Italy, but once again the Money Power had overplayed its hand.

Tradition proved too strong and the Shah had to be brought back again, after which the luckless Moussadek, easily expendable, languished in a Persian jail.

As we shall see, the financial overlords had better luck when they turned their thoughts to getting rid of the British-sponsored Hashemite dynasty in Iraq. The King, Queen and other members of the Royal Family were butchered and the British Ambassador hastened to come to terms with their assassins.

Chapter IX

SUEZ CATASTROPHE

AN even greater humiliation than that of Abadan was the British humiliation at Suez. Here again the World Bank had a part to play, perhaps a larger part than has been revealed.

Egypt had languished under Turkish suzerainty in the days when Turkey, rotted by inertia and corruption, had become known throughout the world as "the sick man of Europe". When British guidance replaced Turkish in the latter part of the last century Egypt was put on its feet and made a going concern, an arrangement favourable to both nations in that Great Britain derived much strategical advantage from being in military control over the Suez Canal, with a hinterland of incalculable value in the event of war. During the First World War full use was made of these assets, and apart from a revolt by Senussi tribesmen the British position was maintained without trouble. In the inter-war period, although there was a devolution which entailed the relinquishment of much authority, Egypt remained a British sphere of influence and the possession of military bases enabled us to retain control of the Canal. During the Second World War our successful operations against the Italians and Germans in North Africa would have been impossible had we not been able to use Egypt as a base and vast assembly-ground for the build up of our forces.

After the second war was over, and bearing in mind the brief which General Marshall took to the Quebec Conference in 1943, it is a matter of no surprise that the special British position in Egypt should have been challenged and strong pressure brought to bear for its termination. The British agreed to concentrate all their forces in the Canal Zone, but this was not enough for those interests which were determined to bring our influence in the Middle East to an end. Acting under duress, the British Government signed a pact with Nasser whereby we were to withdraw our 80,000 troops from the Canal Zone and in return were allowed to retain our bases, worth hundreds of millions of pounds, which could be reactivated in time of war and which meanwhile were to be in the keeping of British caretakers dressed in civilian clothes. It was not a satisfactory agreement, as events were to prove.

The World Bank, with the U.S. and British Governments in tow, was to finance the building of the High Aswan Dam project. The Bank and the two Governments agreed to find the money in given ratios and there was every expectation that the construction would go ahead when suddenly negotiations came to an abrupt end. In return for its loans the World Bank had demanded what amounted to virtual control over the entire Egyptian economy — a demand that, not unnaturally, the Egyptian Government refused to entertain. Thereupon the Bank made known that its support would not be forthcoming and the United States and British Governments obediently followed suit.

During this period, Great Britain had been carrying out her part in the pact with Nasser by pulling out her troops from the Canal Zone and the withdrawal of the last British Tommy was roughly coterminous with the breakdown of the World Bank's negotiations for the financing of the Aswan Dam scheme. Nasser acted at once. Tearing up the pact he had made with Britain, which Britain for her part had already honoured, the Egyptian Government nationalized the Suez Canal, expelled all British pilots and technicians, and made untenable the position of the British civilian caretakers in charge of our bases.

During the summer of 1956 there was a movement of British trucks and tractors across Luneburg Heath in Germany, bound for Hamburg and embarkation. Later they made their way down the centre of England from Tyneside ports for re-embarkation in the South. Something was clearly about to happen. In October, to the general amazement, R.A.F. planes began to bomb Egyptian airfields and other targets while Israeli troops crossed the frontier into Sinai and were soon within ten miles of the Suez Canal.

Meanwhile British and French forces were being assembled in Cyprus. When all was ready, they set forth at night under a naval escort without navigation lights. An astonishing discovery was then made. The expedition found the entire United States Sixth Fleet drawn up in line to stop it, or at any rate so to intimidate it that it would believe it had no option but to turn back. Had British politicians been in charge, that no doubt would have happened, but the convoy was led by a British admiral, a very different breed of man. The admiral gave the command to show navigation lights and the convoy sailed in between the American warships to reach its destination at Port Said and Port Fuad. The attempt at intimidation thus utterly failed.

Nevertheless the Money Power and its agents in the White House and State Department had other means at their disposal to enforce their will. While it had proved impossible to frighten a British admiral, it was all too easy to frighten British politicians. Anthony Eden, then Prime Minister, who had launched the enterprise which he lacked the will to sustain in the teeth of Transatlantic displeasure, announced in the House of Commons that the British and the French had gone back to Egypt temporarily to reoccupy the abandoned bases in the Canal Zone. He repeated with much stress the word "temporarily", but what conceivable use a purely temporary reoccupation could serve was not explained. When he made his speech neither Eden nor anybody else knew quite how apt the word was to prove. The British and French troops established wide perimeters within which to assemble their strength, so all was in readiness for the break-through which would again bring the Canal Zone under Western control. Suddenly the whole movement was stopped dead in its tracks. Within an incredibly short time the United Nations had gathered together a force (which to Canada's shame included a Canadian contingent) which went through the motions of frogmarching the British and French troops out of Egypt. What had happened?

For many weeks the affair was wrapped in mystery. It was obvious that the British and French could have secured their objectives had they been allowed to proceed, and that it would have taken more than a United Nations rabble to dislodge them. As there had been no surrender by the fighting men, clearly there must have been a surrender by the politicians. The Soviet Government, making its traditional snarl, had threatened to bombard Britain with atomic missiles, but only the very simple took the Russian threat seriously.

Not until an afternoon in February of 1957 was any daylight forthcoming. On that afternoon Field-Marshal Lord Montgomery, addressing a senior officers' course at Camberley in Surrey, announced that he could explain what had happened to cause the debacle. Washington, he said, had got in touch with London during the daytime on November 6 and warned the British Government that unless the British and French forces obeyed the "cease fire" which *was to be* passed by the United Nations Assembly that evening (note how these matters are "cooked" in advance) full financial sanctions would be employed against both countries. The nerves of Eden and his Cabinet colleagues collapsed under the strain, and Harold Macmillan, who had previously been in favour of the enterprise, turned abruptly against it and so stepped into Anthony Eden's shoes as Prime Minister.

An officer attending Field-Marshal Montgomery's lecture was so horrified at the thought of an internationalist power which was able to dictate what a British Government should or should not do that he conceived it to be his duty at whatever cost to make as widely known as possible the ultimatum which had put an end to Britain's influence in the Middle East. The officer asked the present writer to publish the information, and this was done. Not long afterwards I received a letter from Lord Perth, then Minister of State at the Foreign Office, telling me that the information was incorrect. I replied requesting that the Minister be good enough to ask Lord Montgomery whether he had in fact given the information to the senior officers' course in Camberley and in due course the Minister wrote to tell me that he had been in touch with Montgomery, who denied that he had made the statements attributed to him "on this confidential occasion". As in the meantime I had been able to check the accuracy of what was said with two other officers who were present at the lecture I was not impressed by the Minister's disclaimer, and it is now common knowledge that the British Government had been dragooned by Washington into calling off the military operations in Egypt precisely as my informants had told me.

The results of the British Government's surrender to the Transatlantic blackmailers were catastrophic. Nasser took over the British bases, British property in Egypt was sequestrated and Britain has never recovered from the loss of "face" attendant upon her humiliation, inflicted by a so-called "friend and ally".

One remarkable fact remains to be recounted. Although the train of events which led to the disaster had been triggered off by the World Bank's demand to control the entire Egyptian economy, followed by its refusal to finance the Aswan High Dam project, the World Bank continued to have excellent relations with the Egyptian Government, and throughout the crisis of the British and French landings and the subsequent evacuation the Bank's special commissioner was at hand and in frequent consultation with President Nasser. What is more, when Russia eventually agreed to undertake the construction of the Aswan Dam — a labour which has not met with conspicuous success — the World Bank and the Egyptian Government remained on the same friendly terms. Strange! Or perhaps not so strange in these days of global conspiracy.

Chapter X

IRAQ AND CYPRUS

THE repercussions of the Suez crisis were many and grave. One of the first was that the Kingdom of Jordan, a British-created state ruled over by a British sponsored monarch, gave marching orders to Glubb Pasha and other British officers who had been in command of Jordanian troops. That alone shows to what extent British prestige had been trampled into the Levantine mire.

Some months later there was a rebellion in another Arab state, ruled over by another British-sponsored monarch — a state in which Britain had large oil stakes. This was Iraq, captured from the Turks by the British during the First World War. It was a very different kind of rebellion from the mild measures taken in Jordan. Baghdadi mobs literally tore to pieces the pro-British Prime Minister, parts of whose body were carried in triumph all over the city. They then broke into the Royal Palace, murdered the King and Queen and their family and hailed as their President the victorious leader of the insurrection, one General Kassem.

The action taken by the British, no doubt on Transatlantic orders, was very curious. They flew troops, not to Iraq, but to Jordan. The United States sent troops into the Lebanon. While these measures were engaging the attention of the world the regicides of Iraq were given time in which to consolidate their power. Moreover, although King Feisal had been placed on his throne by the British, and was entitled to British protection, the British Ambassador, prowling like a hyena in the shadows, scarcely waited for the blood on the hands of the regicides to dry before he extended good-will towards the new dispensation. The British governess of the Royal Family, who had witnessed the murders, was flown to England, held incommunicado from the Press, and then sent to an undisclosed destination. What diabolical interests were being subserved by all this covering-up for, and general acquiescence in, such villainy?

Could it possibly be that New York, with Washington and London in tow, had agreed with Moscow upon the partitioning of the Middle East? That would account for the diversionary moves in Jordan and the Lebanon. It would also explain the instant appearance in Iraq of Russian advisers to replace the British and the great extension of Communist influence, an influence which seems not to have been changed when, a few years later, Kassem himself was overthrown. Naturally, as soon as the diversion had had the desired effect, the troops from Jordan and the Lebanon were quietly withdrawn. Everything was as it had been except that Great Britain had lost its last remaining sphere of influence in the Middle East.

The British and French forces bound for Suez, it will be remembered, had embarked upon the invasion from Cyprus. Long before this time, as part of the policy of eradicating Britain's overseas influence, the island had been marked down as a British strategic centre in the Eastern Mediterranean and plans made for the ousting of the British. When it had been ceded by the Turks it contained a largely Turkish population, but after the war between Turkey and Greece in the early 'twenties, resulting in the devastating defeat of Greece, tens of thousands of Greek refugees from what was then called Asia Minor sought protection under the Union Jack in Cyprus and forty years later Greek Cypriots were more numerous than Turkish Cypriots. Although Cyprus had never in history come under the rule of Greece, Greek Cypriots had a sentimental feeling that the island should become a part of the country of their origin. The parrot cry became "Enosis", which meant union with Greece.

After the Second World War the pro-Communist elements in New York, bankers associated with the Kuhn, Loeb financiers of the Bolshevik Revolution, planned that Greece herself should become part of the Soviet Union's Empire. A rebellion was instigated to bring this about and Greece today would be behind the Iron Curtain but for British intervention — one of the few moves made not only without reference to the American Overlord but in defiance of the Overlord's plan for the ordering of the post-war world. President Roosevelt, when he heard of the landing of British troops near Athens, was furious. "How dare they!" he thundered. As certain actions of Winston Churchill have been criticised in this book, let this action at least be accounted unto him for righteousness.

During the long and difficult period in the late forties, when Great Britain was endeavouring to cope with the insurrection and when American aid under the Marshall plan was going to all and sundry, an exception was made in the case of the Greek Loyalists, and all the time the British bore the burden of supporting the Loyalist cause not a dollar was sent to Greece. It became known, largely as a result of some acrimonious correspondence between the present writer and Mrs. Clare Booth Luce, soon to be appointed U.S. Ambassador to the Vatican, that the embargo had the full approval of Bernard Baruch, the mastermind. Afterwards, the burden on the British being too heavy — that at all events was the excuse — and American public opinion taking a more balanced view after the enraptured acclaim of the Red Army had died down, the United States accepted responsibility for Greece. But Great Britain remained in possession of Cyprus, which had been ceded many years before.

Towards the middle 'fifties there moved a curious figure among the pro-Communist tycoons of Wall St. The figure was draped in the habiliments of a high functionary of the Greek Orthodox Church and wore a beard. For some months this High Priest negotiated with the international financiers and eventually returned to Cyprus with some thousands of dollars in his pocket to begin a terrorist campaign directed, for propaganda purposes, at furthering the cause of Enosis. His name was Makarios and his rank that of an archbishop.

The United States, engaged in encircling the earth with military bases, had been conducting negotiations for the establishment of very large military, naval and air force bases in Greece, and as soon as the signature of the Greek Government had been obtained Radio Athens began to broadcast Enosis propaganda to the terrorists in Cyprus. The main motive of those who stage-managed the event was not to secure the union of Cyprus and Greece, about which they could not have cared less, but to get the British out of Cyprus.

The terrorist campaign soon reached its peak of intensity. It consisted largely of the ambushing of British troops and the shooting down of British troops and their women folk when they were off duty, unarmed and unprepared. Radio Athens continued to broadcast encouragement (despite the fact that it was Britain which had saved Greece from being made captive by the Communist tyranny) and as the murder rate mounted action against the "Holy Man" became an urgent necessity. Makarios was seized and sent in exile to the Seychelles.

In the meantime, however, the dry-rot in the British Government cut ever more deeply, and although a British Minister had declared that Cyprus would remain British "for ever" — a sure sign of impending scuttle — the will to retain the island progressively weakened, until in response to the pressures exerted by the financial power which backed him, together with the representations of a left-wing Little Englander sent there as Governor, Makarios was restored to the scene of his crimes. The Archbishop of Canterbury, in no way concerned with the innocent British blood which had been shed under the auspices of Makarios, invited him to attend the Lambeth Conference of the Church of England in London — an invitation which the archterrorist declined. However, the British Government was now determined to reach an agreement with him. After a meeting of Greek and Turkish Ministers at Zurich there was a London conference at which a tentative agreement was drawn up, in which Cyprus was to enjoy full sovereign independence under a constitution wherein special provision was made for safeguarding the interests of the Turkish minority. Great Britain with great difficulty managed to secure for herself a couple of untenable bases on the island — bases so narrow that they could easily be over-run, and so placed that the British garrisons would have to rely upon the Cypriot Government even for their supply of drinking water. It was an ignominious surrender of the sovereignty which had been an essential feature in maintaining at least some measure of harmony between Greek and Turkish Cypriots.

The agreement was confirmed at a conference in London, where the murderous Makarios had the red carpet rolled out for him, being wined and dined and received in the highest places in the land. That, like the immediate approach by the British Ambassador in Baghdad to offer the hand of friendship to the regicides who murdered the monarch placed by the British on the throne of Iraq, was no doubt the British Government's idea of "diplomacy". "After all, my dear fellow, we must be realists," was their apologia, before and since, for surrendering to enemies with blood-stained hands. When members of the organization founded by the present writer make public protests about the arrival in Britain of such murderers, or leaders of murderous movements, they are arrested by the police, brought before Bow Street magistrates and fined, sometimes quite heavily.

There was one ironical sequel to the ousting of the British from the control of Cyprus. The clauses in the constitution safeguarding the interests of the Turkish Cypriots proved largely inoperative and the Turks, becoming disaffected, organized large-scale riots against the Makarios Government. Makarios, who had been so content with the independence bestowed on Cyprus that his original cry of "Enosis", or union with Greece, was dropped, again invoked the idea of Enosis as a weapon to use against the rebellious Turkish Cypriots. To deal with the mounting lawlessness in the island the United Nations sent in a strong force to keep order and this force, believe it or not, contained a large contingent of British troops. One of the duties of these troops was to fight the Turkish Cypriots who had been their supporters and sympathisers when they were holding the ring for the Turks in Cyprus. After some weeks the British Government decided to recall their contingent, whereupon urgent representations were made to London by the U.N. authorities to reconsider its decision on the ground that only the British were able to cope with the situation.

Why should it be wrong and wicked for the British, under the Union Jack, to maintain order in Cyprus, but perfectly permissible, and indeed desirable for them to do so under the pale blue and white flag of the United Nations? The answer, of course, is that the first role was national and the second international and that no major control in the post-war world must be exercised unless under international auspices — that is to say, under the control of the New York Money Power.

Chapter XI

MOPPING UP THE EMPIRE

BEFORE we travel down the continent of Africa, where the take-over bidders and the leaders of the big financial combines have acted with total irresponsibility and greed for power, it will be as well to take a look at other territories which have been under attack, from within as well as from without, in the gigantic campaign to smash the British world system.

When the Japanese surrendered at Singapore and forces controlled by Admiral Lord Mounbatten took over, battalion after battalion of Indian troops was landed, as though the Indians were the actual deliverers. The over-whelmingly preponderant part in breaking the Japanese in Burma (the nearest theatre of war) was played by the British Army — despite the Hollywood film which displayed its conquest as the work of the Americans under the leadership of the ever valiant Errol Flynn — and it was the hope and expectation of the Britons who had languished for years in Japanese prison camps that they would have the opportunity of welcoming British Tommies, whom they knew had formed the backbone of the assault on the Japanese all the way from Inchon to Rangoon. Yet not one was landed in Singapore until the city was crammed with Indian soldiers. Here was no accident. Mountbatten later explained that British troops were not immediately available for the purpose, which was nonsense. They could have been made available.

Symbolism plays a large part in the armoury of our internationalist enemies. When the liberating forces arrived, the entire population of Singapore turned out to cheer them, the children of all races waving their little Union Jacks. Before long, however, steps were taken to make the people aware that such manifestations of loyalty were not required of them; that their thoughts now had to be directed to the attainment of "merdeka" (independence).

This was related to me in the 'fifties by Mr. Ong, President of the Straits Chinese British Association, when on a visit to London. He said, in reply to my question, that the desired change in the habit of thinking was propounded by British officials themselves, no doubt as the result of some Colonial Office directive. This would suggest that Great Britain's war-time Government, under Transatlantic pressure, had felt itself obliged to give a pledge to wind up its colonial system. I asked Mr. Ong why those loyal to the British connection had offered no resistance to its would-be destroyers. He replied, sadly: "We have been accustomed to look to the British in Singapore and Malaya for our leadership, but now we do not receive it". Clearly the great decadence had already engulfed the British communities in South-East Asia.

The "merdeka" campaign by this time was making rapid progress. It was helped forward by a Baghdadi Jew, David Marshall, who became Singapore's Chief Minister, and then by his successor, Lim Yew Hock. There was a simultaneous, though rather more mannerly, campaign being conducted in Malaya under the auspices of Abdul Rahman. Both campaigns seemed to enjoy the blessing of the Colonial Office in London, which sent out a flashy, publicity-seeking "diplomat", Malcolm MacDonald (son of Ramsay MacDonald) as Governor. Malcolm sought to ingratiate himself with the peoples of Singapore and Malaya by having himself perpetually photographed in bathing trunks or walking hand-in-hand with local belles along the sea-shore. If the policy had been deliberately to destroy the prestige of the British Sovereign's representative, and therefore of the Crown itself, it could not have been better contrived.

What future historians may find surprising is that, although the British Government was fully behind the 'merdeka" movement, the politicians of all parties and races in Singapore and Malaya made anti-British slogans their main stock-in-trade and did so not only without London's protest but in the sunshine of London's approval. British instincts had become perverted by a strange kind of political masochism. How else can one explain such craven obeisance to subversive elements by a great Power on the very morrow of the victory won by its sons in a war of world-wide dimensions? The historians may find another fact no less perplexing. While Britain was being subjected to systematic insult and abuse by the Malayan politicians, British forces were deployed in the jungles of Malaya fighting Communist guerrillas and thereby ensuring the safety of the professional denigrators of their country. I have had much to say about the pressures brought to bear by the malignant New York Money Power, and what I have said is true. But those pressures would have failed but for the treasonable acquiescence of successive British Governments, of British political parties, of the British bureaucracy, of the British Press and Broadcasting Corporation, of the British Churches, of the leaders of British communities overseas, and of the British people themselves, although there may be some excuse for the people in that they had no idea of the brainwashing and other conditioning processes to which they were being subjected.

After Malaya and Singapore had won their "independence", which in days to come they may have cause bitterly to regret, there remained three other territories in that part of the world to be rid of their British "overlord" — North Borneo, Brunei and Sarawak. A plan had long been prepared to take care of this little matter. There was to be formed a Malaysian Federation consisting of

Malaya, Singapore and the three states in Borneo and — with Brunei alone at present standing aloof — the Federation has duly come into being. The full scheme envisaged a South-East Asian Federation, formed by the countries I have just mentioned, together with Indonesia and the Philippines, and it may be that the initial federation of Malaysia, still under some kind of British influence, was not in line with Wall St. policy. At any rate Indonesia, which has been heavily financed by the United States and which has received arms from the so-called Communist bloc, has laid claim to North Borneo and is waging a somewhat cautious "hot war" against its British, Australian and New Zealand defenders. Hostilities are now suspended, but who can doubt that the creation of the larger South-East Asian Federation will be one of the terms of the settlement. That all traces of British influence will be obliterated and that the Dollar Empire will hold sway over the entire region? Indeed, Malaya and Singapore, not awaiting the full consummation, have this year (1967) withdrawn from the sterling area and abolished preferences over a wide range of British goods.

It may seem a long jump from North Borneo to the Central Mediterranean, but when there is an Empire to be liquidated distance matters not at all. The war had not been long in progress when the British Left- Wing, which throughout its existence had vehemently denounced "British Imperialism", was given every reason to be grateful to the "Blimps" (although of course they would never admit it) whose foresight had placed at Britain's disposal such places as Malta, soon to win fame as the George Cross Island, and the Rock of Gibraltar. It was not to be supposed that the liquidators would leave Malta out of account in the course of their systematic laying waste of the British Empire. The method, as always, was that of internal subversion. When the business began, however, the Maltese were so little anti-British that their strongest political party at the time advocated absorption of Malta by Great Britain so that, among other benefits, they would be assured of British citizenship, and all the advantages of the British Welfare State and of Treasury responsibility for the sustenance of their economy. Negotiations were opened with the British Labour Government, but — fortunately perhaps — no agreement was reached. Thereupon Dom Mintoff, the leading proponent of union, turned in his tracks and became a violent anti-British advocate of complete independence outside the Commonwealth. His more balanced opponent, whose policy was independence within the Commonwealth, eventually took over and Malta's independence was negotiated on that basis. Although the British taxpayer was called upon to find many millions of pounds to compensate the Maltese for the closing-down of the British naval dockyards, no vestige of British sovereignty was to remain and in the event of war the island could be offered as a base to any bidder.

Then there is Gibraltar. Franco, like many before him, has repeatedly laid claim to the Rock, and nothing would please the liquidators of Empire more than that it should pass from British to Spanish hands. But a snag arises when the claimant is Franco. After all, did not Bernard Baruch contribute a substantial amount for the formation of the International Brigade, which fought on the Communist side in the Spanish Civil War? Has not Baruchistan proclaimed Franco a fascist monster? In the meantime perhaps the matter may be settled by placing Gibraltar under the command of Nato or even of the United Nations. The one indefensible thing, apparently, is that it should remain under the control of the British, who captured the Rock over two hundred and fifty years ago and have been there ever since.

Apart from Africa, what remains? Well, there is, of course, Aden. Aden has been of immense value in safeguarding Britain's sea-road to the East and her approach to the vital oil-fields without which her industries would come to a full stop and her people would starve. Plans are rapidly being carried out for the complete withdrawal of British forces from the Aden Protectorate and the virtual abandonment of any British role east of Suez – all because the order went forth, when General Marshall was briefed in 1943, that Great Britain was to be left a toe-hold nowhere on earth. In the meantime British soldiers are permitted the privilege of dying to keep the Yemeni raiders at bay.

Such is the pattern. But where in the public life of Great Britain will any spark of anger be found? That the happiness of hundreds of millions of people depended upon the continuance of paternal British administrations cannot be denied; that their happiness has been turned to misery by the withdrawal of those administrations is proved by events. Should there be any British minds brooding upon these things, let them find what comfort they can in the statement of their former Prime Minister, Harold Macmillan, that they "have never had it so good" — a statement supported by his catalogue of washing-machines, television-sets and refrigerators which have found their way into British homes.

To what abysmal depths has a once proud and mighty people sunk?

Chapter XII

DIABOLISM IN AFRICA

WHAT has happened in Africa since the war might have been planned and executed by a criminal lunatic of genius — some diabolist, perhaps, whose derangement took the obsessional form, in one territory after another, of reproducing a pattern in which Western European institutions were perverted with a fiendish delight in sheer mockery. There has certainly been a reckless disregard of the consequences to the human beings who were the victims of this maniacal lust for parody, for extremes of ridicule, and for the debasement and destruction of every civilizational value which had rescued a continent from barbarism and filth.

The first clear indication of what portended was the news that "American" agents were busy in the Sudan working up the anti-British agitation which, in a very short time, was to lead to the granting of independence on the basis of one man one vote. So utterly bewildered were the Sudanese, especially in the south, by the paraphernalia of a general election that steps were taken, under the auspices of British officialdom, to give to the "democratic" processes a kind of kindergarten simplicity. One of the devices was to delineate the difference between the rival candidates by pictorial symbols. Thus the symbol of one candidate was an elephant, of another a spear. Nobody seems to have been disconcerted when it was discovered that the Sudanese imagined they were expected to vote, not for the candidate behind the symbol, but for the symbol itself. This is how a *Daily Telegraph* correspondent described the discussion which he heard when visiting a group of Sudanese tribes-men. Some were in favour of voting for the spear, because the spear was a useful weapon, a manly weapon and a weapon which could be used to kill their enemies or to fend them off. Others agreed that much value attached to the spear but insisted that it would be better to vote for the elephant. After all, the elephant was the biggest of animals, it provided much meat and, above all, the selling of its tusks to European traders was most profitable. For hours, for days, perhaps for weeks, the argument went on as to whether the tribe should vote for the spear or the elephant. One result of the farce was that, when the general election was over, and the victorious party duly installed in office, there was disaffection in the south and ruthless reprisals by the Government caused thousands of Sudanese to flee over the Uganda frontier to seek British protection. It is heartrending to record that military forces and police, led by British officers who were acting in accordance with the direction of the British Governor, rounded up most of the refugees and handed them back to their persecutors. Another result was the clamping-down by the Sudanese Government on all Christian missionary efforts.

The same electoral lunacy was re-enacted in Ghana, as in many other territories. Ghana, however, provided one or two special features of its own. Kwame NKrumah, who had failed his bar examinations in London but nevertheless was given an American doctorate, was at the time in prison serving a sentence for sedition. His future constituents were told that his spirit walked the streets of the constituency at night in the guise of a white cat, and party officials arranged for charabanc loads of Ghanaians to visit the district after dark in the hope of seeing this wonderful sight. NKrumah also told the people that if they voted for him they would be allowed to ride free in perpetuity on Accra's public transport system. NKrumah enjoyed rapid promotion from prison to the highest position in the land. The Independence Day celebrations were honoured by the presence of a British Princess of Royal Blood, who was photographed dancing with NKrumah — a preliminary, it may be, to his reception in England as the honoured guest of Her Majesty and the entrusting to him of the news that another Royal child was about to be born, before any word of the news was made known to the British public. It was on this occasion that he was made a member of Her Majesty's Most Honourable Privy Council— an appointment which he still retained after he had declared Ghana to be a Republic and himself its President. His next step was to terrorise his political opponents, some of whom fled, some were killed and some were imprisoned without trial for ten years. Not that trials were necessarily a safeguard. When Ghana's Chief Justice acquitted three of these opponents of the alleged crimes with which they were charged NKrumah sacked him on the instant, ordered a new trial and the wretched trio were duly sentenced to death. Then Nkrumah himself was sacked – during his incautious absence on a visit to Peking. A subsequent commission discovered that he had insisted on pocketing a ten per cent bribe on all contracts, amounting to scores of millions of pounds, awarded in Ghana.

Nigeria received her own independence, after its disparate medley of races had also enjoyed the glorious "democratic" privilege of voting for pictorial symbols. Its Governor-General — the Queen's representative — was to be one Azikiwe, better known as Zik, who had been Prime Minister of Eastern Nigeria. In this earlier capacity he had used public funds to bolster up the African Continental Bank, of which he was President. A Commission of Enquiry reported that his conduct had not reached the required standard. No matter! Post-war standards being what they are, there was nothing to prevent his subsequent elevation to the position of Viceroy, as it were, of Her Majesty the Queen. Indeed, when Nkrumah's Ghana fell from grace, the British politicians and press began to boost Nigeria as the ideal example of how Western democracy could be made to work in Africa. This task became more than a little difficult when the Nigerians showed that they took their democracy seriously enough to murder during the space of a few days no less than three Prime Ministers (one Federal, the other two Territorial) and thousands of lesser luminaries.

It would be tedious to follow the tracing of much the same pattern throughout what had been British and French administered colonies all over the Western part of Africa. Let us look, instead, at the territories lying in the eastern part of the continent. Forces under British command had driven the Italians out of Abyssinia, Eritrea and Italian Somaliland. The fiat had evidently gone forth that Great Britain was to reap no fruits of victory in the form of spheres of influence, and we were soon scampering at speed from the scene of our conquests. There remained British Somaliland, which we had occupied and defended since Victorian times. Naturally the Transatlantic Lords of Misrule would not tolerate our remaining in this country, but there was a certain difficulty in the handing over of power because the inhabitants were nomadic tribes preoccupied with such matters as grazing grounds and inter-tribal vendettas and they showed no interest in getting rid of their British protectors. Therefore a synthetic "independence" movement was manufactured, largely by British officials acting on Colonial Office instructions, and eventually a comic-opera outfit masquerading as a government was invested with the reins of power, after which what had been British Somaliland was absorbed in what had been Italian Somaliland to form the "independent" state of Somalia, much to the discontent of the Dolbahanta and other tribes which, losing British protection, were soon being dragooned by the central government in Mogadishu and treated abominably by the Abyssinians all along their frontier.

The problem of Kenya, next to be tackled, was a much more difficult one, because the country — unlike British Somaliland — was not a desert but in parts extraordinarily fertile, and its European community consisted of upwards of sixty thousand people, mostly British. These settlers, by hard work, by continuity of purpose and by the exercise of the high European skills, had turned a land previously ravaged by warring tribes, by sickness, by malnutrition, by the practice of evil cults, into a prosperous country run on a civilized basis. What before had been barely a subsistence economy was made into a thriving economy, efficient medical services were introduced to stamp out plague and bring succour to the sick, good roads were laid down, the Africans were taught how to conserve their land against erosion, irrigation schemes were launched, and police and military forces under British leadership put an end to internecine tribal warfare so that the peoples were able to live in peace and contentment.

If the British were to be kicked out of Kenya — and, as we have seen, the elimination of Great Britain's world power was one of Wall Street's main post-war objectives — then it was obvious that these civilizational values had to be shattered and Kenya's harmony wrecked by subversion, bitterness, anarchy and chaos. Means to this end were not wanting.

After the war a member of the Kikuyu, the largest tribe in Kenya, was busily engaged in founding what were called Kenya Independent Schools. His assumed name was Jomo Kenyatta and he had been to Moscow and had lived in England, where he married, as one of his several wives, a White woman. The complacent British administration in Nairobi looked with contented eyes upon the founding of these Independent Schools, either because it had no inkling of their true purpose or because certain key officials approved that purpose. Meanwhile, as we now know, intelligence reports about the secret formation of a vast subversive organization among the Kikuyu and Luo peoples were being sent to the Kenya Government. The Kenya Government chose to discount and ignore them. On terminating his period of office the Governor, Sir Phillip Mitchell, declared that he was leaving a country "prosperous and at peace".

Three weeks later what had long been stirring underground erupted and showed its hideous features to the world. Its name — Mau Mau. The *New Statesman* and other left-wing papers in Britain were pleased to assert that Mau Mau was a figment of the British settler's imagination, but there was nothing imaginary about the thousands of Kikuyu put to death because they chose to remain loyal to the Crown or about the butchering of British men, women and children, among whom was a man who had been a life-long friend of the Kikuyu. A special death was devised for this man, Professor Leakey, who was buried alive upside down with a black goat and a white goat. For good measure his wife and servants were also killed. Recruits were enrolled into Mau Mau at obscene nocturnal ceremonies deep in the heart of the forests or in urban hide-outs. It is impossible to describe in a book what took place on these occasions, because those who took one or other of the Mau Mau oaths, especially those who aspired to the higher ranks, were required to engage in the foulest sexual malpractices, in conjunction with women, sheep and goats — the idea being, apparently, so to degrade members of the cult that, becoming lost to all human dignity and sense of decency, they were conditioned to engineer or participate in infamies fouler than this century had ever before known.

Happening in the times of the great decadence it was only to be expected that Mau Mau would cause only a tame reaction in the Kenya Government. One high official in Nairobi, commenting on the murder of a loyal and revered Kikuyu chief, said that it was a "welcome sign" of the resistance offered by

Kikuyu to the filthy and murderous Mau Mau rebels. A European woman whose only child, a boy in his teens, had been put to death by a Mau Mau gang (whose suspected presence had previously been reported to the authorities) brought to England a petition to the Queen signed by 3,000 women complaining in bitter terms of the fatuous incompetence of the Kenya Government. She was not allowed to present in person the petition, which the Colonial Office sent to the Governor of Kenya for his comments, and the woman, Mrs. Twohey, got no nearer to the Queen than a Colonial Office underling who graciously consented to see her. This event happened even after the Nairobi authorities had begun to bestir themselves when a large number of deeply disturbed Europeans converged on Government House — a demonstration no less effective because the armed askari guard kept the demonstrators at bay. Thereafter the Mau Mau menace, which had terrorised loyal Kikuyu and European alike, was taken more seriously.

The Mau Mau conspiracy, as I have suggested, was the most diabolical rebellion of our times and was conducted in such a way that one would not have been surprised to learn that the Devil himself had managed it. Its actual manager was Jomo Kenyatta, the founder of the Independent Schools. A court of law found him guilty of the charge and sentenced him to several years imprisonment, after which, Kenyans were given to understand, he would be sent to live in a remote, restricted area for the rest of his days. Indeed, a spokesman of the Kenyan Government said that he would never be allowed to return to the normal life of the colony. After Kenyatta's sentence had been served and he was exiled to a remote part of the country, a subsequent British Governor, Sir Patrick Renison, described him as "a leader to darkness and death". That, anybody might suppose, would be the end of Kenyatta as a politician.

But not at all. The international forces of subversion had other plans. Although I have received no credible information that New York subsidies were forthcoming for Mau Mau purposes, there is absolutely no doubt that once the rebellion had been put down by the British, "American" funds were made abundantly available to enable the African "nationalists" by other means to carry on the campaign which Mau Mau had started — the campaign to get rid of British rule. There were comings and goings between Black politicos and Kenyatta in his distant Kipinguria exile, followed by visits to Kipinguria by Kenya's White politicians. One of the latter, whose periodical had been suppressed because it was too "right-wing", came back to announce that he thought it highly desirable that Kenyatta should again take part in the public life of Kenya.

Before long a house near Nairobi was got ready as a residence for the convicted manager of Mau Mau, White toadies concerning themselves to see that it was adequately furnished. After this the "leader to darkness and death" was not only released but being received in London. A year or two later the entire country was handed over to one who had been pronounced unfit to return to the normal life of the country, and when Independence Day arrived the Queen's Consort flew out to Nairobi to bestow the Royal cachet on Kenyatta and to watch the Union Jack being hauled down. Following what was now an accepted tradition, Prince Philip was photographed dancing with some Black bibi, the wife of one or other of Kenya's ministerial overlords. Not long afterwards Jomo Kenyatta attended a Commonwealth Prime Minister's conference and dined with the Queen. Truly could it be said that the Devil had come into his own.

The loyal British and the loyal Kikuyu had been abandoned by the British Government and Mau Mau, despite its extreme depravity, became a heroic legend. Could any criminal maniac, stage-managing all these events, have wished for any more exquisite consummation of his dreams?

Chapter XIII

LUNATICS AT PLAY

THE masquerade of the African in the guise of a politician able to take over the running of a modern state, together with the highly complex skills and institutions inseparable from it, has nowhere been demonstrated in a more ludicrous light than in Zambia, formerly known as Northern Rhodesia. When British rule was brought to an end here as everywhere else, in accordance with the master plan, some exceedingly quaint devices were thought up to show, in respect of modernity, to what extent Africans are not only "with it" but beyond it. What other country in the world, for example, boasts a Minister of the Heavens? I quote a report from the Lusaka correspondent of the *Northern News*: "The Scientific Executive Board of the National Academy of Science, Space Research and Philosophy announced today that it has been decided to put off plans to blast off several rockets at the independence day celebrations. Mr. E. F. Muku Nkoloso, the organization's director-general, said the reasons were because the rockets would cause a terrifying earth tremor and because the top officials of the same body were now fully engaged with the heavy task of making preparations for the Unip annual conference. He said : 'We want the independence celebrants to devote all their minds and energies to making the independence celebrations a miraculous historical event in Zambia. The other reason for putting off the blast of the rockets is that the rock-bang will contaminate the heavens'. Meanwhile Mr. Nkoloso said that the young Minister of the Heavens, Mr. G. M. Simbumwe, has been appointed to mount guard where the rockets are dumped — to avoid spies from reaching them. Instead of blasting rockets to mark the birth of Zambia, a space march with acrobats will be displayed." The reader may think that this is satire, but that would be a mistake. Such play-acting represents a kind of reality to the African mind and is intended to impress both Zambians and the world at large that Zambia is in the forefront of those countries now reaching forward to the conquest of space.

In a later report Minister Nkoloso appears content with the more modest title of Minister of Space. The first "space woman", however, had been accorded the title "Sister of the Heavens" and Nkoloso solemnly declared that he will land her on the moon during 1965. Her training included being rolled down an anthill in a barrel every day, because — the Minister explained — this "simulates the conditions of a moon-landing". Nkoloso himself swung from a tree, being convinced that "this is training for feeling weightlessness". His twelve space cadets were dressed in green satin jackets and yellow trousers. Asked if that is their space uniform, they replied: "No, we are the Dynamite Rock Music Group when we are not space cadets". The capsule which the Minister of Space intended to use for the landing of his space woman on the moon was being built out of dustbins soldered together. The launching mechanism? Believe it or not, a sapling bent back and then to be released! All that the Minister required to see this great scientific venture well endowed was a favourable response to his application to U.N.E.S.C.O. for a grant of £7,500,000. So mad is the world that he might have got the money. At all events a supposedly responsible American journal sent him a wire begging him not to launch his space woman until one of its special correspondents, hastening to the scene, had arrived at the launching site. Laughable though such antics may seem, in a deeper sense they hold more cause for tears than for laughter. They are a true reflection of an aspect of the African mind to which almost an entire continent has been entrusted, and that aspect is by far the mildest and most innocuous.

If it be supposed that Zambia has a monopoly of this sort of light-headedness, let us for a moment slip across the frontier into Nyasaland to hear an extract from a speech to the Nyasaland Legislative Assembly by Minister Chisiza before he fled for his life:

"Mr. Speaker, Sir . . . Sons and daughters of Malawi . . . Ngwazi has given me permission to speak to him, and through him to you. Are you with me? Here we go. Halleluja. Amen. You have done it. You have made it. It is real. It is true. Federation is dead — Kwacha! Forward we march, buttressed by a long tradition of courageous deeds, held together by an enduring patriotism and down-to-earth nationalism, led by dynamic Ngwazi Kamuzu Banda, the Lion of Malawi, Father and Founder of the Nation, Architect, and Builder of the State — Dr. Kamuzu Banda. Inspired by the achievements and sacrifices of our heroes, determined to fight on the soil of Motherland freedom, we dedicate ourselves to Ngwazi and to exerting all our efforts in order that Malawi, Motherland, shall bloom, in spite of the wounds inflicted upon her by the Gorgon monster — Federation, alias Imperialism, alias Colonialism. Oh ye Gods of Africa, hear me! I have a message from Ngwazi Kamuzu Banda — hear me! 1963 goes in the annals of history with the soul, spirit and carcases of the Gorgon monster, Federation and the architects. Oh ye Gods of Africa, this time I have a message for you from Mother Africa, and this is, let the souls of these devils, Gorgon Monster and the architects, go to hell. Ngwazi Kamuzu Banda, whisper to me, Sir, do me that favour. Did you say that independence is just around the corner? Yes, Sir, Thank you, Sir. May I take this message over to the Gods of Africa? Very good, Sir. Ye Gods of Africa, I have got a message for you from Ngwazi Kamuzu Banda. He says independence is just round the corner. Oh what's that? Sir, the Gods of Africa told me that they already know the date and time, and on that day they will send to you the souls of all your sons and daughters who died in service of Motherland."

Comment would be superfluous.

Here, for good measure, is an "order to cheer" sent to Nyasaland natives in advance of one of Banda's journeys : "The Ngwazi Dr. Kamuzu Banda, the Messiah and Redeemer of the Malawi people, saviour of the untenable soil of Malawi, the founder of the nation, the builder of the state of Malawi, the life president of the ruling Malawi Congress Party, the first Prime Minister of Malawi, Minister of National Resources and Surveys and indeed, the man of the people of Malawi, will drive in his usual splendour triumphantly from the state house, Zomba, to the presidential palace at Mount Pleasant, Blantyre, on Wednesday.

"The Ngwazi has just returned from his recent and first earth-rocking political tour of the central and outer regions since he assumed the hard-won office of premiership.

"To show their usual national pride and dedication to Ngwazi Kamuzu, Kamukwala, Katsitzi, all Malawians will join this route from Zomba to Blantyre, the Ngwazi will be met by frenzied crowds of dancing and singing people, and the cheering crowds at his palace will accord him with the usual ovation by the Amazon army (league of Malawi women)."

Phew!

Lest the reader suppose that such hyperbole is confined to Central and Southern Africa, I quote the following gem from *West Africa*:

"In Accra the Minister of Education, Mr. A. J. Dowuona-Hammond, said recently that a nation without culture is not worth living in. It was the duty of all not only to revive but also to improve upon the arts of hairdressing in the country, adding 'hairdressing can help make Ghana great as far as art is concerned'. The Minister who was addressing the second meeting of the Ghana Hairdressing and Beauty Culture Association, said that the formation of the association was of vital importance 'because it will sustain our cultural heritage. I urge the association to stand firm with the assurance that the Government is always prepared to help you to preserve our cultural heritage'."

I defy any satirist to beat that!

Zambia offers more than the moon-madness of a Minister of Space who happens to be the country's chief witchdoctor. Here, as throughout the rest of Black Africa, there is systematically applied the only political art which the African can master — the art of relentless intimidation, which often enough does not stop short of murder. During the electoral struggle between the followers of Kenneth Kaunda and those of Harry NKumbula, if any man not carrying the correct party card fell into the hands of a gang from the opposite camp he would be mercilessly beaten up and perhaps be lucky to escape with his life. Nor were such pleasantries the monopoly of the political parties.

After Kaunda had won the election and headed the Zambian Government, there was a head-on clash with an inoffensive religious sect led by one Alice Lenshina, whose principle it was not to be involved in any form of political activity. This did not suit the Government, which now demanded the political allegiance of all Africans in the territory, and several Lenshina villages were attacked. Members of the sect had the effrontery to defend themselves, an attitude which Kaunda found altogether intolerable. I quote from a source which cannot be divulged, but which I assure readers in unimpeachable: "When the security forces were approaching a Lenshina village, then occupied by its inhabitants, they received instructions from Lusaka (that is, from the seat of government) to hold off for twenty-four hours. When they came back at the end of that time, it was to find that a Unip (Kaunda's supporters) raiding party had visited the place in the interim. All forty-seven in the village were dead. A few had died swiftly through being burned alive in their houses which had been fired when they had taken refuge in them and barricaded the doors. The rest, men and women and children, had taken many hours to die. The men had been trussed, emasculated and their members thrust into their mouths. The women had had their breasts and private parts treated with burning faggots. The leader of the expedition is known to be an African Government officer, then on leave. Yet no action is to be taken against him or other members of the Unip raiding party. Y (a British police officer), who had seen close-up victims (Kikuyu loyalists) of the Lari massacre in Kenya by the Mau Mau, said this raid put Lari in the shade. Many European police who had considered staying on are now resigning, sickened by what has occurred. Some can hardly bear even to speak of things they have seen. Yet the Governor has raised not one finger either to protect European security personnel from being required to continue in the Lenshina areas or to arrest excess". A British Government officer who had shown courtesy to Alice Lenshina after her surrender was violently taken to task by Kenneth Kaunda, which reveals who must on any showing be held responsible for the raiding party's infamy.

Should the reader be inclined to think that such outrages occurred in some remote and savage hinterland which had never had the advantage of coming under Western influence, he should remember that this is a country in which European skills have been used for the building of fine towns and which the great Copperbelt industry has made prosperous. What is more, shameful though it be to record the fact, it was here that Britain's Princess Royal was sent to be present at the lowering of the Union Jack and to dance — following many a sorry precedent — in the arms of the unspeakable Kaunda.

Mention of the Copperbelt recalls to mind that this is one of the scenes of activity of Harry Oppenheimer's "Anglo-American" empire and of the Rhodesia Selection Trust, which also has strong American affiliations. Harry Oppenheimer's other interests include control of De Beers diamond monopoly, which extends from Kimberley in South Africa to South Kasai province in the Congo and even further north, and which has been entrusted with the selling rights of diamonds produced in the Soviet Union. Among these interests must be included a huge participation in the Witwatersrand gold mining industry, the virtual control of almost all the English-language newspapers in South Africa, that country's dynamite factories and other concerns too numerous to mention. Oppenheimer also financed in South Africa the founding of the Progressive Party, which advocates the staged integration of White and Black and the staged surrender of power culminating in Black Government.

Oppenheimer's De Beers empire was founded by Cecil Rhodes, whose struggle for control of the diamond monopoly in its later stages was financed by the House of Rothschild. At this time the Rothschilds, looming so immense on every financial horizon, had begun to discover the advantage of forming "fronts". If it did not retain an interest in creating the world's diamond monopoly, if it did not go with Rhodes to the Witwatersrand, the largest goldfields ever known, if it did not march behind Rhodes into Southern Rhodesia, and after the death of Rhodes associate itself with the exploitation of the Copperbelt and of the mineral wealth of the Congo, then these things would be so out of keeping with the family's eye for the main chance as to be incredible. As it happens, Evelyn de Rothschild, of N. M. Rothschild & Sons, is a London director of both De Beers and "Anglo-American".

This tracking down of financial interests is not a diversion. Although it is true that the combining of the two Rhodesias and Nyasaland to form the Central African Federation was the result of a campaign financed by the Oppenheimer complex, almost certainly with the Rothschilds in the immediate background, the collapse of the Federation still left it in financial domination of Northern Rhodesia, or — to give the territory its new name — Zambia. What, then, has been its response to the happenings which I have recounted? It could afford a tolerant smile at the idea of launching a "space-woman" upon the moon by means of a sapling, but the torturing to death of the members of a Lenshina village is a very different matter. Does it, like the craven British Government, remain in cahoots with Kaunda, the instigator of such diabolism? There is no evidence to the contrary.

In other words, Oppenheimer's backing in Southern Rhodesia of Welensky and "racial partnership", his support for the Progressive Party in South Africa and the determined stand made by his newspapers against the idea of White government both north and south of the Limpopo, can be equated with the acquiescence (to say the least) of the United Africa Company (on the board of which is to be found Lord Rothschild) in the granting of "independence" to Kenya, Tanganyika and the other East African territories, and of its affiliated Unilever interests in the handing over of power to Black Governments in Ghana, Nigeria, the Congo and the other West African territories.

Now the fact is that the anti- White propaganda trail throughout the length and breadth of Africa has been blazed by American functionaries both official and unofficial. Adlai Stevenson, one of the Money Power's chief stooges, made several visits up and down the Continent always stressing one all-important point — "American" aid would be forthcoming in abundance on condition that countries asking for it applied the principle, suicidal in the African context, of 'one man one vote'. Nixon, when U.S. Vice-President, undertook a short "air safari" from Ghana to Uganda and the Sudan before returning to Washington, where he presented to President Eisenhower a long report in which he depicted Africa solely in terms of Africans and Americans, without reference to the Western nations which had tamed these savage lands and made them prosperous. He wrote that it was the historic destiny of the United States "to lead dependent peoples to freedom". The freedom, that is, to live under their own barbarous despots and at the first sign of discontent to die the sort of death suffered by Kaunda's Lenshina victims or experience the no less dreadful and even more widely spread horrors which have resulted from the leading to "freedom" of the Congolese peoples and the Zanzibar islanders. Naturally Nixon did not put it like that; probably he was naive enough not even to have seen it like that. Instead, he called for the setting up on American soil of many more Information Offices, and these agencies have got on with the job of "liberation".

While men like Nixon may have been naive and while men like Stevenson were not more than parrots, totally ignorant of what their propaganda meant in terms of human life and death, the same naivety and ignorance cannot be attributed to

Harry Oppenheimer or to concerns such as Unilevers and the United Africa Company. They knew, and today must know even more clearly, that the only form of government of which Africans are capable, once European supervision has been withdrawn, is the rule of terror. Why, then, have they acquiesced in the handing over of Africa, in which they have held predominant economic interests, to tyranny? Is it because, in the face of a gigantic American take-over bid, they have felt impelled to compete on American terms for the favour of African demagogues? Or is it because they have agreed to merge their interests with those of the take-over bidders and accepted as part of the pact that European authorities be replaced by African authorities, who — savage though their methods of government may be — are more malleable than upright officials in the Colonial Service of the Western European nations? The fantastic sequence of events in the Congo suggests that the second explanation is the more probable, but the one absolute certainty is that European leadership has been eliminated over most of the African continent with a lack of conscience in the vested interests concerned amounting to diabolical wickedness.

Chapter XIV

CONGO INFAMIES

WHEN the Belgians handed over the Congo to African rule, they did so in style. Their King flew to Leopoldville to attend the "independence" ceremony — an occasion which must have been as humiliating to him at it was to other Belgian patriots. What had caused this particular abdication? There had been for some time a state of civil war between two powerful Congolese tribes which Belgian and Belgian-commanded troops were endeavouring to stop, but the consequent unrest in a well-run colony, which had long enjoyed peace, enabled local agitators backed from abroad to carry on a subversive campaign against the Belgian Administration. Even so, the determining factor was not pressure exerted on Leopoldville but pressure of the kind with which we have become all too familiar exerted on Brussels. The Congo had to be laid open for a vast takeover bid. It happened with break-neck speed.

Before laying down the reins of power the Belgian Government had entered into an agreement with its putative successor, the party headed by the notorious agitator, Patrice Lumumba (who had done a stretch in prison for dishonesty), whereby Belgian troops would remain in the territory for some time before beginning a staged withdrawal and Belgian officers would remain in command of Congolese forces. The agreement was torn up as soon as the transfer of power had been effected. There was an officially instigated mutiny of Congolese troops in the vicinity of Leopoldville and the Belgian officers, apparently having taken leave of their senses, surrendered their weapons to the mutineers as a token of "good-will". Thus encouraged, the mutineers began an orgy of raping the wives and daughters of the officers and all other European women in reach, including nuns. The rapings were multiple and were followed by other unspeakable outrages inflicted on the same women and girls. Soon the mutineers flocked into Leopoldville and began to intimidate the Europeans in that city. Although the lawlessness had all the appearance of an amok-run, it was noticed that at a certain time each day the rabble of soldiery would withdraw, thus giving the impression that it was subject to an undisclosed discipline and under the orders of an unseen command.

While these terrible things were happening, Patrice Lumumba was in negotiation with an agent from Wall St. called Detweiler as a result of which— to the surprise of all and to the dismay of some — Lumumba made over to Detweiler the entire mineral wealth of the Congo. The next event was the arrival in London, en route for New York and Washington, of both Detweiler and

Lumumba, having made the journey from Leopoldville, incredible though it may seem, in an R.A.F. machine. No Member of Parliament thought it worth while to enquire how the R.A.F. came to be used for a mission completely outside its own scope and purpose. Arriving in New York, Lumumba spent happy days choosing his Cadillac and when he reached Washington there awaited him a hero's welcome, which included his reception by the President and a Congressional grant of $20,000,000 to see his regime suitably launched. It would seem, however, that the President and Congress were misled. The financial interests represented by Detweiler, whoever they may have been, were obviously not the intended beneficiaries of Belgium's withdrawal from the Congo. Many years may elapse before the mystery is resolved. The one thing certain is that soon after his return Patrice Lumumba was murdered.

Meanwhile, with astonishing rapidity, the United Nations assembled and despatched to the Congo a multi-national force, and innocents the world over imagined that it had been sent to restore order and prevent further outrages against Belgian women and children. Nothing could have been wider of the mark. When news of the outrages reached Belgian European troops in the remote garrison towns of the Congo they began to march towards Leopoldville, and other districts in the hands of the mutineers, for the purpose of protecting their fellow-countrymen and women from the reign of terror to which they had been subjected. The United Nations rabble arrived in time to put a stop to this errand of mercy. Instead of itself providing protection, the force made a token gesture of establishing the U.N. "presence" in Leopoldville and the Secretary-General lost no time in making known the real intention behind its despatch. He issued a peremptory order to the Belgian troops, then hastening to the aid of their countrymen, to return to barracks. This order was swiftly followed by another, ordering the Belgian troops to leave the country. Transport facilities were provided on the instant, the Belgians were sent home and the U.N. force was left to maintain watch and ward over what was now the property of the take-over bidders. The "front" of these usurping interests has since been exposed, but the interests themselves still remain largely hidden from public view.

What we do know is that on the eve of "independence" the House of Rockefeller greatly extended its holdings in the Congo. As it did so in conjunction with Belgian companies, including *Union Miniere*, how it reacted to the next move — the secession of Katanga, where *Union Miniere* was dominant — is still a matter for conjecture. It could have wished the secession to become permanent or it could have desired Katanga to be brought back under the authority of the Central Government at Leopoldville.

Two things are certain. *Union Miniere* approved — it must have initiated — Tshombe's action in launching the separatist movement in Katanga. The second certainty is that other outside interests at least as powerful, and perhaps much more powerful, were determined that the Congo should be administered as a single unit and that Katanga must therefore abandon all idea of being run as an autonomous state. This second complex of vested interests had the power of determining how the United Nations should be used. It was decided to launch its polyglot force upon an invasion of Katanga.

Before this decision was taken — and it could only be taken at the highest international financial level — there was an obvious attempt by the contending financial powers to reach a settlement. Tshombe's visit to Leopoldville alone is sufficient evidence of the attempt. *Union Miniere* was influential enough to secure his release from prison, into which the Leopoldville politicos had flung him, but not influential enough to prevent the series of catastrophic events that followed. When it was clear that the interests behind Tshombe intended to stand firm, the United Nations — although its constitution disallows it to interfere in matters of domestic concern — marched in. What is more, the international policy-makers who decreed that the invasion should be launched had sufficient power to force a reluctant British Government to supply the invaders with one thousand pound block-buster bombs to drop on *Union Miniere* installations should that infamy be considered desirable. There followed bitter fighting between Central Government troops and the United Nations force on the one hand and Tshombe's men stiffened by a sprinkling of Europeans to whom the opprobrious name of "mercenaries" was given. Many unspeakable atrocities were committed, some of the United Nations' units proving themselves by no means inferior to the Congolese in the infliction of barbaric cruelties. Although in the event Britain's block-busters were not dropped, the United Nations bombed towns, shelled hospitals and in general waged an all-out war against Katanga's civil population. The end result was that Tshombe's men were defeated, Katanga was brought under the authority of the Central Government at Leopoldville and Tshombe fled, to become one of the outcasts of the world.
He found temporary refuge in Belgium and later in France but his first application for a visa to come to Britain was refused.

The end result, have I written? So it seemed at the time. But it was by no means the end. There was soon to be a miraculous change in the situation. The British Government, having formed the opinion that Tshombe was an undesirable visitor, suddenly discovered that he was a most desirable visitor and granted him a visa. Here was a portent of what was to come. Tshombe went back to the Congo, not to be Prime Minister of Katanga, whence he had been kicked by the United Nations, but to become Prime Minister of the Congolese Central

Government at Leopoldville! What had happened to cause this astonishing rise in his fortunes? Obviously no development in the Congo. Either *Union Miniere*, with its Oppenheimer and concealed Rothschild affiliations, had managed to turn the tables on the immensely strong financial interests which had enlisted the United Nations to fight for them or there had been a deal, involving a "cut-in" and the elevation of Tshombe as, among other things, a *quid pro quo*. Of the two explanations the second is the more probable.

Even this was not the end of the business. There would seem to have been a third financial power contending for the masterdom of the Congo — a power excluded from the deal which led to the settlement I have postulated. It could conceivably have been the power on whose behalf Detweiler secured from Patrice Lumumba concessions covering the entire mineral wealth of the Congo. At any rate Tshombe had not been long in his new office when a serious rebellion broke out in Stanleyville and the surrounding territory and there is no doubt that the dead Lumumba was its patron saint. It was to the Patrice Lumumba Stadium that the rebels would drag their wretched victims by the hundreds, that the huge crowds gathered there, by their acclaim or their denunciation, could decide which man or woman should live and which should die a savage death. It was the name "Patrice Lumumba" that the rebels used as their war-cry when they sallied forth to kill.

In dealing with one aspect of this rebellion the United States revealed the ambivalence of its policy. The reader will remember that while the thought of British troops maintaining order in Cyprus under their own flag was intolerable to Washington and its masters, the thought of British troops serving there under the flag of the United Nations was found entirely acceptable. Much the same situation, although only for a brief period, obtained in the Congo. After the U.N. interregnum, the United States stepped in to purloin the territory from which Belgium had been ejected. American opinion, however, was gravely disturbed by the report that the rebels in and around Stanleyville had captured over a thousand White hostages, many of them missionaries. What was Washington to do? If American troops were sent to their rescue, the United States- — as though it had not already created a world-wide Dollar Empire, backed by military bases — would be accused of "Imperialism", and of course that would never do. The solution was ingenious. Despite the fact that Washington's first priority, when the Belgians relinquished their authority, had been to secure the expulsion of the Belgian troops, there had now arisen an occasion when Belgian troops could also serve in an acceptable role. Belgian paratroops were accordingly assembled in Ascension Island, a British possession, and then dropped on Stanleyville by American planes. They rescued a certain number of hostages and Washington by making this gesture was able to appease public opinion at home. But there had also to be appeased certain Wall St. elements backing the rebellion. On that account, I suggest, it was necessary to ensure that the Belgian paratroops were used only to make the gesture and not to quell the revolt. Whatever the explanation, the fact is that they were withdrawn within a few days, with less than half their rescue mission completed. This incident, indeed, reveals something more than the ambivalence of American policy. It shows that Great Britain, Belgium and the United States itself are all in essence mere satrapies of the International Money Power, no matter to what extent the Money Power at any one time may be rent by internal rivalries.

The Stanleyville rebellion establishes another strong probability. Whereas the "mercenaries" in the nominal service of Tshombe when he was Katanga's Prime Minister were secretly recruited, once he was made Prime Minister of the Congo they underwent a great improvement in status and were openly recruited in Rhodesia and the Republic of South Africa. Whose was the influence which made this possible? To my mind there can be only one satisfactory answer — the influence of Harry Oppenheimer, head of the vast complex of interests which holds most of Rhodesia's bonds and which dominates the gold, diamond and newspaper industries in the Republic.

We shall see in the next chapter how little disinterested was the United Nations in the Congo operations. I hope that the present chapter will have established that anybody who really believes that the basic struggle there was between rival African factions should betake himself, if not to a mental hospital, then certainly to a kindergarten for politically retarded simpletons.

Human life, however, is full of imponderables and poor old Tshombe's vicissitudes were not over. Either he put a foot wrong or another violent row now occurred in the boardrooms of New York, London and Brussels. It was not long before he was again "out" and this time he was followed by his patrons, *Union Miniere*. President Mobutu was given the task of declaring the company "nationalized". The Government would hold 55% of the new consortium's shares, Anglo-American (through Tanganyika Concessions Ltd.) would be allowed to retain its 17% while the remaining 28% would be put out to tender at home or overseas. It seems unlikely that many Congolese would be able afford to get killed in the rush. The Government's share would of course defray the costs of the unseen American administration. Another exquisite example of a take-over bid.

Chapter XV

U.N. IDEALS AND THE REALITY

MANY well-meaning people in the world, whose lives are filled with "good works", will support any institution provided only that its declared aims are benevolent and high-sounding. They accept such institutions at their face value, without mental reservations about the application of their principles. The backing given to the many United Nations' Associations scattered about the Western world establishes the truth of this statement. The United Nations would seem to be tailor-made to receive such support. In the first place it is international and the propagandists have long been at work to give the word "international" the connotation of being disinterested and devoted to the interests of mankind as a whole. Then there is a general impression, sedulously fostered, that the United Nations stands for peace on earth. Finally, it is looked upon as the champion of the under-dog and the implacable foe of every kind of tyranny. So well have the propagandists done their job that any suggestion that it acts tyrannically on its own account and that, so far from serving the under-dog, it is an instrument wielded by the harsh hand of an international overlord, is discounted as ridiculous and those who discern its true purpose are dismissed as cranks and fanatics.

Were it not for this all-pervasive form of liberalism, which has substituted emotionalism and woolly-mindedness for true thinking and an accurate perception of the malignant forces behind the conventional facade of a well-ordered world, it would have been impossible for the West to lapse into its present state of putrescence or for the overseas territories, brought with such labour within the purview of civilization, to be abandoned once again to savagery and the hungry maws of the jungle. Not the least grievous aspect of the tragedy is that the men and women who allow themselves to be deluded by fine phrases into acting as the enemy's fifth column, in almost every country to which the rot has spread, are mostly people of irreproachable character, innately decent and abundantly kind at heart. The battle for the victory of the spirit of man would be won with relative ease were it but possible to convince these eminently worthy altruists that by thinking nothing through to its logical end, and by their willingness to judge institutions by their professed aims, they are a living example of the truth that the ideal is the enemy of the real.

The true nature of the United Nations can best be assessed by examining the work on which it has been engaged and its manipulation by the unscrupulous international power-elite. There is no clearer example of this manipulation than that provided by its "presence" in the Congo. The outrages by U.N. forces to which I have briefly referred may be written off to human vices and to the savage, or semi-savage, contingents which were included for the U.N.'s professed purpose of upholding the rule of law. But the cold calculation of those who did the manipulating belongs to quite a different order of wickedness. Those of us who follow as best we may the workings of the power-elite knew very well that the United Nations had not interested itself in Congolese affairs for love of curly Congolese heads, but had it not been for the revelations of Congressman Bruce of the United States we might have had to wait many years for the information I am now able to relate.

Congressman Bruce did a signal service by making known to the U.S. House of Representatives many of the interests involved in the dirty business in the Congo and by bringing to light the intricate relationships between those interests and functionaries of both the United Nations and the State Department. These disclosures suggest that the new part-owner of the former Belgian Congo is a multi-sided concern called the Liberian American Swedish Minerals Company. Basing his case on meticulous research Congressman Bruce enables us to trace some of the ramifications of this titanic firm, which was formed by combining the International African- American Corporation and the Swedish syndicate of large companies called the Swedish Land Company Syndicate. For some reason known only to themselves, but perhaps not unconnected with the nationality of Dag Hammarskjoeld, the New York wolves chose to work behind a largely Swedish facade. As the Congressional Record setting forth the Bruce disclosures is closely knit and too involved for easy reading I will try to simplify the issue by breaking down and listing the component parts of the interests behind Lamco (the aforementioned Liberian American Swedish Minerals Company) : I begin with the two already mentioned and proceed with the analysis as far as it can be taken :

International African-American Corporation

Swedish Land Company Syndicate

Grangesberg Company

Skanska Cement A.B.

Svenska Entreprenad A.B. Sentab

Liberian Iron Ore Ltd.

Ifoverken

Bolidens Gruv A.B. (a large shareholder in Svenska)

The U.S. Anaconda Group

The Chile Copper Company (Anaconda Group member)

It may be that to the general reader the names of these companies do not convey very much, but those of many of their officials should mean a great deal.

Who is aware, for instance, that a director not only of the Grangesberg Company but also of the U.S. copper corporation Anaconda Mining is Bo Hammarskjoeld, the brother of the late Dag Hammarskjoeld, U.N. Secretary General at the time of the occupation of the Congo and the first attack on Katanga? Nor is this the only coincidence — not by a long way. One Sture Linner was appointed by Dag Hammarskjoeld to be resident U.N. representative in charge of technical assistance in the Congo. The appointment was made on the day Linner officially severed his connection with the International African-American Corporation, of which he had been executive vice-president, general manager and manager consultant. Eleven days later he was promoted to be in charge of the Congo operation in all its totality. Beyond all reasonable doubt the appointment and subsequent promotion were in anticipation of the U.N. attack on Katanga.

Associated with Linner in the International African-American Corporation was an American named Fowler Hamilton, later the Administrator of the Agency for International Development in the U.S. State Department. Naturally he resigned his directorship on entering the State Department, but was it not more than a coincidence that he should have been replaced as director by another member of his law firm, Melvin Steen? Here is Congressman Bruce's comment: "The man for whom Linner had worked in Lamco, Fowler Hamilton, was now in the foreign policy making agency of the U.S. Government, the Department of State, as head of our entire foreign aid department. It is also interesting to find a high officer in the department of State associating with a combine in which Sture Linner had been a key man". Then there is Mr. Sven Gustaf Schwartz. In 1961 this Mr. Schwartz, after much coming and going between Leopoldville and America and Europe, was appointed by the United Nations as senior consultant on natural resources and industry in the Congo. Although he had enjoyed U.N. facilities before April of that year he had not been in U.N. service. In whose interests was he then employed? The answer is not far to seek. As we have seen, Skanska Cement A.B. was one of the components of the Lamco Syndicate, the combine up to its eyes in the nefarious intrigues and skulduggery of the Congo operations, and Sven Schwartz was a director not only of Skanska but also of Ifoverken, another member of the combine.

Congressmen Bruce admirably summarizes the position up to this point :

"Now it was apparent that Sture Linner, who directed the operations in the Congo that saw two bloody assaults on Katanga and the *Union Miniere* installations, had had several bosses in Lamco who turned out to be in positions to make policy in the Congo. The top man in the U.N. was the brother of one of Linner's bosses, Bo Hammarskjoeld. The man whom the U.N. Secretary General, Dag Hammarskjoeld, appointed to give the word on what would be done with the Congo's mineral and other natural resources just happened to be another boss of Linner's in Lamco, Sven Schwartz. As we have seen, another of Linner's former bosses, Fowler Hamilton's law partner, Melvin Steen, now sat in the same director's seat that he held before he went into the State Department, and Hamilton's firm still represented the American partners in the Swedish-American combine, I.A.A.C."

A charming set-up!

It so happens that in December 1961 it was the duty of Mr. Schwartz to make a four-month study of mining in the Congo for the U.N. Consultative Group for National Resources and Industry and to draw up a report. Among the recommendations was the possible nationalization of the Katanga mines. But although the report bore Schwartz's name it was not in fact written by him but by another Swede, Borge Hjortzberg-Nolund. And who was Mr. Hjortzberg-Nolund? Believe it or not, an alternative director of Lamco and general adviser to the president of the Grangesberg Company. The tie-up of this Swedish front with Washington is manifest in the position held by Fowler Hamilton. This, however, is not the only nexus. Hamilton's law firm has two names, Cleary, Gottlieb, Steen and Hamilton (Fowler Hamilton) in New York, while in Washington it is known as Cleary, Gottlieb, Steen and Ball. And the last-named person turns out to be none other than George Wildman Ball, Under-Secretary of State in the Kennedy Administration. Thus two Americans of the American-Swedish Corporation, Lamco, as Congressman Bruce points out, are very highly placed in the policy-making agency of the U.S. Government — the State Department. (An additional light on the way the world is governed lies in the fact that the firm, now known as Cleary, Gottlieb and Steen, is listed at the Justice Department of the U.S. under the Foreign Agents Registration Act as being the agent for the Common Market, the European Coal and Steel Community and the European Atomic Energy Community.)

Count Charles Terlinden, writing in *La Libre Belgique* of 12th December, 1961, had this to say:

"As early as August, 1960, while sojourning in Stockholm on the occasion of a scientific congress, we were informed by a reliable source of the existence of a Swedish-American concern headed by a very high official of the Swedish Foreign Ministry and set up for the purpose of gaining control over the non-ferrous metals of the Congo. A relative of Mr. Hammarskjoeld was the king-pin of this trust, the real aim of which was, by having control of Katanga copper production, to put it into a state of suspended animation so as to boost copper stocks, the control of which was in the hands of American high finance."

A similar comment was made by the *Star Ledger* of Newark, New Jersey, which wrote:

"Last June a group of private Swedish and American financiers formed a new combine for exploitation of Katanga's natural resources. As those resources are tightly held by *Union Miniere*, it might seem that the combine's chances of success were exceedingly slight. But the private Swedish-American group apparently had advance information that led it to believe the mining monopoly soon would be broken. It considered this information so reliable that it promptly filed incorporation papers in Switzerland and deposited about $l00m in Swiss banks in preparation for a Katanga take-over.

"As long as Katanga remains independent under pro-Western President Tshombe, *Union Miniere* probably will retain control of the mining industry, including some of the world's largest and richest copper deposits. But if the Tshombe Government falls and Katanga again becomes part of the Congo republic, the mineral monopoly will be finished. At this point, the new combine plans to move in.

"Katanga and Northern Rhodesia produce about one-fourth of the free world's copper supply. The three combines in Katanga and Northern Rhodesia co-operate closely in all phases of copper production and marketing. No outside firm stands a chance of cutting itself in as long as the present Governments of Katanga and Northern Rhodesia remain in power. . . ."

Congressman Bruce and his supporting authorities insist upon the part played in the Congo, particularly in Katanga, by American High Finance, but while they are willing to expose the "front" men and their disgusting intrigues they all lay off the Big Boys of Wall St. The Congressman, somewhat disappointingly, suggests that the ultimate control lies elsewhere, declaring :

"The individual who may be the central figure in the international combine is Marc Wallenberg, senior, a Swedish banker. He is the chief officer of the entire complex. He is a director of at least two of the Swedish companies in the Swedish Lamco Syndicate, a vice-chairman of Stockholm's Enskilda Bank, which serves as financial adviser to the Lamco combine, and also chairman of Telefon AB L.M. Ericsson."

As no Swedish financier or financial combine can hope to dominate the wolf packs of New York we are entitled to reject out of hand the idea of Marc Wallenberg's supremacy. I wrote in the previous chapter that the "front" of the usurping interests in the Congo has since been exposed, but that the principals themselves still remain largely hidden from view. That remains the position.

As the reader will have noted, certain developments have taken place since the *Star Ledger* made its remarkably percipient prediction that "if the Tshombe Government falls and Katanga again becomes part of the Congo Republic, the mineral monopoly (of *Union Miniere*) will be finished. At this point the new combine plans to move in". The Tshombe Government did indeed fall, and it may be that the new combine had started to move in as planned. But the return of Tshombe and his elevation to the Premiership of the entire Congo Republic would suggest that *Union Miniere* was able to call upon the support of prodigiously strong financial interests, with the result that the interloping combine was cheated of its "killing" and had to be content with a deal. Should there have been no deal, perhaps we might be able to pin-point the promoters of the Stanleyville rebellion. However, these are matters of conjecture. What is certain, as we have seen, is that *Union Miniere* has lost out to its rivals through the use against it of "nationalization" as recommended by Mr. Schwartz of Lamco and of that organisation so beloved of idealists known as the U.N.

The fact remains, as Congressman Bruce has established, that the participation of the United Nations in the Congo take-over was very far from being a noble and disinterested crusade, but instead a most ignoble racket involving Big Business crooks, venal functionaries, political pimps and panders and servants of the Devil. How many of the dear old ladies, of both sexes, who organize fetes and sales of work for this or that United Nations' Association have the slightest inkling of the truth? Alas, not one. It is impossible to stress too often that the ideal is the enemy of the real.

Chapter XVI

THE BATTLE FOR RHODESIA

SOON after the influx of the United Nations soldiery into the Congo, and no doubt under its cover, there was a serious rebellion against Portuguese rule in Angola, a territory efficiently governed by Portugal during many centuries. Ghanaian soldiers, who may have been unofficially detached from the Ghanaian contingent sent to the Congo, were reported to be among the prisoners captured when the Portuguese authorities, taking strong counter-action, gained control of the situation after the insurgents had committed the most appalling atrocities. The putting down of the rebellion was the first serious rebuff encountered by the take-over bidders in their otherwise successful conquest of the African continent and, all the more because of its belief in the importance of symbolism, the Transatlantic power behind the campaign of subversion cannot be expected to accept its defeat as final. As this book is being written the author has had reports of the systematic building-up of subversive forces, both within and without Angola, to mount a more powerful rebellion against Portuguese rule.

One of the most important reasons why it is considered essential to terminate Portuguese rule in West Africa, as in East Africa, is the desire to isolate and then to destroy Southern Rhodesia, one of the two remaining bastions of White civilization in Africa wherein the White communities are large enough, for the present at least, to manage their own affairs without the support of metropolitan countries and, indeed, in the teeth of their displeasure. The proposed "liberation" of Mozambique, the Portuguese territory on the East Coast, has had to be slowed down because the African leader, Hastings Banda, despite his megalomaniac rantings during his campaign against British rule, has possessed the practical insight to understand the necessity of maintaining friendly relations with a neighbouring country controlling Nyasaland's access to the sea. Hence the hope of the subversives to use Nyasaland as an advanced base for the attack on Mozambique as outlined by Kanyama Chiume is now placed in cold storage. This unsuspected caution of Hastings Banda has made him also realize that without the British taxpayer to underwrite his Budget the economy of Nyasaland (Malawi, to give the territory its new name) would speedily collapse. That is why the fiery lieutenants who helped to build his legend, Chipembere, Chiume, Chisiza and the others, were encouraged to rebel against him and are at present in exile, plotting his downfall from adjoining countries. As things are, even with the help of the British taxpayer, Malawi has sunk deep into the doldrums. There is no longer any normal police activity and the general picture is one of administrative chaos. As for Mozambique, the Frelimo (or "freedom-fighters") there, flanked by a non-cooperative Malawi, operate a long way from the Tanzanian frontiers and are dependent for access and egress upon Swaziland, where they enjoy the shameful support of some members of the British administration but are handicapped by the fact that the Protectorate is an enclave, so that supply and escape routes involve an air-lift or a hazardous journey through South Africa.

Rhodesia — Southern Rhodesia to give it its legal title — found itself, on the break-up of the Central African Federation due largely to the bad faith of the British Government, faced with decisions vitally affecting its own future. Although a British colony, it had enjoyed self-government since 1922 and now reverted to that status. British governmental pressures, however, were applied with a view to extending the present limited African franchise in stages until it would be possible for a Black government to be rapidly installed. Rhodesians, composed mostly of British stock, being descendants of the men who had civilized this land and tamed its savage tribes, were determined that it should not revert to savagery. They turned against their "progressive" elements who in greater or less degree advocated the integration of White and Black, and when a right-wing government of their choosing, composed of the Rhodesian Front, showed signs of temporising with the multi-racialist opposition they summarily dismissed their leader and replaced him as Prime Minister by Ian Smith, a likeable, quiet, almost dour man with a magnificent war record — a man whose strength of character and dislike of compromise have made him a national hero.

There were three choices confronting Ian Smith — the retention of the *status quo*, which would give the British Government opportunities for further interference on the question of franchise, a negotiated independence under the Crown, which would certainly involve concessions to London, or a unilateral declaration of independence, which would leave Rhodesia free to regulate its own affairs and take whatever consequences might accrue. The present writer, who can claim some following in Rhodesia, has urged the Rhodesian Government to proclaim its allegiance to the British Crown and tell the U.K. Government to go to hell. Developments were precipitated when the British electorate returned the Labour Government to power, and Harold Wilson, almost on the instant, threatened Rhodesia with a formidable list of sanctions should independence be declared unilaterally. Ian Smith met these menaces with two measures. One was to call the chiefs, the traditional rulers of the African peoples, to a great *indaba*, or conference, at which — having no love of the African demagogues who spread dissension through the land — they spoke with one voice in favour of the Smith Government and the unilateral declaration of independence. The second was to hold a referendum which would give the

White electorate the opportunity of endorsing or rejecting the idea of unilateral declaration should negotiations with Britain fail.

At this point the local branch, as it were, of the International Money Power intervened. These interests, which held nearly all the Rhodesian bonds, brought out a statement, only a few days before the referendum, in which was set out every possible economic disadvantage which could attend unilateral action. Thereupon the Government, to the astonishment of many, announced that the referendum would not be mandatory. As a mandate confers only the power to act, without imposing an obligation to act, it is difficult to know why the announcement was drawn up; except perhaps to make any voters who had been worried by the attempts of the Money Power to scare them feel happier in their minds. The referendum went overwhelmingly in Smith's favour, but as it conferred no mandate, but merely expressed a general opinion known to exist, its utility is not altogether clear. Next came a general election which resulted in the Rhodesian Front making a clean sweep of all European seats — a magnificent victory.

It seemed impossible for the implication of that result, confirming as it did the result of the referendum, to be ignored. Yet no action that could conceivably be called precipitate followed. At the time the distance between the British and Rhodesian Governments seemed so great that talks and "talks about talks" between the two merely increased the tension without helping in any way to secure the amendment of the 1961 constitution, which provided for African rule within the foreseeable future—a provision shown by both the referendum and the election to be now abhorrent to the Rhodesians. It was clear that no amendment would be possible until the country became independent and that if independence could not be negotiated it would have to be unilaterally declared. Visits to London by Ian Smith and to Salisbury by Harold Wilson proved fruitless but still the talking continued.

Not until November 11, 1965, did Salisbury decide that there should be no further procrastination. On that day, while affirming loyalty to the British Crown, Ian Smith on behalf of his country made its unilateral declaration of independence—U.D.I., as it is now known. The reaction of the British Government was swift and shameless: it declared economic war on Rhodesia. There was at once put into operation a system of sanctions, designed to starve her into submission. That the first to starve would be the four million Africans so beloved by Harold Wilson (and by many thousands of others whose sentimentality was more genuine than his could ever be) was not regarded as a factor in the situation. Great importance was attached to the employment of oil sanctions and the Royal Navy, engaged in blockading the port of Beira, was required to do unbelievable things, almost amounting to piracy on the high seas.

But all to no avail. South Africa, behaving with impeccable rectitude, had affirmed that, the dispute being between Britain and Rhodesia, there was no need for any disturbance in trading relations with her northern neighbour. Even Harold Wilson, notwithstanding the follies engendered by outraged vanity, drew back from the final absurdity of ordering a blockage of the Republic's extensive coastline, and so the Rhodesians continued to receive their oil supplies—not enough to avoid rationing, it is true, but more than enough to keep her economy ticking over.

Inside Rhodesia, morale soared. Everywhere one went, outside the capital, one encountered the fighting spirit of a grand people—a people full of bitterness and anger at their betrayal by Britain, to whom no country has ever been more loyal, but now determined to stand their ground to the last, even as Alan Wilson and his Shangani patrol stood their ground against the Matabele until there was no survivor left alive to fight. Only in Salisbury did one begin to entertain certain misgivings and there only in governmental circles. As there had been a long period of something that seemed perilously like dithering between the referendum and U.D.I., so has there been a long, and still continuing, period between U.D.I. and fulfilment of the purpose for which, one must assume, U.D.I. was made—the perpetuation of White rule.

I asked Ian Smith about it in April, 1966. The question made the Rhodesian Prime Minister decidedly angry. "Have we not got enough on our plate," he asked, "without giving London and the United Nations another weapon to use against us?". I replied that I saw his point, albeit in my view the U.N. attitude, being bespoke, was not susceptible to any other influences. I also said that I saw the point of view of those members of the Rhodesian Front, by no means the least enthusiastic of his supporters, who were asking: "What has U.D.I. brought us except an economic boycott?" My remark was not well-received. I was told that the Right-Wing support could be taken for granted: the task now being to woo the Centre. It seemed to me that the referendum and election showed that the centre had been wooed and won, and that what was being attempted was an appeasement of the unappeasable financial Left, which observation led the Prime Minister's private secretary to remind him that he was ten minutes late for his next appointment.

The months dragged on until October, when Commonwealth Secretary Bowden went to Salisbury for earnest confabulations with Mr. Smith and his colleagues. While I held no brief for the British Government and utterly despise its policy (my sympathies being one hundred per cent with the Rhodesians), I am convinced that Bowden brought back to London outlines of a general agreement which convinced Wilson that another talk with Mr. Smith would finalize matters. Hence his suggestion of the conference on board H.M.S. *Tiger*. Among the reasons which led to this willingness to resume negotiations must have been Bowden's account of how he and the Rhodesian Prime Minister had discussed ways and means of ditching the Rhodesian Right Wing—"ditching" being the actual word used when the Commonwealth Secretary reported to the House of Commons. He added that Ian Smith told him that over thirty people were an embarrassment to him.

The *Tiger* conference's "working document" embodied acceptance of the British Government's six cardinal principles, the first of which was that there should be unimpeded advance towards majority (that is to say, Black) rule. Many of us, and here I am sure I speak for all my own friends in the Rhodesian Front, imagined that to amend the 1961 Constitution so as to impede this advance was what U.D.I. was all about. As Mr. Smith asserted that the British proposals had been accepted some months before the *Tiger* conference we were obviously mistaken.

Nor were the six basic points the only contents of the "working document", which detailed the methods whereby they were to be implemented. The Legislature was to be dissolved. Providing that there was recognition of the Governor's authority, the Governor would recognise an interim Government headed by Ian Smith until such time as the views of all Rhodesians were ascertained (four months was the period allowed for this purpose) on condition that the Governor appointed to the Cabinet five members, of whom two were to be Africans.

Asked by Harold Wilson whether this would mean raising the number of Cabinet members from thirteen to about seventeen, the Rhodesian Prime Minister replied that on the contrary he would reduce the number to twelve. This would establish a ratio in his favour of only seven to five. Wilson then enquired whether such a step might not involve several resignations, whereupon Smith said, "No–I will move in first". In other words, presumably, he would do his own sackings. Another condition was that the Governor, as Commander-in-Chief, should take over the control of Rhodesia's military and police forces, with an advisory council of five (including a British Government representative) to assist him. This would mean, in effect the exchange by the Smith regime of a *de facto* power to act for a somewhat dubious and perhaps temporary *de jure* recognition. As he was about to leave the *Tiger* Mr. Smith was asked whether he would recommend the "working document" to his Cabinet. He said that he had still to convince himself about it, yet the fact remains that, without committing himself or his Government, he signed the pernicious thing. Asked later why he had done so, he gave the curious reply on British television: "Mr.

Wilson was very keen to have a signed document to record this rather memorable meeting, with the signature of Sir Humphrey Gibbs, so I did not want to upset the little thoughts he had in his mind and providing it did not commit me I agreed to sign." Of all the extraordinary statements made by politicians, that is far and away the most extraordinary known to me.

Back in Salisbury Mr. Smith and his Cabinet worked all through the day and far into the night examining the document, in the process contacting London to secure amplification of various clauses. What finally decided the issue, to the best of my information, was that Wilson—foolishly from his own point of view insisted that the appointments to the council advising the Governor as Commander-in-Chief would not be a matter for the Rhodesian Government, thereby ensuring that it was divested of its military and police powers. Although additional reasons were publicly announced, I have good reason to suppose that this was the determining factor which led to the Rhodesian Government's rejection of the "working document."

At any rate the document was rejected. The enraged Harold Wilson, declaring that never again would he negotiate with Salisbury until it had accepted majority rule – a daft statement if ever there were one – did what he was pledged not to do: he handed over the problem to the United Nations by urging the employment against Rhodesia of mandatory sanctions – a request which the United Nations forthwith granted. At the time of revising this book (February 1967) these sanctions have had no markedly adverse result on the Rhodesian economy, being honoured more in the breach than the observance, and produced no disturbing political effect except for a rather unpleasant squeal from Capetown's *Die Burger*, regarded as the mouthpiece of the Cape Nationalists, complaining that her refusal to return to "legality" could be an embarrassment to Rhodesia's neighbours. The withdrawal of South African facilities would of course make the Rhodesian position untenable.

The Rhodesians themselves for the most part remain in good heart, very few of them realizing how narrow was their escape from disaster as a consequence of the *Tiger* confrontation. Ian Smith has fortified their morale and rallied many of the waverers by assuring them that "one man one vote" would not come in his lifetime or in that of Harold Wilson. It caused them to forget that he had said, early in November 1966, that the existing system enabled Africans to take over the government, adding: "The record shows that they will not be ready for it by the next election and perhaps not for five years after that." (Eight glorious years of crowded life for White Rhodesians under siege!) Instead, they remembered the rousing cry soon after Smith's replacement of Winston Field: "If we can maintain White government in my lifetime there is no reason why it should not be maintained for ever." The important word there perhaps was the initial one—

the little word "if". I make this point because some months later Mr. Smith was speaking of his conviction that twenty years hence Rhodesia would be "a fully integrated nation" and still later—in fact the week before the *Tiger* conference—that Black rule was inevitable and he then reduced the time-factor to a period of eight years or less. "Inevitable." It is the false concept of inevitability which has led to the abdication of the White man throughout the world.

Thus we find in Ian Smith, not the plain blunt man which most of his followers believe him to be, but a complex and even enigmatic character. As a man, he is forceful and transparently honest: as a politician he is, what all politicians under pressure seem to become, an expediency-merchant, equivocal and apt to bend political principle to what may seem to be the advantage of the moment. This characteristic is the more marked in that Ian Smith, to what extent consciously one does not know, has allowed a totally false image to emerge from the tremendous legend built around him. That image is of a mighty champion of the Right-Wing—and it simply is not true. Smith is not even a Right-Winger. He is a man of the centre and, if anything, a shade left of Centre. His political antecedents are liberal. His present attitude, as shown by his acceptance of an unimpeded advance to African rule, is liberal. His view of the future, a fully integrated Rhodesian nation in 20 years, is liberal. Whatever doubts and misgivings he may have about the hand-over, within a measurable period of years, they are for all practical purposes obliterated by his overwhelming sense of inevitability. It is sincerely to be hoped that events will conspire to make him change his mind, because if ever a man were born to lead, and to become a noble leader, it is Ian Smith.

I have written at length about the battle for Rhodesia because I believe it to be a battle destined one way or another to change the course of history. Nor am I alone in this belief. The *Daily Telegraph* has unearthed a secret organisation called Interform, operating in Europe and at least until the time of its exposure, using a numbered, account in the Union Bank of Switzerland at Zurich. It represents a consortium of governments which contribute funds on the pledge that their identities will not be revealed, and it is also financed by one of the large American Foundations. Its function is to act as a propaganda machine for the purpose of making mandatory sanctions effective – and this only as a prelude to the attack on South Africa, which is regarded as the ultimate prize.

Rhodesians have every reason to hold successive British Governments in odium, but the wiser will bear in mind that the Governments themselves are under pressure from the same conspiratorial forces as those gunning for their own country, and that an institution such as Interform, with its abundance of funds, is only one of countless mechanisms used to press home the assault.

The editor of *Die Burger* should also condescend to give these matters some thought, since complacency in South Africa about the plight of the Rhodesians must mean that the front-line in the battle for Western civilization will be withdrawn from the Zambesi River to the Limpopo River and the enemy will be athwart the gates of the Republic.

The last attempt at a settlement was made by Lord Goodman, on behalf of the Rothschild Empire and the British Foreign Office. The terms agreed were parity and a crash programme to give Africans a qualifying vote. Thanks to the stupidity of their leaders the agreement was turned down and civilisation in Rhodesia for the time being saved.

Chapter XVII

WHERE STANDS SOUTH AFRICA?

THE politics of South Africa for upwards of one hundred and fifty years have been bedevilled by a clash between Briton and Boer, which until recently was the name (it means farmer) given to the people of Dutch and Huguenot descent. Bitterness reached its peak during the turn of the century when the so-called Boer War was being waged, largely through the instigation of the cosmopolitan millionaires on the Witwatersrand. If the British Government had not been prevailed upon to coerce President Kruger's Republic it would only have been a matter of time before the grievances of the "Uitlanders" (foreigners), some of them real enough, were redressed. As things fell out, the Boer War left in its wake feelings of hatred which not even the Act of Union, which in effect placed the whole of South Africa under Afrikaner (Boer) control, was totally to eradicate, and which are still a factor in the South African situation. English-speaking South Africans often enough imbibe with their first milk a dislike and distrust of the Afrikaner, and the Afrikaner children as often inherit a hatred of Britain and a desire to keep English-speaking South Africans at arm's length in the higher echelons of government. Both attitudes are as unnecessary as they are deplorable. When two virile peoples (and not so long ago the British were a very virile people) confront each other in the conquest of new lands a head-on collision is perhaps inevitable, but where their successors settle down in occupation of the same country it is a sign of adulthood for the bitterness of an earlier time to be dropped and co-operation on a basis of practical (as distinct from theoretical) equality to be practised. English-speaking South Africans should understand that Afrikanerdom once had much cause for bitterness, and that such emotions are not easily expurgated, while Afrikaners for their part should recognize the large part played by English-speaking South Africans in the development of what is now their common country and that it was the British who finally broke the power of the Xosa, Zulu, Matabele and other warlike tribes which, undefeated, would have made the growth of Western civilization in South Africa impossible.

Until a few years ago the feud between the two components of the White population dominated South African politics and to a certain extent it still does. The general tendency is for English-speaking South Africans and Afrikaners who advocate co-operation between the White races to vote for the United Party and for Afrikaners who tend to think in terms of Afrikaner nationalism to vote for the Nationalist Party. But the creation of Bantu movements aiming at Black government has modified these attitudes. Although most members of the United

Party are as conservative as any member of the Nationalist Party, and as determined not to come under Black domination, the Party failed to make clear where it stood on this vital issue. In consequence, the Nationalist Party came to be regarded by many English-speaking South Africans as the only bastion which could be relied upon to uphold the principle of White leadership and the maintenance of Western standards, and many personally known to me transferred their allegiance to Dr. Verwoerd. Others switched over after South Africa, having attained republican status, left the Commonwealth because of the insufferably insolent attitude adopted by the dusky politicos and parvenus of the "newly emergent nations" such as Ghana and Nigeria. English-speaking South Africans were as incensed as any Afrikaner at this treatment of their Prime Minister, who maintained his dignity in the face of a barrage of insults, and many decided to back him, if need be against the whole world.

Since then the Bantu policies of both the main parties have been more clearly defined, to the perturbation of some Britons who are the friends of South Africa and of a few South Africans who understand the implications of the policies and are not blinded by their party loyalties. When the Nationalist Party policy was first fully explained to me by the editor-in-chief of *Die Burger*, the leading Nationalist newspaper in the Cape, my Nationalist friends were amazed, and perhaps a little incredulous, when I related what had transpired at the interview. Here was the argument. South Africa had never been a unitary country, until unity was imposed by British Imperialism. That is itself a false premise, but no matter. The time had now come, the editor-in-chief told me, for South Africa to resolve itself into the various nations which lived there. Hitherto I had always understood that the Bantustan idea was to encourage devolution so that the Africans might be allowed to develop along their own lines in their own tribal areas and under their own tribal leaders. It had not occurred to me that the tribes would each be elevated to nationhood, so that there would be about eight Black nations and one White nation occupying what is now the Republic of South Africa. I sought reassurance from the Permanent Under-Secretary for External Affairs that this was not Government policy and was given that reassurance.

Yet next year the same official, leading the South African delegation to the United Nations, depicted the future Bantustans precisely as outlined to me by *Die Burger's* editor. As Mr. de Wet Nel, Minister for Native Affairs, had in the meantime given an explicit promise that the Bantustans would enjoy sovereign independence, and as Dr. Verwoerd had endorsed that pledge, I cannot say that I was surprised. Today most of my Nationalist friends, Afrikaner and English-speaking alike, speak precisely the same political language. They use the word I detest more than any other in the context of our times — the word "inevitable".

Had the Nationalist Government, which has dealt with so admirably firm a hand with subversion and sabotage, reserved to itself in the proposed Bantustans power of police, military command, control of foreign policy and final control of the purse, it would have produced a policy which gave Africans the maximum chance to develop in peace and concord and with the assurance that neither they nor White South Africa would be menaced by the rise of African tyrants and the establishment of hot-beds of terrorism and subversion. Frankly, I regard with the greatest alarm the proposal that what is now the prosperous and well-governed Republic of South Africa should be replaced by eight Ghanas or Tanzanias interpenetrating as enclaves, or in places surrounding, such parts of South Africa as may be set aside for White habitation. Where the implications of this policy have been fully understood there is undoubted alarm at the thought of eight Black republics, each with its own absolute control of military and police, each with its own representatives in the U.N. Assembly, each with the power to negotiate with the World Bank and each heavily indebted to the Transatlantic Money Power. The argument is then put forward that the time factor in creating the Bantustans will be under the control of White hands but this is a fallacy which events everywhere else in Africa have exposed. In no country has control over the time factor been maintained, with the result that developments designed to cover a period of years have everywhere been compressed into as many months and sometimes into as many weeks.

Nor is the United Party policy the more acceptable. It boasts that instead of eight Bantustans it will allow eight Bantu representatives to sit in Parliament. Once the principle is conceded that Bantus have the right to participate in legislating for the conduct of affairs in a highly complex Western State, which has to rely for its existence on highly developed skills far beyond the reach of the African mind, then eight becomes a purely arbitrary figure and what is conceded in principle is the right of Bantus to participate in accordance with their numbers — in other words, to take over the country. No, the only solution which seems to me to make sense is the creation of Bantustans with the vital powers I have mentioned kept in firm White hands.

One is not encouraged to think that the Nationalists will revise their policy by the knowledge that during recent years Rothschild finance has been pouring into the country, and that big Afrikaner firms, supporters of the Nationalist Party, are being drawn within the gigantic Oppenheimer complex. I have heard Nationalists declare that this development represents nothing more than the Afrikaner staking his claim to a fair share of the country's wealth. As South African Jewry, although only a small fraction of the White population, controls between 70 and 80 per cent of South Africa's economic activity a more probable outcome could be the absorption of Afrikaner businesses by the International Money Power.

It is not a happy thought to those who, having studied international developments through many years, can claim to know the form.

There are many things upon which South Africa has every reason to congratulate herself. The present mood of complacency is not one of them. Any idea that the policy of either party will conciliate a manufactured "world opinion", which has been made proof against appeasement, belongs to the world of wish-fulfilment. It seems there is not even a general understanding that the very word which describes the policy of separate development and which is intended to reduce racial friction, is employed as a weapon against the users — the word "apartheid". As the Oppenheimer Empire, which controls virtually every English newspaper in the country, does not allow an edition to appear without making some use of the weapon there is no excuse for supposing that similarly inspired newspapers everywhere on earth will allow the weapon to rust.

Nor is it the English-speaking Press alone which is responsible for the spread of "liberal" opinion in the Republic. It should be explained that liberalism in South Africa has a connotation which it does not carry in other countries. The Communist Party being banned, it is the custom of many Communists to adopt the liberal label, with the result that South Africans have come to hold the label suspect. The suspicion is not invariably justified—these are genuine liberals who hold Communism in as much abomination as does anybody else. But whether or not they are genuine, the liberals expound ideas which are rightly held to be subversive of civilized life in South Africa.

There is no recognition of the fact that what they call differences in the colour of the skins of the various races go much deeper than mere pigmentation. They are totally ignorant of psychological factors which create profound differences between racial attitudes, aptitudes, character and habits. They do not even begin to suspect, what scientists not bespoke are able to prove, that the differences are genetical and therefore basic. The liberal endeavour to set aside these differences as though they did not exist, if successful, could only lead to the conditions which prevailed before the imposition of the White man's law— murder and rapine on a continent-wide scale. But economically it would have, as it has had elsewhere, the advantage of facilitating the task of the take-over bidders, native puppets being much more malleable than civil servants brought up to observe a strict ethical code.

It so happens that as ever more alien money flows into South Africa, the more menacing becomes the spread of liberal propaganda and the more bitter and all-embracing the attack on those who dare to call attention to it. The universities today, with only one or two exceptions, are hot-beds of subversion. Every newspaper slant is a subversive slant. Magnates at one time considered bulwarks for the cause of nationalism are going to extraordinary lengths to show sympathy with subversives, as witness the action of a powerful tobacco company in sending abundant supplies of cigarettes to comfort Joshua Nkomo and his terrorist followers placed under restriction by the Rhodesian Government. (One can only hope that such gifts are not a portent that Rhodesia is to be allowed to bite the dust.) The tycoon at the head of this company, traditionally a financial pillar of the National Party, on opening a branch of his tobacco outfit in Kenya, where Kenyatta's former deputy Joseph Murumbi is to be chairman, told an astonished audience that there was no incompatibility whatever between African nationalism and the South African policy of *apartheid*. The liberal infection seems even to have spread to official circles. Dr. Carel de Wet, until recently South Africa's charming and able ambassador in London, said, on leaving his post to become a member of the Cabinet, that if there was one country in the world which desired to see all African peoples free and independent, that country was South Africa. (Dr. de Wet should have been a witness of what Mau Mau did during the Lari massacre, or of the treatment given by Kaunda's specially briefed thugs to Alice Lenshina's villagers.)

It so happens that a small but very brave and well-informed periodical, the *South African Observer*, edited by Mr. S. E. D. Brown, had for several years been exposing subversive elements at work within the country, without drawing fire upon itself from any quarter. However, when it began to investigate some of the affiliations of members of such institutions as the South African Foundation and then to give details of the new link-up of Oppenheimer and Afrikaner business interests, whoever it is who masterminds such operations obviously echoed the words of Captain Corcoran : "Why, damme, it's too bad." He ordered a massive bombardment, with all the artillery at his command.

The *Sunday Times* in each of two issues devoted the front page to attacking Brown and the *South African Observer* under huge banner headlines. Its lead was followed by every daily and Sunday English-speaking newspaper in the country. As Harry Oppenheimer's empire embraces the over-lordship of the English-speaking press, that was not surprising. Nor was it altogether surprising that Piet Cillie, the liberal editor of *Die Burger*, should have been swift to give covering-fire. Their colleagues in the other provinces have always thought of the Cape Nationalists as being a bit "soft". What was truly amazing was that, with the honourable exception of Johannesburg's *Ons Vaderland*, the entire

Afrikaner Press, instead of defending Brown, joined in the vicious attempt to silence his little paper and drive him out of public life.

The implication of the onslaught is not a pleasant one to contemplate. It means that beneath all the shadow-fighting on the surface are basic interests which, once exposed to view, will be defended with the utmost unscrupulousness by those whose job it is to guard them. It means, in other words, that there is in South Africa a secret government which has the power to summon to its defence virtually the entire newspaper-world of the Republic, Afrikaans as well as English-speaking. What is more, when it operates above ground through its various agencies, one may be sure that the language spoken will be the language of liberalism.

It is not to be supposed that the official Government of South Africa, composed as it is of strong men, can relish the thought of sharing power with a subterranean government—a government which in any real crisis would not hesitate to reveal its full strength both nationally and internationally. The Republic's superb Security Service can be trusted to deal with subversion on all ordinary levels, but to deal with it on the level of High Finance would seem to require extraordinary precautions. It is a problem involving the issue of National life and death, and as such do I commend it, with the greatest respect, for the consideration of Mr. Vorster and his colleagues and of all the many South Africans endowed with the capacity to think.

Chapter XVIII

SUBVERTING THE WHITE COMMONWEALTH

I HAVE paid much attention to the application of irresponsible, and indeed impossible, policies to Africa because that continent has become the great battlefield of our times and because it is there that the techniques of the take-over bidders may most clearly be seen. It should not be thought, however, that the programme implicit in the brief General Marshall took with him to the Quebec Conference in 1943 left out of account the nations which shared the same British ideals and which acknowledged allegiance to the British Crown. The eyes and thoughts of these vigorous young countries had at all costs to be turned from London to New York and Washington.

It was during the term of office of President Truman that the first serious efforts were made to weaken the bonds between Australasia and Great Britain. Foster Dulles, when Truman's ambassador-at-large, was entrusted with the carrying out of the bi-partisan policy which embraced this particular task. As at the time it would have been ludicrous to have tried to stampede the Australians and New Zealanders into entering into an exclusive defensive pact with the United States to meet a Chinese menace, the Anzus pact was presented as a measure to insure the Australasian nations against a revival of Japanese military power, Washington having signed a treaty of peace with Japan. Proposals were made by Canberra and Wellington for Great Britain to be asked to become one of the partners in the Anzus set-up, but on being strongly opposed by Foster Dulles on behalf of his masters they were dropped and Britain was excluded from partnership. As it would have been a natural thing for the United Kingdom to join a defensive alliance which vitally concerned her daughter nations in the Pacific — nations which had come to her aid with unsurpassed valour in both world wars — it is legitimate to ask why the United States should have insisted upon her exclusion. The only explanation offered at the time was that Australia and New Zealand would otherwise have been drawn into Britain's defensive arrangements for Malaya, but as both countries have since freely participated in those arrangements it does not meet the facts. Beyond doubt the true explanation was that the internationalist policy required Australasia to be progressively weaned from the British nexus and drawn into the orbit of the Dollar Empire.

In later years the pretence that the Anzus pact insured Australia and New Zealand against a resurgence of Japanese power was quietly dropped and the menace of Communist power substituted. One of the aims of the U.S. policy, under pressure from armament firms interlocked with Wall Street's financial houses, was that the weapons of war of all satellite countries (among which the British nations were marked down for inclusion) should be brought into line with American armaments. Whenever there appeared to be a hitch in this process of standardization, it was reported that Communist submarines had been sighted in Australian waters making surveys of the coast-line, whereupon the hitch would be resolved on the instant and standardization of arms continued according to plan.

There have been several other pointers to the spread of "American" influence, because members of the international power-elite attach much importance to symbols. As I have written, once a symbol is derided or replaced, the reality for which it stands is also derided or replaced. One instance followed the Australian Government's decision to apply the decimal system to its currency. Prime Minister Menzies announced that the new basic standard of measure would be a "royal", roughly equated with the British ten-shilling note and the South African rand. The "royal", as it happens, was an old English coin and its modern usage in Australia could be expected to symbolize that country's allegiance to the Crown. Then Menzies went on a visit to the United States. On his return he declared that the standard of measure would not be called a royal but a dollar, which he surprisingly asserted was in accordance with the wishes of the overwhelming majority of the Australian people. As the Australians had not been consulted, and as many are known to be strongly opposed to the introduction of the dollar, the only logical conclusion one can reach is that Menzies had succumbed to American "suggestion" during the course of his visit. As a cynic he probably thinks that nomenclature is a small matter, of no real significance. If so, he is profoundly mistaken.

Then there is the steadily growing campaign, in both Australia and New Zealand, against so-called "racial discrimination". After a disastrous experience in the early days of the influx of Asians, Australians laid down their "White Australia" policy to which they have long adhered. Only in recent years has it come under serious attack and from the same fifth columnist quarters as operate all over the globe. Unseen hands appear to have planted "liberal" professors in Australian and New Zealand universities as they have been planted the world over — as, for instance, in London, Birmingham, MacGill in Canada, Salisbury in Rhodesia, Cape Town, Witwatersrand and Grahamstown in South Africa and most of the universities in the United States. In the same way it is extraordinary how similar are the views expressed in Australian newspapers to those which appear in almost the entire British Press, in Canadian newspapers, in English-speaking newspapers in South Africa and Rhodesia, in Scandinavian and other European newspapers and in papers published throughout the length and breadth of the United States. The same observation may be made about the pulpits of almost all the denominations of churches in every part of the globe. Patriotism and the safeguarding of national interests, together with the natural tendency to stand by the men and women of European lineage wherever they may be, are systematically discouraged and scorned. In place of these traditional values the malign doctrines of internationalism are preached, and children are being brought up in the unnatural and poisonous belief that racial integration is among the most desirable of all human objectives. Brock Chisholm, the first Director General of the World Health Organization (one of the United Nations' agencies), declared that the ideal skin for a human being is a coffee-coloured skin and U.N.E.S.C.O. (another United Nations' agency) has brought out several publications to proclaim the lie that there is no fundamental difference in aptitudes between the different races of mankind. Nobody is encouraged to observe the end results of racial integration in places such as Brazil, the Cape, and the West Indies. Irresponsible and wicked though the doctrines of U.N.E.S.C.O. undoubtedly are, that does not alter the fact that the Organization's agency in Great Britain is the Ministry of Education, or the fact that New Zealand's Department of Education has taken the lead in disseminating propaganda hostile to national sovereignty and in favour of internationalism and the mixing of the races.

The importance attached to symbolism by those who have decreed the destruction of the British world has been nowhere more evident that in Canada. My first example may perhaps be traced to a development outside the main internationalist assault on the British world system. The Canadian Government, taking everybody by surprise, announced that officers and ratings of the Canadian Navy would be put into uniforms different from those of the Royal Navy, so that Canadian seamen would have to endure none of the odium incurred by British Jack Tars when visiting foreign ports. It was difficult, indeed impossible, to imagine what the officers and men of the Royal Navy had done to deserve this alleged odium. Then all was made clear. At that time the British Government was still trying to ensure some sort of a future for the Palestinian Arabs by restricting the number of Jewish immigrants. The result was that Zionist newspapers in every land were shrieking abuse at the British, whom many of them charmingly called "the new Nazis". The Canadian Government of Mackenzie King, which had become increasingly under Jewish influence, joined in the attack by offering this gratuitous snub to the Royal Navy. As the differentiation of naval uniforms was also calculated to weaken the bonds between Canada and Britain it was doubly welcome to the international power-addicts.

The second example had nothing to do with Palestine, because at the time of its occurrence the United Nations, on the motion of a Canadian stooge, had long since recognized the parvenu state of Israel. There appeared on Canadian dollar bills a delineation of Her Majesty in whose hair was shown, beyond all possibility of mistake, the traditional face of the Devil. This was in the middle 'fifties. As a result of a campaign of protest started by the present writer, the Canadian Government was obliged to call in all issues of the offending bill and replace them with one of a modified design from which the Devil's face was deleted. A little later Canadian post office vans and other property were observed to have had removed from their title of "Royal Canadian Mails" the word "Royal". There was another storm of protest and once again the Canadian Government gave way, so that the word "Royal" was restored. Such attempts to remove or tarnish the symbols affirming the common destiny of the peoples of Canada and the peoples of Great Britain were certainly not accidental. They were intended to further the fulfilment of a deeply laid plot.

Unfortunately the most recent battle of the symbols has resulted in a victory for our internationalist enemies. The national flag of Canada since this great country became a nation has always incorporated the Union Jack. Following the determined efforts of Prime Minister Lester Pearson, Canada now possesses a national flag which makes no acknowledgment of the British connection. It was Lester Pearson who, as Canadian delegate to the United Nations, proposed the recognition of Israel. It was Lester Pearson upon whom, when he was External Affairs Minister, Israel conferred its Medal of Valour, although nobody seems to know precisely for what act of valour he was rewarded. It was Lester Pearson who, as Canadian Ambassador to Washington during the war, was described by the ex-Communist agent, Whittaker Chambers, as "an easy touch" for information. Do I go far astray when I venture the opinion that Lester Pearson is not only the trusted henchman of the declared United States Government in Washington but no less the chief agent in Canada of the Secret Government in New York?

It may be said with some truth that the examples I have cited of the attack on Canada's traditional symbols follow rather than precede the realities of the Canadian situation. Soon after the war, when the possibilities of nuclear conflict were being ruthlessly exploited for political ends, Canada's defence system was to a large extent merged in the defence system of the United States for the purpose of the joint defence of North America. This was the first real inroad upon Canada's national sovereignty. The command was to be essentially a United States command and the United States was to control a series of alarm and other stations extending over Canada's entire breadth. What is being served by this set-up is only incidentally the defence of Canada: it may more accurately be described as the use of Canada as the advanced base for the defence of the United States of America.

There is another use being made of Canada's armed forces. Recruiting posters depict groups of Canadian soldiers keeping the peace in distant lands under the pale blue and white flag of the United Nations — incidentally or perhaps not, the Zionist colours. Thus the appeal to recruits is not even to help in the defence of their own country, let alone in the defence of the British heritage to which Canada owes so much and to which she has given so much. The high ideal held before them is to form part of a cosmopolitan rabble which has included raping Ethiopian soldiery and contingents from many other barbarous countries. Canadian troops, as I have mentioned, were even sent to Suez to go through the motions of shepherding their former British comrades-in-arms out of the area. It is bad enough that Canadian authorities should have no pride in Canada's share of the British heritage: it is even worse that they should have no pride in Canada. Is it supposed that internationalist influences have upheld the standards of efficiency and discipline which obtained when Canadians were still allowed to be content with, and proud of, their British origins and associations? Let this extract from a letter sent to me by a trusted Canadian contact furnish the answer: "The demoralization of the Navy due to the integration drive can be seen: ships are laid up because there are not enough men to man them; the officers are resigning in a disastrous flood; the men are undisciplined, unruly and belligerent. The ships are dirty and sloppy and the crews, when ashore, present a sight which can only be termed sad in the extreme. All this has happened in spite of extraordinarily high pay scales. How far the rot has seeped into the other Services is hard to say but I am told that it is a factor there, too".

The attack on the economies of the British and Commonwealth countries will be discussed when I deal with attempts to drive Great Britain into the European Common Market. Enough has been written to establish that the undermining of the British world and the destruction of national traditions in the White Commonwealth, so that internationalist values may be exalted in their stead, have led to the debasement of standards, to abject mental aberrations and to a spiritual impoverishment which has only to be taken a step further to result in the total collapse of Western civilization.

Chapter XIX

ENFORCING "UNITY" IN EUROPE

DESPITE Lenin's dictum that the Western European nations could best be attacked on their peripheries, determined assaults have been made on the metropolitan countries themselves, mostly by the exerting of pressure to secure the so-called "pooling" of national sovereignties. Such unions must lead to vast administrative units acting in a sphere far removed from the ken of ordinary people, so that whatever small control the electorate may have over national governments is watered down to vanishing point in the larger administrations. Democracy, always subject to the pressures of vested interests, even in small municipalities, becomes nothing more than a name in the ordering, or disordering of affairs in gigantic political combines.

The merging of the nations is no new idea. Paul Warburg in the early 'twenties was calling for a United States of Europe, which he probably saw as a Communist outfit responsive to the dictates of Wall St. In the late 'thirties much support was forthcoming, from interested as well as idealistic sources, for the plan ascribed to Clarence Streit of an Atlantic Union, which was to be a federation of the fifteen or so countries with an Atlantic seaboard. At that time Hitler's Germany was used as a bogey to try to make the countries concerned federate. When Germany was defeated, the promoters of Federal Union, in no way abashed, made the Soviet Union the bogey in her place. The British Broadcasting Corporation, which in any choice between nationalism and internationalism has always backed the internationalist cause, plugged the Federal Union scheme in programme after programme, not even neglecting the Children's Hour, and every offer by the present writer to secure men of national fame to put the other side of the case was declined. Atlantic Union (of which Lester Pearson is a champion) still remains one of several schemes for the staged "advance" to World Government. The creation of the North Atlantic Treaty Organization is itself a functional approach to Atlantic Union.

Then there was the Strasbourg approach, which worked, and perhaps still works, for a Federated Europe as one of the stepping-stones towards the federation of the world. Lack of immediate success does not mean the abandonment of the plan. Strasbourg is still the spiritual home, and indeed the capital city, of the European federalists. Among Britons who repose their hopes in developments planned by embryonic Strasbourg institutions are Lord Boothby and Mr. Christopher Hollis, former Conservative M.P. for Devizes, both of whom, curiously enough, are far from being uninstructed in the machinations of the Money Power.

Functional institutions in Europe are already fully operative. The first was the merging of French and German iron, steel and coal interests under a central authority exercising wide powers, to be followed by the European Common Market, which is the most ambitious scheme as yet adopted. The European Common Market began as a relatively simple device for the adoption of a common tariff policy and free trade between the participating nations — France, Germany, Italy and the Benelux countries. These measures alone did not satisfy the promoters. There had to be a cut-and-dried Constitution and one was duly drawn up and promulgated in an agreement known as the Treaty of Rome. The Treaty of Rome made serious inroads upon national sovereignty, as was to have been expected. It provided, with only very tenuous safeguards, for the free movement of capital and labour across the frontiers of the signatories. It required the municipal law in all the participating countries to be standardized, and as "municipal law" was not defined it could be made to cover pretty well the entire corpus of laws in each of the countries. It legislated for the standardization of professional qualifications, which could only mean for the more advanced participants the lowering of standards, which could have a very deleterious effect, especially in the medical field. In brief, it was, in accordance with internationalist intentions, a blue-print establishing the foundations of the United States of Europe.

The British Government was under strong pressure to bring the United Kingdom into the Common Market. As participation would have dealt a very heavy blow to Britain's agriculture, and also to Commonwealth primary producers receiving preferential treatment in the British Market, the Macmillan Administration proposed the creation of a Free Trade Area (not to be confused with the subsequent E.F.T.A. organization) in which Great Britain, apart from making special dispensations for British farmers and overseas producers, would join the European Common Market and bring its tariff policy into line with that adopted by the Market.

This would have meant joining the British economy to competitive economies, and as the reservations intended to safeguard the British farmers and overseas producers must soon have been jettisoned, the complementary economy covered by the Imperial Preference system would have been abandoned and the British market flooded by products from Common Market countries with a lower standard of living. Indeed, at the outset Continental manufactured goods would have flowed into Britain duty-free, whereas manufactured goods produced by Canada, Australia, New Zealand and other British or partly British countries would have been obliged to jump a tariff wall. Apologists for the Macmillan scheme said that this would affect only ten per cent of their trade, but ten per cent often represents the difference between profit and loss.

Canada had become so alarmed by the infiltration of United States interests, and by the founding in Canada of United States subsidiaries, that John Diefenbaker won an election on the promise of diverting to Britain a substantial percentage of Canadian trade. That he did not carry out the promise when he became Prime Minister, and even reworded the promise to give it a totally different meaning, could be attributed to "politics", a dirty word, or it could have been caused in part by the changing attitude of the British Government which made clear that sooner or later it would be willing to plunge into the European Common Market without reservation or safeguard.

However this may be, the Australian and New Zealand Governments had so little faith in the British Government to resist international pressures and not to rush into the Common Market as an act of complete surrender, that they sent trade missions all over Asia in search of buyers of their primary, and also some of their secondary products. In the nature of things this had to be a two-way process. Japan was not slow to grasp the implications of the changed policy and has already made a start in exploiting it by acquiring interests in Australia and establishing industries in New Zealand. The Chinese, working through Hong Kong, are engaged in much the same pursuit, and public opinion in both Australasian countries is being conditioned to accept these developments by the incessant propaganda of White professors, divines and newspapers preaching the unholy doctrine that Australians and New Zealanders, instead of looking to Great Britain for their future, should wholeheartedly embrace what is called their "Asian" destiny.

Unless these policies are soon reversed, the end result can be foreseen. Dependent financially and strategically upon the United States, Australasian producers have only to rely upon Asian countries to buy the bulk of their exports for the White Australia policy, already undermined, to be trampled into the dust by huge invasions of Asian immigrants, and for New Zealand, even more rapidly, to become the scene of a yellow or brown flood in which the Europeans would be almost totally submerged. The reversal of these policies depends upon a resurgence of the British spirit in the United Kingdom.

Because the British Labour Party, true to accepted political standards, tried to make capital out of the Conservative Government's approaches to the European Economic Community, there is an erroneous belief that it rejects the principle of Britain's adherence to the Common Market. How far this is from the truth may be judged by the welcome given to it by Harold Wilson when the subject was first mooted in the House of Commons:

"We therefore regard this plan, if appropriate arrangements can be made in the negotiations so that we can enter it, not as a generalisation of a free-economy, but as a change of policy which will require very fundamental changes of internal policy in this country. This is our chance, our one chance, to increase investment, and in our view this will mean more controls, more positive Socialist planning measures, more positive use of public ownership, not only to increase the volume of investment in this country, but also to direct that investment more purposively into the industries we most need to expand."

The Labour Party, therefore, would look upon entry into the Common Market as an opportunity of advancing the cause of Socialism. Indeed, as this revised version is being written, Messrs. Harold Wilson and George Brown are traipsing around the Common Market capitals to use their personal charm in advancing the cause as ambassadors in whom Great Britain can take as much pride as though they were Sir Toby Belch and Sir Andrew Aguecheek!

I doubt whether Mr. Macmillan's motives would have been very different. In the 'thirties he was associated with a body known as Political and Economic Planning (P.E.P.), which advocated the association of Government with private enterprise to form industrial and commercial mergers as the most efficient method of production and distribution. Human happiness was not a factor worthy to be considered. The small man might be proud and happy to own a factory or a shop, but it would be so much the worse for his pride and happiness if "efficiency" demanded that he become a charge-hand in a huge industrial enterprise or a shop-walker in a big chain-store. The moving spirit behind P.E.P. was Israel Moses Sieff, who is reported to have referred to Roosevelt's New Deal as "our plan in America". Although the doctrine preached by P.E.P. was called "rationalization" to distinguish it from the Fabian Society's policy of "nationalization", close liaison was maintained between the two organizations. It is quite clear that the programmes of both were part of the drive for political and economic monopoly which has become the twentieth century's obsession. Among the innumerable business mergers of recent months has been the acquisition by the Thomson Empire of *The Times* newspaper and the swallowing up of the famous Rootes interests by the American Chrysler firm – both sad events, inimical to Great Britain.

What has this to do with the European Economic Community? A columnist of the Conservative *Daily Telegraph*, John Appleby, an enthusiastic supporter of the Common Market, seems to have been taken behind the scenes by its promoters and made privy to their true intentions. "It is in the minds of the sponsors," he wrote in the *Daily Telegraph*, "that there would be a merging of productive facilities until there might be, for example, only two motor manufacturers for all six countries". What is this if not an extension to Europe of the Macmillanite and P.E.P. doctrine of rationalization? It is certain, moreover, that any rivalry between two such motor manufacturers would be more nominal than real. Both would be subjected to the same overall control. Appleby then wrote: "To this end it is part of the scheme that the countries concerned should set up a European Commission to run the market. It would have powers of trust-busting." The first sentence is intelligently prophetic. Such a governing body was duly set up. But what of the second sentence? Only in a brain-washed community would it be possible for a responsible newspaper's readership to accept without a hoot of derisive laughter the idea of a trust-forming commission of management having powers of trust-busting. Which are the trusts to be formed and which are the trusts to be busted?

At a moment in time when the British Government was hesitating as to whether it should continue to strive for a negotiated entry into the Common Market or make an unconditional surrender, President Kennedy and the Secretary-General of the European Economic Community simultaneously issued fiats that Britain would be refused participation unless she accepted the Treaty of Rome and all its implications — in other words, made unconditional surrender. Professor Hallstein, Secretary-General of the European Economic Community, made no secret of the purpose the Common Market is intended to serve. It had been placed before the peoples of Western Europe purely as a measure to increase and facilitate trade, but Hallstein knocked that idea on the head. "We are in this," he declared in a public statement, "not for economics but for politics". People who, like the present writer, had insisted upon this truth from the first, naturally received no apology for the derision cast upon us when our thesis was thus openly avowed!

President Kennedy's standing in what was supposed to be a European venture escaped questioning. That, however unconsciously, was realistic. Kennedy laid down the law less as the President of the United States than as the bespoke fugleman of the Secret Government in New York, which had incubated the plan for the European Common Market and which has every intention of running it — for the dual purpose of blazing the trail for World Government and at the same time of introducing Communism by stealth.

Then came President de Gaulle's famous "Non". The possible reason for it, and other related matters, will be considered in the next chapter.

116

Chapter XX

DE GAULLE AND WESTERN DEFENCE

I KNOW many people, some of them intelligent and well-informed, who regard President de Gaulle as a redoubtable opponent of the Money Power. They may be right, but I am free to form my own mental reservations. The use of the term "Money Power", let us not forget, is a kind of shorthand, a necessary over-simplification. It should not be regarded as an all-seeing, all-powerful cabal which never knows internal dissensions or which, because of these dissensions, never sets in motion divergent strands of policy to secure the same ends. That there is an overall policy objective I believe not to be open to doubt. It may be glimpsed in occasional revelations, but fully comprehended, at least in outline, by its continuity. The Final Act of Bretton Woods, which gave birth to the World Bank and the International Monetary Fund, the Dumbarton Oaks Conference which created the United Nations and all its agencies, the Havana Conference which produced the General Agreement on Tariffs and Trade, and many similar assemblies of hand-picked functionaries were not incubated by hard-pressed Governments engaged in waging war, but by a supranational Money Power which could afford to look ahead to the shaping of a post-war world that would serve its interests. There has always been room for rivalries between the different financial groups of which the Money Power is composed and for divergent views about the ways and means whereby the overall objective may be reached. There is beyond question a continuing conspiracy, but its method is more empirical than doctrinaire.

When de Gaulle, as a Major-General in the French Army, arrived in Great Britain after Dunkirk, there was no obvious military reason why he should be placed in command of the Free French forces. He had the reputation of being an expert on tank warfare, although it did not approach that of our own Major-General J. F. C. Fuller, whose services the craven British Government, terrified of the "Left", refused to employ because he had given expression to some very forthright right-wing views. De Gaulle, it is true, did not suffer from this disability. But his name had never been one to conjure with in France, and when the heroic French fighting soldier, General Giraud, escaped from German custody and made his way, via Gibraltar, to join the Allies in North Africa, his fame entitled him to the Free French leadership — an appointment which would have sent a thrill of pride and expectation throughout France. Instead, to use a popular slang expression, he received the "frozen mitt". Why? One reason could be that he had no very high regard for the international power elite. Another, and one more germane and perhaps even related, was that he lacked the patronage upon which de Gaulle was able to rely.

When Charles de Gaulle landed on British soil his patron was already there, waiting to welcome him. The name of this patron? Guy de Rothschild, head of the French branch of the family which operates in Paris under the title of Rothschild Freres. Biographers of the Rothschilds assert, with more coyness than accuracy, that Guy de Rothschild was able to undertake several confidential missions for de Gaulle — an enchanting piece of camouflage. In truth, de Gaulle was a Rothschild nominee and the association has continued ever since.

When the Allied victory was won de Gaulle became the Prime Minister of France. During the period of his premiership, Sisley Huddlestone, who lived in France throughout the war and its aftermath, computes that at least ten times more Frenchmen were put to death, on the pretext of being "collaborators", than were killed from the beginning to the end of the French Revolution. It was during this period, too, that the great soldier and patriot Marshal Petain — whose only crime had been to try to secure for France the best possible terms after the French armies had been overwhelmingly defeated — was put on trial and flung into a prison fortress for life. Contrast Petain's fate with that of Thorez, leader of the French Communist Party. Thorez was tried *in absentia* for broadcasting from Moscow in 1940 urging Frenchmen to lay down their arms (this was while the Berlin-Moscow axis was rotating) and sentenced to death. Did the patriotic de Gaulle ensure that the sentence was carried out? He did not. Instead he made Thorez Deputy Prime Minister of France. This was doubtless the sort of thing the noble Bastard in *King John* described with scorn as "commodity".

De Gaulle was destined to have a much longer period in which to practise "commodity". He retired from public life and waited for many years for his recall. It duly came. The French Generals in Algeria, alarmed by the progressive betrayal of French interests in North Africa by successive governments in Paris, staged a successful rebellion, and because of the fame and patriotism attributed to General de Gaulle as leader of the Free French, he seemed the obvious choice to consolidate the results of the rebellion, unite France, and stand unflinchingly for the maintenance of *Algerie Francaise*. So at least the Generals believed. They were mistaken. After a year of temporising, during which de Gaulle "liberated" all the rest of French Africa, he surrendered Algeria to Ben Bella, implacable enemy of France and the blue-eyed favourite of Moscow, Peking — and, need one add, Washington. When the Generals again protested they were ruthlessly hunted down and subjected to the harshest penalties.

118

It may be said that President de Gaulle (that now became his title) is a romantic French patriot who engaged in "commodity" because of the *force majeure* employed by the international conspirators. Perhaps so. But I doubt whether there is much of the romantic in M. Pompidou, his Prime Minister and right-hand man. Before being elevated to the Premiership, Pompadou was the chief functionary — can the reader guess? — of Rothschild Freres, who had been from the first de Gaulle's patrons. And who can doubt that the Gaullist policy in North Africa was in alignment with the international financial objective of separating the Metropolitan countries from their former colonies and spheres of influence?

Against this must be placed the fact that when Great Britain, thoroughly softened up, was prepared to enter the European Common Market at any cost, the Rothschild- de Gaulle combination said "Non". More accurately, what it said was "Not yet". I do not find this difficult to reconcile with the declared international policy of waging war against national sovereignty and seeking to destroy national independence. When the United Kingdom sought entry into the European Economic Community Great Britain still had ties with the British nations overseas — ties which remain. They have been continually weakened by the stresses and strains of international pressure, but as long as they exist there is still the possibility of a great British revival. The possibility may seem remote and every year traitorous policies make it ever more remote as one by one the overseas bonds are loosened or destroyed. Given patience, it is thought, they may soon completely disappear. That would be the time for Great Britain, made naked and afraid, to be admitted into the Common Market, less as an equal than as a captive. President de Gaulle may consider such a development to be a French interest. If so, it would be a very short-term view. But one strand of international policy-making could well derive from a belief that top priority has to be given to the smashing of the British world, about which there would be no divergence of view among the conspirators.

Whether this can best be done before, and not after, Britain's admittance into the Common Market, is a matter on which opinion could very easily diverge.

Much the same considerations might apply to de Gaulle's apparent indifference to the requirements of those who created the North Atlantic Treaty Organization as an instrument of power for the governance of the Western World. It is not difficult to visualise a situation in which the promoters of Nato might wish to give the impression that members of the alliance are not strictly regimented — always provided, of course, that the apparent rebellion does not go too far. The gestures of independence made by de Gaulle have done nothing to weaken the Nato structure. Should this view be considered far-fetched, then an alternative explanation could be that the Money Power in New York is so engrossed in the task of giving the British world-system its *coup-de-grace* that for the time being French attitudes are not of much importance and can be dealt with when the more immediate objective has been attained. Of the two explanations the first seems to me the more probable.

However French attitudes may be interpreted, there is very little doubt about British attitudes. There are no indications that British Governments have kicked against the pricks and endeavoured to rescue the British defence system from the entangling alliance. Instead, every move has been to allow it to become ever more entangled. Field-Marshal Lord Montgomery, a fine soldier but a child in the sphere of international politics, long ago proposed that the R.A.F.'s famous Bomber Command should be integrated with the United States Air Force, with Headquarters on the American side of the Atlantic. This naive proposal assumed that alliances are what they have never been before — permanent. It assumed, further, that Great Britain would never again wish to use air power as a sovereign nation. Such a line of thought would coincide with the intentions of the promoters of Nato, not only because of the power over the West which the alliance confers on them, but because the alliance is one of the foundations on which they hope to build World Government. In this context it is interesting to recall the strange speech made by Winston Churchill at Aachen when he suggested that, subject to certain provisos, it might be possible for the Soviet Union to become a member of the North Atlantic Treaty Organization — a truly Baruchian proposal. As the Western nations had been induced to accept Nato as an alliance for the containment of Communism, the idea that the Soviet Union should join it to help in containing itself was, to say the least, novel.

It so happens that the Montgomery proposal for the merging of Bomber Command with the United States Air Force, although naive, was not very different from what actually took place. The allegedly Conservative Government of Harold Macmillan placed almost all our bombers under Nato — that is, American — command and the greater part of our Fighter Command as well. Even this was not enough for the international conspirators. Although under Nato command, the components of the Nato force were still national contingents liable to recall, as President de Gaulle had shown. How could the power to recall be circumvented? New York's back-room boys soon worked out the answer. Let there be mixed-manned fleets and air-crews. Let every Polaris-carrying submarine be manned by a polyglot crew under an American commander. Let every H-bomb carrier be similarly crewed. What matter if in the result efficiency went to hell! The main objective would be achieved — such omelettes could never be unscrambled. No British politician of any pride or patriotism, one might think, could possibly acquiesce in the fragmentation of the Royal Navy or the Royal Air Force, both first-class fighting services, to help in the creation of a cosmopolitan rabble at sea or in the air. Yet Alec Douglas-Home, first as Foreign Secretary and then as Prime Minister, enthusiastically pressed for British participation in the scheme, on the curious ground that thereby Great Britain would be able to speak in weightier tones in the council-chambers of the world, which was a proposition contrary to every logical conjecture.

Then came Harold Wilson at the head of the Labour Government. What solution had Wilson to propose? It was staggeringly simple. Great Britain must forgo every means of nuclear defence at her disposal and invest the whole power of deterrence in the United States. The Labour Party, to judge by its speeches during half a century, is opposed to the capitalist system. Yet here it was, tumbling over itself in its haste, offering sole monopoly of nuclear deterrence to the greatest capitalist country on earth. How does one explain such fantastic anomalies? The only answer that makes any sense is that economic pressures, possibly applied to exploit Britain's imbalance of payments or other vulnerable economic situation, turn every British Government into a Wall Street lackey. It is not a situation we should continue to tolerate. We can produce out of our own resources sufficient power of nuclear deterrence to make an attack on Great Britain, from whatever quarter, a deadly dangerous enterprise. We can, in co-operation with the other White Commonwealth countries, so harmonise our various economies as to make ourselves invulnerable to alien pressures.

If a British Government had the guts to devise these measures and stand by them it is more than possible that the other Western European countries, all of them sick of domination by Wall Street, would join with us to form a real Western European alliance that was free from the influence of the pro-Communist lending houses of New York. But such a Government could only be born out of national resurgence, and signs of that rebirth are all too tenuous and few. Signs of it in France are as illusory as was de Gaulle's statement in 1959 that never in his own life would the F.L.N, flag fly over Algeria. Indeed, when the French President adumbrated his scheme for a European Federation extending all the way from the Atlantic to the Urals, he might seem expressly to have renounced the national idea. Is it not remarkable today how all roads, in whatever direction they may start, lead through phased developments to the attainment of One World?

At the time of writing, despite Harold Wilson's charm turned on at full pressure, the French "non" still stands, which would suggest the appropriateness of conferring at least the O.B.E. on President de Gaulle "for services rendered".

Chapter XXI

DEMORALIZATION AT HOME

REFERENCE was made in the first chapter to the deplorable deterioration of morale in Great Britain and there have been references in subsequent chapters to the abject laying aside of national sovereignty by politicians entrusted with the conduct of her affairs. These are themes which must now be further developed to establish their connection with the overall plan to destroy all our values and so to disarm and emasculate us that we become unable to protect ourselves when Communism advances to claim the British people, with the rest of mankind, as serfs subject to the tyranny of a One World State. Let us, for example, take another look at Harold Wilson's declared policy of abandoning our power of nuclear deterrence so as to invest the United States of America with the sole means of defending us against the menace of nuclear attack. Even if the United States were on our side, as over and over again she has shown herself not to be, this would be a shameful — indeed a traitorous — abandonment of the power to survive as a nation in our own right. The United States is not on our side for the simple reason that she is not even on her own side, but a cat's paw for alien interests to use as they please. Many American patriots are aware of this truth and do their best to make it known. Many have been smashed in the process.

If Harold Wilson does not know the facts of the American situation he must be an exceedingly ill-informed man. It is difficult to credit such ignorance. There are some matters of the utmost gravity of which he cannot fail to be aware. The most important of these was the acceptance by President Johnson of the policies of the late President Kennedy. Too little is known in Britain about the real nature of these policies. It was under the Kennedy dispensation that work began on the rehabilitation of soiled reputations such as those of Owen Lattimore, J. Robert Oppenheimer and many another whose allegiance had been judged more than doubtful by competent authority. The U.S. Senate Internal Security Sub-Committee had described Owen Lattimore as "a conscious, articulate agent of the Soviet Conspiracy". The U.S. Atomic Energy Commission decided that Oppenheimer had contributed large sums of money to the Communist Party, that his wife, his mistress and his brother were Communists, that he had lied to Security investigators about Communist attempts to obtain nuclear data, and that he had recommended an identified Communist for a job on the top-secret A-bomb project. What did Kennedy do? He approved the grant to Oppenheimer of the 1963 Enrico Fermi award of $50,000 in tax-free government funds and later in the year President Johnson duly made the presentation.

These were only pointers, but they were significant. Nobody supposes that Kennedy and Johnson acted under the Kremlin's orders. The headquarters of the conspiracy were much nearer home. How many people remember that after the signing of the Test Ban Treaty in Moscow in 1963, Kennedy described it as a further measure to implement Bernard Baruch's plan, drawn up nearly twenty years before, for the centralized, internationalist control of every form of atomic energy? How many people remember that, in his speech to the opening session of the United Nations in 1961, Kennedy proposed a plan "for the general and complete disarmament of the United States?" This new policy was set forth in a subsequent State Department document. I quote from John A. Stormer's excellent book *None Dare Call It Treason*: "Under the official, published three-stage disarmament plan, nuclear tests would be banned, production of nuclear weapons and their delivery systems would be halted, existing stocks of weapons and atomic warheads would be transferred to the United Nations, development of anti-missile missiles and similar defensive weapons would be abandoned. . . . Conventional armed forces and weapons would be reduced by transferring control over U.S. and other troops to the United Nations so 'no state (including the U.S.) would have the power to challenge the progressively strengthened United Nations Peace Force' ". All existing nuclear weapons and control of conventional forces to be transferred to the United Nations! I ask the reader whether this proposal is or is not part of the international conspiracy. I ask whether it is or is not a policy of treason and suicide involving, not the United States alone, but the whole of Western civilization and Christendom. One may legitimately enquire why — in the name of Heaven why— a monument should be erected to Kennedy, master of double-speak and a tool of the Money Power, in — of all places— Runnymede, the Thames-side site of the signing of Magna Carta in 1215. Is it a symbolic attempt to slur over the clause in Magna Carta which sought to protect the English people against Jewish usury?

It is to a country pledged to the abolition or transference of its nuclear weapons that Harold Wilson proposes to surrender Britain's own power of nuclear deterrence. Does this indicate, or does it not indicate, that Wilson is himself "a conscious, articulate agent" of the all-enveloping internationalist plot?

What I now mention may seem as thistledown in comparison with the mighty and disastrous developments of the last two decades and with the still mightier and still more calamitous events which, having been planned, are now in the wings awaiting their cue to enter the public arena. Reference has been made to bands of Mods and Rockers who in every part of Britain represent the gregarious instinct in Great Britain's youth and whose presence there is a perpetual demonstration of the decadence in our midst. Members of one or other of these factions — I have never troubled to find out which — make a cult of wearing their hair down to their shoulders so that it is impossible from the back to distinguish between male and female. Only a front view, showing a fringe of beard round pallid faces and weak, watery eyes, reveals the sorry simulacrum of the male sex. The Labour Government of Harold Wilson has now decreed that members of Great Britain's fighting services, which have a superb record in battle, are to be released from the tyranny of having their hair cut, thereby giving them the freedom to cultivate locks which reach down to the shoulders and beyond. The sight of a Guards' battalion on the march, hitherto a splendid spectacle of British manhood at its physical best, may now be something to turn away from in dismay and revulsion. According to officialdom the new "freedom" will bring the fighting services into line with modern custom. It is more likely to make them sickly and decayed. The proposed nuclear disarmament of Britain is a policy of constructive treason, but I doubt whether in the long run its deleterious effects will be greater than the spiritual disarmament and debasement of those who are supposed to be its defenders against enemy attack.

The supreme treason in the British Isles, however, is the creation of a colour problem in a White nation where no such problem has existed throughout the hundreds of years of its existence. In the 1955 elections the present writer and some of his colleagues went to Bromley to challenge Harold Macmillan about this issue, which even then had assumed alarming proportions. In reply Macmillan said that he, too, was very much concerned about the situation which had been created, but added that Britons could go anywhere in the British world on the strength of a British passport. This we denied, whereupon Macmillan, then Foreign Secretary, assured his audience that he knew all about it, having made a special study of the subject. We responded by reciting some of the innumerable countries where entry visas were needed and residence permits and financial deposits essential. Defeated, he tried to change the subject.

Next year Macmillan became Prime Minister, with power to move and secure the passage through Parliament of measures to put an end to coloured immigration. He did nothing. While he posed and strutted upon the stage of public life further hundreds of thousands of coloured people poured into the British Isles from the West Indies, from West Africa, from India and Pakistan and from many other countries, thus casting derision upon Harold Macmillan's professed "concern", the expression of which obviously had no meaning other than to delude the British people. Today the coloured invasion has spread throughout England, being encountered even in the remotest country villages. Finally, when the problem got out of hand, an Act was passed which purported to restrict the influx of immigrants from the "Commonwealth" — that is to say,

White immigrants as well as Black and Brown — but its provisions were easily evaded and still they came. At Smethwick, however, during the General Election of 1964, Patrick Gordon Walker, former member of the Labour "Shadow Cabinet", lost the seat to a Tory candidate on the question of coloured immigration, and again when he stood for Leyton. The politicians, to whom votes are all-important, now began to perceive that it was necessary to take some kind of a public stand, in their propaganda if not in their actions, against the coloured invasion, and Peter Thorneycroft, a prominent member of the previous Conservative Government, spoke to a Conservative gathering of the need not only to tighten up controls but to return to their country of origin certain types of immigrant. Thorneycroft had suffered a spell in the political wilderness by resigning from the Government on a relatively minor matter which concerned a difference on financial policy. Why, if he felt so strongly about the creation of the colour problem, did he not resign on this major matter, affecting in perpetuity the breed of men produced in the British Isles? The answer could be that the vested interests sponsoring coloured immigration had become so strong that anybody rash enough to offer real opposition might well be committing political suicide.

There is something to be said for the coloured immigrants — at any rate for those arriving from the West Indies. If British Governments in the inter-war years had not encouraged West Indians to concentrate on export crops at the expense of produce for home consumption, and then coolly switched imports into Britain of commodities such as sugar from the West Indies to Cuba and elsewhere, there would be less temptation for their sons and daughters to leave their sunny lands and shiver in misery throughout the long English winters. There is also a case, though slighter, for the Indians of Kenya, betrayed by the British Government, to move into Britain, as many of them— fearful of what an African Government portends — have already done, India apparently having no attraction for them.

Even so, the main duty of the British Government and the British people is to honour the British past, to protect the British present and to legislate wisely for the British future. This duty entails sending back whence they came, with generous help which elsewhere is now being systematically misapplied, the bulk of Great Britain's coloured population. It is no part of my case that these people are inferior in general, but only that most of them are inferior in the context of British skills and standards. The result of their impact must be a lowering of these standards. Their ideas of quiet neighbourliness, of sanitation, of overcrowding and of health are only some of the factors which cause disquiet. British people, who have paid for their own health services, often wait for months to be admitted to hospitals because so many beds, indeed entire wards, are occupied by coloured people cashing in on the National Health scheme. The incidence of tuberculosis and venereal disease has risen enormously as a result of their influx, their almost habitual crowding of several families into a single room, as well as the habits of many of them, create sanitary conditions which the British have come to regard as disgusting and intolerable. Their participation in crime is out of all proportion to their numbers and there are complaints that they make the night hideous with their revelry. By far the worst aspect of their presence, however, is the interbreeding which inevitably results. This does permanent injury to the British stock, because genes thus transmitted remain for ever. If there be any doubt about this, let the reader dwell on the seemingly intractable colour problem in the United States, on the situation created in Brazil, on conditions of life in the West Indies and on the hopeless difficulties and frustrations, rending to the heart, of a large coloured population in the Cape. To have allowed the same sort of problem to arise in the British Isles has been at best callous negligence and at worst downright criminality.

So disastrous has been the flooding of the country by the sea of coloured immigrants that one wonders what economic motives have prompted its sponsors. To pass the kitchen entrance to many of the chief catering firms when there is a change of shift provides part, if only a small part, of the answer. The dominating motive may well have been not economic but political — the conspiratorial plan, everywhere being carried out, of securing the mongrelization of mankind. More will be said about this later. What has here to be stated, with the greatest possible emphasis, is that the mixing of White and Black or Coloured people results in hordes of unhappy half-castes who feel that they belong nowhere, whose tendency is to embrace the vices of both racial stocks and not to strive after the virtues, and who must eventually, through no fault of their own, bring to an end the tremendous history of achievement which is the heritage of the European nations.

"Criminality", have I described the sponsorship of these migrations? I understated its significance. The movement at base is not merely criminal: such destruction of the happiness and contentment of peoples still unborn is more than criminal: in the truest sense of the word it is diabolical. What is more, it is aimed at the destruction of the great British nation and system of nations. In times past men were hanged for treasons much less full of menace than this treason, but the men responsible for it will go, not to the block at the Tower of London, but to the British House of Lords.

Chapter XXII

BURGESS, MACLEAN & CO.

SO many well-informed American writers have probed and put on record the work of powerful forces engaged in subversion within the boundaries of the United States that it would be superfluous for me to do more than take an occasional glance at their activities, to show how closely related they are to the general pattern of events elsewhere. Only one quotation is needed to establish that the attack on nationhood in America is being pressed home as ruthlessly as it is in Great Britain and elsewhere. In 1962 Mr. J. Edgar Hoover said: "Too often in recent years patriotic symbols have been shunted aside. Our national heroes have been maligned, our history distorted. Has it become a disgrace to pledge allegiance to our flag — or to sign a loyalty oath, or pay tribute to our national anthem? . . ." This work of denigration is no mere fashion: it is calculated policy.

While I admire the courage and tenacity of the American patriots who expose what is happening behind the American scene, I sometimes wonder whether some of them are not so engrossed in studying the minutiae of the trees that they fail to see the wood. Mr. Robert Welch, for instance, the founder of the John Birch Society, contrived to write a brilliant and devastating exposure of Eisenhower without once mentioning the name of Baruch, who was his patron and his mentor. Similarly, in *None Dare Call It Treason* I find Mr. Stormer quarrelling with the authors Gavian and Hamm for quoting what Mary Lease wrote: "Wall St. owns the country. It is no longer a government of the people, for the people, and by the people, but a government of Wall St., by Wall St., and for Wall St. The parties lie to us .... the people are at bay; let the blood-hounds of money who have dogged us thus far beware". Comments Mr. Stormer: "Gavian and Hamm do not counter-balance this quotation by pointing out that nearly every American family has a stake in Wall St. Over 25 per cent of American families own stock in industry directly. Almost all others share in some way through private insurance policies, company pension plans, or union welfare programs whose assets are invested in Wall St." All this is perfectly true. The same things from time to time are said for and against the City of London, which is also used as a sort of shorthand.

But such criticism to my mind circumvents the real issue. Of course, both in Wall St. and the City of London there are operating responsible firms with no inordinate lust for power. It cannot be denied, however, that these are also the haunts and headquarters of world power-addicts and the investments of the general public are not directly a factor in the situation. Apart from their monopoly of the issue of credit, such as that vested in the Federal Reserve Board, the big financial firms build up their own fortunes and their power mechanisms by the use of other people's money — a practice as old as usury. The question to be asked, more often than not, is not who makes the investment but who controls the investment when made. It is in that control that power resides.

This fact is implicit in many American treatises, but rarely explicit. In tracking down the masters of Dean Acheson, Alger Hiss and Harry Dexter White, for instance, Right-wing writers are too realistic to seek for them in the Kremlin. Instead, they look at figures like Felix Frankfurter and Henry Morgenthau Junior, knowing that even these men are not the principals and probably suspecting that the principals are to be found much nearer to the centre of Wall St. than in Moscow. In the same way, asked to name the master of Franklin Roosevelt, Harry Hopkins and Dwight Eisenhower, nobody would be so foolish as to answer "Stalin". Bernard Baruch would be a much better bet.

Even so, American patriots have done such fine service in exposing subversive activities that it would be churlish to dwell too long on this strange omission — an omission perhaps not so strange when one takes all the factors into account. Nothing even approaching this work of exposure has been done in the United Kingdom, where there is ample scope for it. Every aspect of the Hiss affair, for instance, has been exposed to public view, whereas in Great Britain the defection of Burgess and Maclean, while it made headlines for many a day, escaped real probing except for the efforts of the present writer, whose means of disseminating the facts were not extensive.

It is known that at the time of his escape from Britain Maclean was being shadowed by the British Secret Service. There was no Parliamentary bloodhound to sustain a barrage of questions as to how a shadowed man was able to go on a trip to the Continent and then disappear from view. Was the shadowing called off on superior orders to allow him to make his get-away and so avoid the disclosures of a public trial? It had long been known that both Maclean and Burgess had been practising homosexuals, but there was no Parliamentary bloodhound to demand an answer as to why they should nevertheless have been given sensitive posts in the Foreign Office. That both men had powerful patrons was not difficult to deduce, but no British newspaper dared mention the fact that Guy Burgess had once shared Lord Rothschild's flat — a circumstance which, though it in no way implicates Lord Rothschild, was surely of some significance and interest. When, long afterwards, the Left-wing British M.P. Tom Driberg was allowed by the Russians to visit Burgess in

Moscow he came back and wrote a book on the subject, stating among other things that Burgess had been asked to give financial advice to a member of the Rothschild family, an event not without its amusing side. As there is nothing more cowardly than smearing by innuendo and association, let me make clear the reason for my mentioning of the Rothschild name. It is not to suggest that the Rothschilds sponsored Burgess. It is to suggest that a man moving in such circles has no need of sponsorship.

There was nothing in the way of a real disclosure until a British Socialist M.P. let it be known that he had warned Hector McNeil, Minister of State for Foreign Affairs, that Burgess, whom the Minister was employing as his private secretary, was a Communist agent. Although Burgess was thus at the very heart of Great Britain's foreign affairs network, the Minister made no use of this warning and allowed the agent to carry on. Then a very peculiar thing happened. When the Burgess-Maclean story was about to break, Members of Parliament were streaming back to London from all over the world in readiness for a new session — with one exception. Hector McNeil alone was outward bound. Taken ill a couple of days after embarking, he was flown by seaplane, not back to England for treatment, which would have been the natural thing, but to New York. A week or two later he died in a New York hospital. The captain of the ship in which he sailed, when interviewed, declined to comment. I do no more than state the facts and make no insupportable deductions. Among these facts, beyond question, was that the death of Hector McNeil took place at a very convenient time, which averted all possibility of questioning and scandal. When an M.P., summoning up his courage, did raise the matter in the House of Commons he was rebuked for his lack of sensibility and told that the dead man was not there to answer for himself.

Those conversant with the course of McNeil's illness may perceive nothing strange in the way it terminated. Not being conversant with it I can only say that I find his death very strange — as strange — though in quite a different context — as the death of James Forrestal, Secretary of the U.S. Navy, who had opposed the formation of the State of Israel and who had placed on record Neville Chamberlain's complaint that the Jews were pressing him to make war on Germany. Forrestal is said to have jumped from the top storey of a psychiatric ward of a naval hospital. I had always thought that among the functions of psychiatrists was the responsibility of ensuring that patients sent to them for observation did not jump to their deaths. There may be rational explanations of these events. I can only record that I am not aware of them. About yet another death there was no mystery whatever. Bang Jensen, a Hungarian official of integrity on the staff of the United Nations, possessed confidential information on what could be a matter of life or death for his country's Freedom Fighters. He was instructed by his U.N. superiors to pass on the information to them. He refused on principle, because it had been given to him in confidence. Knowing some of his superiors and their affiliations it is certain that he would have kept the information to himself even had it been otherwise acquired. The refusal, as may be imagined, was not well received.

Sensing danger to himself, Jensen made known to those closest to him that on no account would he ever take his own life. He was found dead in a New York park. The verdict, it need scarcely be said, was "suicide". Jensen was murdered.

These deaths may be considered important enough to warrant my digression. There has still to be recorded the sequel to the Burgess, Maclean and McNeil episodes. At the time of the exposure of Burgess and Maclean the British newspapers were making the most of a theme which they called, dramatically enough, "The Third Man". This was supposed to be the man who had warned Maclean that he was under suspicion. Some years later a British agent — or at any rate a Briton in receipt of British pay for supposedly acting as a British agent — disappeared from his post of duty in the Middle East and reappeared in the Soviet Union. His name was Kim Philby, and his father was the famous Arabist St. John Philby. The son was a Communist agent, disloyal to his country and his pay. Here was the opportunity for the British newspapers neatly to round off their thesis. "The Third Man" had been discovered in the person of Philby. Nevertheless the *denouement* was improbable. Why should Philby have known that Maclean was held suspect? Who told him? Is it not more likely that the warning had come from a much higher quarter? It is even possible that it came from the United States. Maclean and Burgess had both served on the British Embassy staff in Washington. So had Philby. McNeil, the protector of Burgess, was on his way to New York when he became fatally ill. Indeed, although the three Communist agents sought sanctuary in Russia, their ties with America were much closer and more intimate.

Here, indeed, is the chief feature in the pattern of world conspiracy which we have been tracing throughout this book. The "cold war" was a device, not to divide and rule, but to confuse and unify. The United States and the Soviet Union have been partners in every act of conspiracy. Together they equipped such countries as Indonesia. At Suez the Russians did the growling while the Americans did the dirty work. So it was at Abadan. People are taught to be aware of the Russian, and even of the Chinese, menace in Africa, whereas the usufruct of every "liberated" country in the Continent has been seized by the United States on the instigation of its pro-Communist masters. There is little doubt that this seeming duality is not in fact dual but represents two arms of the same power- instrument. And there is still less doubt that unless the contrived dichotomy is tackled in detail, exposed as fraudulent, and denounced as a pestilence-laden plot, there will be no freedom for the world but only a world doped, stupefied, brainwashed and made ready for spiritual death.

Chapter XXIII

THE CONSPIRATORIAL BUREAUCRACY

WHEN writing of conspiracy, the writer feels that to make good his case it would be only fair to the reader to furnish the names and addresses of its principals. This is rarely possible, because the essence of conspiracy is that it be incubated in secrecy and the conspirators do not defeat their own ends by avowing their objectives. Even so, the face of a master-mind is sometimes revealed. The face, for example, of Bernard Baruch, who for fifty years and more had moved across the stage of world affairs as a shaper of world policy. For the rest, we do know quite a lot about the agents and agencies used for furthering the conspiratorial design, and it is possible that among them may be some of the policy-making principals, the actual directors of the conspiracy. It is perhaps fairer, and more realistic, to regard the functionaries and the institutions I am about to discuss as part of the bureaucracy of the projected new order rather than as the governing body. I begin with some facts about the Council on Foreign Relations in the United States and its related body, the Royal Institute of International Affairs (Chatham House) in Great Britain. The reader should be informed that well-meaning people, innocent of power-addiction, will be found, among others of whom the same cannot be said, in the membership of both bodies.

The Royal Institute of International Affairs was conceived during the treaty-making at Versailles. As originally planned it was to have been the Anglo-American Institute of Foreign Affairs, but no doubt for the sake of appearances the proposers eventually decided that there should be two bodies instead of one, with no ties between them visible to the ordinary eye. While Chatham House alternates between coyness and the "come hither" look in matters of publicity, its American opposite number — the Council on Foreign Relations— has been only too glad to avoid the limelight. In 1958, however, Mr. Joseph Kraft told the readers of *Harper's Magazine* a little about the Council. Although the tone of the article was innocent, it contained many revealing passages, such as the fact that the Council "quietly incubates a surprising share of both the men and the ideas which make policy for the United States". Its membership, "indisputably important", included at the time "the President, the Secretary of State, the Chairman of the Atomic Energy Commission, the Director of the Central Intelligence Agency, the board chairmen of three of the country's five largest industrial corporations, two of the four richest insurance companies, and two of the three biggest banks, plus the senior partners of two of the three leading Wall St. law firms, the publishers of the two biggest news magazines and of the country's most influential newspaper and the presidents of the Big Three in both universities and foundations, as well as a score of other college presidents and a scattering of top scientists and journalists." If a surmise be permissible it is that the part played by the finance houses has here been played down. That much is apparent from the revelation that Paul Warburg and Otto Kahn, of Kuhn, Loeb and Co., were members of the Council's first board. It is improbable that the direction has passed out of Kuhn, Loeb hands.

Much is explained by the existence of the Council on Foreign Relations. Its function is clearly to frame — or at any rate to co-ordinate — the policy behind the policy. Not without reason was Mr. Kraft's article headed "School for Statesmen", allowing, of course, for latitude in the use of the word "statesmen". Here are two quotations which were used by Mr. Kraft:

"Whatever General Eisenhower knows about economics," says a Republican member of the Council who participated with Eisenhower in the 1949 Council study on European recovery, "he learned at the study group meetings." Another participant in the same group recalls that "Eisenhower came with a vague predilection in favour of building up Europe. When he left, European aid was a ruling conviction."

So that is where Bernard Baruch sent his protege to learn the ropes! Nor was Eisenhower the only student. We were told that in 1947, "just before taking over as Under-Secretary of State to George Marshall, Robert A. Lovett asked the Council staff to arrange for him a briefing session on U.S. foreign policy problems." It must surely seem odd to the uninitiated that a designated American Under-Secretary of State should look for his instruction on the affairs with which he will have to deal, not to his own Government, but to a private body. Those who have studied such matters are not surprised. Perhaps the real status of the Council on Foreign Relations is much higher than that of the White House and the State Department combined.

Mr. Kraft showed us what happened on the outbreak of war. "Whenever we needed a man," John McCloy, the Council chairman who served Stimson as personnel chief, recalled, "we thumbed through the roll of Council members and put through a call to New York". Here is something of even greater significance. "The Council provided for the U.S. Government the first organized framework for post-war planning. Less than a fortnight after the guns began pounding in Europe, and a full two years before Pearl Harbour, Armstrong and the Council's executive director, Walter Mallory, journeyed to Washington with a proposition. State lacked the appropriations to set up a planning division ; Congress was bearish about any official move that hinted at U.S. intervention;

there was a danger that, if it finally did get going with a sudden jolt, post-war planning might get out of the hands of State. Why not, they asked, let the Council begin the work, privately, with the understanding that its apparatus would be turned over to State as soon as feasible? Secretary Hull was in favour. Accordingly, in December 1939, the Council, with financial aid from the Rockefeller Foundation, established four separate planning groups. ... In 1942 the whole apparatus with most of the personnel was taken into the State Department as the nub of its Advisory Committee on Post-war Planning Problems. Up to that point, the five groups had produced a total of 150 planning studies." That indeed was to take time by the forelock! Who can doubt where Bretton Woods was conceived? Or Dumbarton Oaks? Or the Yalta Conference? Or the attacks on the British and other Western European Empires?

Mr. Kraft gave the case against the Council and then tried, not very convincingly, to knock it down :

"But it is undeniable that the Council, acting as a corporate body, has influenced American policy with wide-ranging effects upon the average citizen. Set against the total public, the Council can hardly be called a representative body; its active membership is, by force of circumstances, Eastern; and, by any reckoning, either rich or successful. Its transactions are remote from public scrutiny, and, in fact, refractory to any detailed examination. Thus, in theory at least, the Council comes close to being an organ of what C. Wright Mills has called the Power Elite — a group of men, similar in interest and outlook, shaping events from invulnerable positions behind the scenes."

What is wrong with the theory? That the Council does not accept Government money. Not a very cogent argument, Mr. Kraft, since on your own showing the Ford, Rockefeller and Carnegie Foundations are only too pleased to furnish the cash!

Another of Mr. Kraft's innocent remarks was that the Royal Institute of International Affairs is "a separate institution with no American ties". Did he mean that the Ford, Rockefeller and Carnegie Foundations, which have all helped to finance Chatham House, are not American but international? If so, his point may be conceded!

A complaint often put forward by those who say there is no such thing as an oligarchy ruling the world is that it would be impossible for a few men to influence the actions and thoughts of many thousands of other men holding important positions in various parts of the world. Quite apart from the fact that poison can, and does, spread by word of mouth and the printed word, without any direct contact between the originator and the person influenced, it is possible to show that friends and "employees" of members of the oligarchy have direct contact with literally thousands of leading politicians and bureaucrats the world over.

The names of members of the Council listed below are from its 1952 report. It can be seen that the ideas and policies of these members can be spread by personal contact, on committees, at embassies, clubs and parties; by pamphlets and periodicals of limited circulation, put out by groups like the Institute of International Affairs; by reports from special advisory groups; by memoranda circulated by bureaucrats; by technical and scientific reviews and so-called scholarly periodicals; until finally they reach thousands of people who are flattered to be receiving "inside" information not yet available to the public, but have no inkling of the source of this information.

The names are as follows: John J. McCloy of Chase Mantattan Bank, a former President of the International Bank; Lewis Strauss (Kuhn, Loeb), Eisenhower's Secretary of Commerce at the time; Eugene Black, President of the International Bank; Herbert Lehmann, banker; Harold Stassen, a member of the Eisenhower circle; Nelson Rockefeller, David Rockefeller and John D. Rockefeller III; Averell Harriman, international banker; David Sarnoff, of Radio Corporation of America; Benjamin J. Buttenweiser, banker; Clarence Dillon (born Lapowski), of Dillon, Read, international banking house; General Lucius Clay; David Lilienthal, first chief of the U.S. Atomic Energy Commission; Walter Lippmann, the columnist; Henry Luce, of *Time, Life* and *Fortune* magazines; Eugene Meyer, international banker; Edward R. Murrow, commentator; Alexander Sachs, of Goldman, Sachs and Co.; John M. Schiff, grandson of Jacob Schiff; Eric M. Warburg, Fred M. Warburg and James P. Warburg of the famous banking family; Felix Frankfurter; Dean Acheson; Paul Hoffman, of the Eisenhower circle; Robert J. Oppenheimer, of atomic energy fame. There were dozens more, men like John Gunther, Ralph Bunche and Adolf Berle; university men like James B. Conant, army and air force men, publishers, journalists, heads of radio and TV networks, big bankers, little bankers, men known to the public as "right wing" and men who have defended and protected Communists.

The Council on Foreign Relations is only one of a number of organizations which connect up with the U.N. and with similar networks in other countries, the whole system covering most of the globe. In the *Saturday Evening Post* in December 1958 there was a long description of the "public service" carried out by a group called The Advertising Council. It was headed "Persuaders in the Public Interest". The Public Policy Committee of the Advertising Council included four powerful men who were also members of the Council of Foreign

Relations — Paul Hoffman, Benjamin Buttenweiser, John J. McCloy and Eugene Meyer. Another member was Ralph Bunche. The magazine *U.S. News and World Report* for December 1958 had this to say about Paul Hoffman : "A veteran dispenser of U.S. foreign aid was picked to run the United Nations' new fund for underdeveloped countries. He is Paul G. Hoffman, administrator of the U.S. Marshall Plan from 1948 to 1950."

Lewis Strauss, investment banker, and former chairman of the U.S. Atomic Energy Commission, was a member of the Council on Foreign Relations in 1952, and may still be a member. In 1957 he was appointed co-chairman of the National Conference of Christians and Jews, alongside a Catholic financier James F. Twohy and a Protestant industrialist Benjamin Fairless. This same Lewis Strauss became U.S. Secretary for Commerce. The *U.S. News and World Report* said that Strauss "is said to be preparing an 'imaginative' plan for developing trade in the non-Communist part of the world on a much-expanded basis".

According to *Williams Intelligence Summary* another member of the C.F.R., Benjamin Buttenweiser, is a trustee of the Baron de Hirsch Fund and of the American Jewish Committee. Williams says: "Buttenweiser and wife protected Alger Hiss in their home during his second trial and still condemn those who criticise Red Spy Hiss". It is pleasant to see people stand by their friends, but it is also instructive to see who their friends are. In this particular case we have, apparently, a direct connection between Kuhn, Loeb and Alger Hiss, for Buttenweiser was a member of Kuhn, Loeb a few years ago and probably still is. In any case he still moves in those elevated circles.

The 1952 report of the C.F.R. said that : "In response to a suggestion of officials of the State Department, the Council organized a series of three meetings on foreign economic policy to aid in the re-examination of our policy in preparation for the new Eisenhower administration." The "foreign economic policy" here referred to is the same economic policy decided on by the usurocracy before the beginning of the Second World War. It was worked out in detail by men like Harry Dexter White, Dean Acheson and various appointees of White during the war years, and was acted upon again in 1958 at the annual meeting of the International Monetary Fund at New Delhi. Substantially the same group of men as make up the C.F.R., or else their underlings, attended the secret meeting of bankers and planners at St. Simon's Island in February 1957.

Readers will notice how these groups are always concerned with "economic policy". One of the overall plans was sketched in 1958 by a Special Studies Project of the Rockefeller Brothers Fund. Convertibility of sterling and currency changes on the continent are part of the same plan, and will make it much easier for money to be transferred according to the demands of the usurocracy's programme of world development.

An example of the concern for economic policy was clearly given in 1959 during the speech made by the then Senator John Kennedy in his capacity as Chairman of the newly created Senate Foreign Relations Sub-Committee on African Affairs, in which official capacity he promised Africans a visit in the autumn of 1959. He promised Africans a vast increase in American aid. "It is not enough to say that private capital should take the lead in Africa," Kennedy said. "The Development Loan Fund is our best tool for African economic policy today." In other passages of his speech he mentioned that "we dare not think of Africa in terms of our own self-interests or even our own ideologies . . . the people of Africa are more interested in development than they are in doctrine. They are more interested in achievement of a decent standard of living than in following the standards of either East or West . . . perhaps the most effective way to provide financial help for investment, development and personnel might be through multilateral co-operation with African, European, American and other countries in an African Regional economic plan." He also mentioned an "African educational development fund". He finished his speech by quoting the words of George Washington — ordinarily a calm and solid figure — who declared he felt irresistibly excited whenever in any country he saw an oppressed people unfurl the banner of freedom.

Kennedy might have quoted with advantage Washington's dictum that nothing is more foolish than to expect real favours between nations.

On this side of the Atlantic, Britain has its Chatham House brigade of internationalists who will happily co-operate in surrendering our national sovereignty as long as the Rockefeller and Carnegie and Ford subsidies hold out. It was a Director of Studies at Chatham House, Professor Arnold Toynbee, who told an internationalist conference that "he and they were engaged in removing the instrument of sovereignty from the hands of the local national states, that they were, in fact, doing with their hands what they were denying with their lips".

Chatham House has long been a hot-bed of "One World" propaganda. During the war, when private sea and air passages were almost impossible to obtain, the Royal Institute of International Affairs, a quite unofficial body, had no difficulty in bringing to London from all over the world private individuals to form a sort of Commonwealth Conference. This fact in itself was suspicious. The Press was barred from the proceedings, but some of the proposals submitted became known. One was that Imperial Preferences should be abolished. Another demanded that the Dominions should come within the purview of the Foreign

Office, as though they were foreign countries. Henceforward I began to take a very close interest in Chatham House. It was not long before I discovered that it was a platform for internationalists militantly opposed to national sovereignty and any concept of Commonwealth or Empire which had any meaning except to deceive. The next discovery was that the big American Foundations were pouring money into its various projects. After I had landed many body-blows upon the Institute in the columns of *Truth*, the Secretary-General asked me to lunch, during which he said: "I want to assure you that, because of its constitution, Chatham House is debarred from formulating its own policy". I replied: "I do not doubt you. Chatham House does not need to have policies of its own when it can choose men of known views to comprise its research groups and write its publications." The Secretary-General seemed not to know the answer to that one.

When Mr. (later Sir) Ivison Macadam was the Secretary and Director-General of Chatham House, I asked him why he never arranged for the case for British nationalism to be heard at Chatham House. He replied: "Why not come along yourself?" "With the greatest of pleasure," I said, "providing I am allowed to debate with Professor Arnold Toynbee." Mr. Macadam told me he saw no reason why not. I smiled, perhaps a little cynically. That was the last I heard of the invitation to address Chatham House.

Mr. Macadam left the Royal Institute at the age of sixty because he found that out of its then paltry income of £123,000 a year it did not pay him enough to bring up his four children, one of whom was at a university and another at Eton. However Mr. Macadam did not appear to have had any fears for the future. Such was his altruism that he wanted to spend his leisure time raising more money for Chatham House. The Rothschilds and the many other plutocrats who subscribe to its funds may perhaps be persuaded to wipe out his reproach that the Institute's income was too small to finance "enough good ideas". What ideas? Perhaps at that time there was some dust-up behind the scenes of the Royal Institute. Not so long ago the Astors adopted towards it a proprietary air as though they possessed the title deeds to Chatham House. At the time of Macadam's departure, their organ, the *Observer*, became very critical towards the Institute, particularly on account of its racial policy. Perhaps Chatham House, notorious throughout the last two decades as the spawning-ground of internationalism, was too tardy in producing the perfect plan for the mongrelization of mankind. No doubt there were also other troubles. Mr. Kenneth Younger, for instance, told a Press conference: "The research programme of Chatham House has grown to such large dimensions that a real direction of studies is essential." That sounded very much like a straight left to the jaw of Professor Arnold Toynbee, who was also resigning after many years as Director of Studies. The use of the word "real" would imply that the Professor's function was unreal. It may be that Toynbee, the avowed enemy of national sovereignty, gave too much of his time to his self-confessed habit of denying with his lips what he was doing with his hands — a strange confession, one would have thought, for a man of repute to make. Perhaps, too, he expended too much vigour in inflating bags marked "history" with gusts of heavy speculation and sending them soaring into the impalpable inane.

The policies of the Royal Institute have the great advantage of being predictable. One knows for certain that in every controversy presenting the choice between a national and an international solution, the national solution will go to the wall. There have been several instances of this. One which readily springs to mind was the crisis created by M. Spaak's rebellion against his own Monarch. It was M. Spaak, the internationalist, and not the King of the Belgians who was invited by Chatham House to come to London to state his case. The conferences sponsored by the Royal Institute are invariably international. It has previously been mentioned that during the war Chatham House invited private individuals to form a sort of Commonwealth Conference, which proposed that Imperial Preferences should be abolished and that the Dominions should come within the purview of the Foreign Office. These proposals were restated at a Commonwealth Relations Conference in New Zealand sponsored by the Royal Institute in 1959. According to the periodical *New Commonwealth* "a most forthright declaration of intent was made. There was an extremely realistic approach to the problem of closer association between the Commonwealth and the European Common Market and Free Trade Area. The position taken in the White Paper that the British Government 'could not contemplate entering arrangements which would in principle make it impossible for the United Kingdom to treat imports from the Commonwealth at least as favourably as those from Europe' was no longer tenable now that the European Economic Community had come into existence." The declaration of intent was furnished in the Conference's suggested solution. This was that of a new trading relationship of the United Kingdom. Great Britain would admit (in the teeth of every pledge!) some horticultural products from Europe. She would lose some preferences in Commonwealth markets and would have to reduce tariffs on manufactures imported from the "Six". Britain's gain would be entry into the European market. The Commonwealth countries would give up some Commonwealth preferences in the United Kingdom market. They would admit manufactured goods from the "Six" on at least as favourable terms as those from Britain. Their great "gain" would be securing the economic well-being of one of their main customers, Great Britain. The "Six" would be asked to accept entry of Commonwealth products as at present and to admit Britain to the Common Market, but would gain entry both to the Commonwealth and United Kingdom markets.

At the time of the conference I surmised that one of its main purposes would be to help irrigate Asia and Africa with dollar loans and aid. That remains my conviction. It almost certainly had other purposes no less disturbing, among them the furtherance of the attack on race. Nobody with any knowledge of the sources of inspiration which actuate the Royal Institute could doubt that, in the field of race relations, this bespoke body would not be influenced by the lessons to be learned from the centuries of experience in South Africa or the Southern United States, but would go all out for social integration. There was accumulative evidence to support this view. Mr. Garfield Todd, former negrophile Prime Minister of Southern Rhodesia, led the Central African delegation to the New Zealand conference in 1962. Mr. Michael Wood, the president of the multi-racialist Capricorn Africa Society, was the representative of Kenya. To be told that Marshal of the Royal Air Force Sir John Slessor headed the British delegation might seem incongruous enough until one learned that Sir John was the chairman of the London Committee of the Capricorn Society. Did Chatham House invite to New Zealand anybody who was not a Capricornist or at least sympathetic to the Society's aims? Mr. A. L. Adu represented Ghana. As Mr. Adu organized the conference of "Independent African States" in Accra in 1958, it would have been almost worthwhile travelling all the way to New Zealand to have heard him speak on the structure and function of the Commonwealth!

In the middle 1950's, Chatham House was responsible for another unofficial Commonwealth conference. This served no conceivable good purpose and one very bad one, in that it provided a platform for the Pakistani Prime Minister to launch a concealed attack on South Africa. It would be interesting to know who financed the venture. Soon after the Pakistani conference, Chatham House sent a mission to Canada "to discuss political and economic affairs". What kind of political and economic affairs? There was little reassurance in the fact that the mission was led by Colonel Walter Elliot, the "Conservative" M.P. who was a leading light in the World Parliamentary Association for World Government. Included in the mission, incidentally, was the managing director of Lazard's, the international banking house. It seems that Chatham House will not easily be weaned from its addiction to the internationalist cause and the champions of that cause.

As in the case of the Council on Foreign Relations, Chatham House can also spread its ideas through the persons connected and sympathising with its aims. An article in the *Daily Telegraph* in 1958 read as follows: "Professor Blackett, the President of the British Association, seems a curious choice to speak on nuclear weapons and defence at Chatham House next month. His subject is labelled as 'Comment on Kissinger, Kennan and King-Hall'. Although he is regarded as one of the leading thinkers on nuclear defence and is a well-known strategist, Professor Blackett has acknowledged and outspoken Left-wing views. He seems out of place in non-political Chatham House."

That passage, believe it or not, was headed: "Political Naivete". I assure "Peterborough", the writer of the article, that his was the naivete. One can imagine no visitor likely to be more at home at Chatham House than the near-Red Professor. Again in 1958 during the Cyprus crisis there were talks on the B.B.C. following the Parliamentary announcement that the island should retain international status for seven years. The Turkish representative asked what particular virtue resided in this period. Why not five or six or any other number of years? He could have been fobbed off with the answer that everything in Mau Mau ritual went in sevens! Indeed, the British representative furnished by Chatham House replied that the British Government had refrained from giving Greeks and Turks grounds for quarrelling about the ultimate solution, as it could not itself know what the world would be like seven years hence. He might have gone further and said that the Government could not know what Cyprus would be like seven hours hence, since the announcement led to an immediate recrudescence of Turco-Greek throat-slitting. However, it was not difficult to see what the Chatham House spokesman had in mind. It was what the British Government had in mind. Long before seven years had elapsed the promoters of One World would have been expected to have made sufficient progress in Cyprus for the problem of the sovereignty of Cyprus to have become totally irrelevant. It is at the present time occupied by United Nations troops.

Through the written word, too, Chatham House spreads its ideas. Chatham House commissioned Professor William Hardy McNeill, an American, to write a book entitled *America, Britain and Russia — The Co-operation and Conflict*. Reviewing this book, Mr. Max Beloff wrote:

"Nevertheless, as he rightly points out, the most enduring result of the Grand Alliance has been the new relationship between Great Britain and the United States; and this work provides a most valuable illustration of the steps by which this came about and throws a new light on the statesmanship of Sir Winston Churchill, who perhaps alone could have induced his countrymen to accept second place even to so generous an ally. Sir Winston emerges as incomparably the major statesman of the period, as indeed he should."

A remarkable passage. Perhaps Professor McNeill was happy at this result of Sir Winston's "incomparable statesmanship". Chatham House probably rejoiced at it. It may have induced thoughts of ecstasy in Mr. Beloff's mind. But what did Churchill himself think of this description of his triumph? And what were the thoughts of those of his fellow-countrymen whom he did not reconcile to the idea of the subordination of our ancient Kingdom to America?

Even the *Sunday Times*, which is supposed to be nationally minded, is involved with Chatham House. In 1953, under the editorship of Mr. H. V. Hodgson (a Chatham House "One World" boy), the correspondent who commented on the changed structure of NATO command, which resulted in an American Air Deputy's being appointed to the American Supreme Commander in Europe (a Briton was ousted from the post to make this possible), wrote: "It is not generally realized that the reason behind it was that full information about new weapons, particularly atomic weapons, cannot be given by the United States even to senior officers of Allied forces. And, lacking full knowledge, any non-American deputy supreme commander would be at a disadvantage. The British point of view is that American control may be expected to give the best results. It should lead to the fullest co-ordination of air and land power, including the use of strategic air forces for tactical purposes." If that were true, then the British Chiefs-of-Staff needed their heads examined. It was more likely, however, that the "British point of view" was the *Sunday Times* "point of view". Indeed, the Left-wing *New Statesman*, writing of the *Observer*, has expressed its preference for the *Sunday Times*. In 1958 the *Sunday Times* again came down on the side of the internationalist cause. Speaking of the Middle East, the paper declared that "no Middle East policy is worth anything unless it includes Israel. We are sometimes told that we should refrain from mentioning Israel for fear of offending the Arabs; but since we are bound by the most solemn pledges, including the U.N. Charter, to defend Israel's independence and integrity, there is no harm but only good in making that obligation explicit and precise, in terms of an open Anglo-American guarantee to defend Israel's *present* frontiers." That looked after the sacred beast of the Middle East. But there was more to Middle Eastern policy than that. The *Sunday Times*, after discussing how we should woo the murderous regime in Iraq, wrote : "It follows that no Jordanian intervention in Iraq should be countenanced; King Hussein, who still seems to be hankering after such adventures, should be told that this would be flatly counter to the purpose for which British troops were sent to his aid." That this was accepted policy has been proved by events. Even so, it was a pity that the *Sunday Times* (or was it Chatham House?) did not see fit to disclose the purpose for which British troops had been sent to King Hussein's aid.

Almost the last source to which one would normally think of going in search of a fair presentation of the problems of race relations in South Africa is *International Affairs*, the journal of Chatham House. Such a fair presentation was given by Mr. H. V. Roberts in 1958. Mr. Roberts appeared to put the apartheid question in proper perspective and the article contained much common sense. However, the final sentences showed why Chatham House allowed it to be published. They read: "The achievement of racial harmony in South Africa would be of immense benefit — not only to the Western world in its present struggle against Communism, but also to the world of tomorrow in the adjustments that each nation will have to make in its own sovereignty. It is in this task that I hope the informed members and staffs of Institutes such as Chatham House will be able and willing to play their part." From this part of the article it would appear that Mr. Roberts is in favour of World Government, and this alone would explain why Chatham House, which is one of the foremost enemies of racial and national pride, permitted the publication of his paper, even with its array of inconvenient and bravely stated truths.

There were no false hopes to be harboured, either, when it was learnt that the Royal Institute had appointed a Board of Studies to make "an extensive study of race relations in Central Africa". Everything we knew about that body warned us to expect a report in which the follies of the Capricorn Society would be exalted into sacred principles. There would be no word about the exclusive role played by White leadership in preventing the complete collapse of Africa into age-old barbarism, and indeed there was no secret made of the fact that the investigation was intended "as a first step in a wider study of racial problems in the world". Who can doubt that the "wider study" formed a part of the campaign of the international policy-makers to break down racial barriers and so mongrelise the human race.

Let there be no doubt about it, the Royal Institute of International Affairs, although enjoying the Royal cachet, is far more responsive to the views of bodies such as the Rockefeller and Carnegie Foundations than it is amenable to the pursuit of distinctively British interests. Precisely the same comment may be made about the U.S. Council on Foreign Relations concerning American national interests.

Chapter XXIV

PRINCE BERNHARD'S SECRET SOCIETY

IF the facts concerning the Royal Institute of International Affairs and the Council on Foreign Relations be accepted, it will be seen that the proper study of political mankind is the study of power elites, without which nothing that happens can be understood. These elites, preferring to work in private, are rarely found posed for photographers, and their influence upon events has therefore to be deduced from what is known of the agencies they employ. There are dozens of such agencies, and financial support received from one or other or all three big American foundations — Rockefeller, Carnegie and Ford — provides an infallible means of recognizing them. One of the most blatant of these agencies, despite its adoption of a secret society technique, is the Bilderberg Group, which seems to have been inspired by an important event. In the year 1908, secret agents of the New York Money Power and their Washington fuglemen had themselves transported in the dead of night to Jekyll Island off the coast of Georgia. As the result of their plotting there was created, four years later, the means whereby the Money Trust was enabled to seize control of the entire American economy through the mechanism of the Federal
Reserve Board. In February 1957, a similarly hush-hush conference took place at St. Simons Island in the same region. A "summary" of the proceedings was entered by Senator Wiley, champion of the Left-wing, in the appendix of the Congressional Record. It referred to "the preservation of peace" under the auspices of Nato, which revealed nothing. The composition of the gathering, however, was revealing. Nobody with Right-Wing views was permitted to attend. Wiley was accompanied by Fulbright, both of the U.S. Foreign Affairs Committee. Sulzberger of the *New York Times* was there. So was the mysterious Gabriel Hauge, said by the *Wall Street Journal* to be "the expert who tells Ike what to think". So was the only less mysterious George Kennan, former Ambassador to Russia. So were the representatives of the Rockefeller Foundation and the Carnegie Endowment for International Peace. A Supreme Court Judge was reported to have been present, although he did not register. Westbrook Pegler, the courageous American columnist, believes that he was Felix Frankfurter, the patron of Dean Acheson and Alger Hiss among other dubious proteges. There was also Lord Kilmuir, who as Sir David Maxwell Fyfe figured among the prosecutors at Nuremberg, and whose appearance was that of a more improbable-looking Scot than could be imagined. What these agents of Financial Jewry were plotting was nothing to the benefit of the sovereign independence of the nations of the Western World.

144

The following people were also present : —

J. H. Retinger, Polish Charge d' Affaires in Russia, 1941 ; Joseph E. Johnson, President, Carnegie Endowment for International Peace; Hon. F. D. L. Astor, Editor, *The Observer*, U.K.; G. W. Ball, Attorney, Cleary, Gottlieb, Friendly and Ball U.S.; Fritz Berg, Chairman, Federation of German Industries, Germany; M. Nuri Birgi, Secretary-General, Ministry of Foreign Affairs, Turkey; Eugene R. Black, President, International Bank for Reconstruction and Development; Robert R. Bowie, Ass. Secretary of State for Policy Planning, U.S.; McGeorge Bundy, Dean, Faculty of Arts and Sciences, Harvard University; Hakon Christianson, Chairman, East Asiatic Company, Denmark; Walter Cisler, President, Atomic Industrial Forum, U.S.; Pierre Commin, Secretary, French Socialist Party; B. D. Cooke, Director, Dominion Insurance Company, U.S., Arthur H. Dean, Law partner of John Foster Dulles, formerly of Sullivan and Cromwell, U.S.; Jean de la Garde, French Ambassador to Mexico; Thomas E. Dewey, Attorney, former Governor of New York, U.S.; Sir William Eddlitt, Air Chief Marshal, Royal Institute, U.K.; Fritz Erler, Socialist M.P., Germany; John Ferguson, Attorney, Cleary, Gottlieb, Friendly and Ball, U.S.; Lincoln Gordon, Professor, Consultant to Nato's "Three Wise Men"; Sir Colin Gubbins, Industrialist, U.K.; Lawrence R. Hafstead, Technical Adviser, Atomic Energy Commission; Jens Christian Hauge, Socialist M.P., Norway; Brooks Hays, House Foreign Affairs Committee; Denis Healey, Labour M.P. (now Minister of Defence), U.K.; Arnold D.P. Heeney, Ambassador to U.S.A., Canada; Michael A. Heilperin, Economist, U.S.; Henry J. Heinz, President, H. J. Heinz & Company, U.S.; Leif Hoegh, Banker, Norway; Paul G. Hoffman, Former Director, E.C.A., U.N. Delegate, U.S.; C. D. Jackson, President, Time Inc., Former Special Assistant to the President, U.S.; Wm. H. Jackson, Former Special Assistant to the President, U.S.; Per Jacobson, Man. Director, International Monetary Fund, Sweden; Georg Kurt Keisinger, Director of Special Studies, Rockefeller Foundation; Pieter Liefnick, Director, International Monetary Fund, Netherlands; Imbriani Longo, Director-General, Banco Nazionale del lavoro, Italy; Paul Martin, Minister Health and Welfare, Canada; David J. McDonald, President United Steelworkers ; Geo. C. McGhee, Director, Middle East Institute; Ralph E. McGill, Editor, *Atlanta Constitution*; Alex W. Menne, President, Association of German Chemical Industries, Germany; Rudolf Mueller, Lawyer, Germany; Robert Murphy, Deputy-Under- Secretary of State U.S.; Frank C. Nash, Attorney former Assistant Secretary of Defence, U.S.; Geo. Nebolsine, Attorney, Coudert Bros, U.S.; Paul H. Nitze, Director, Policy Planning, State Department, U.S.; Morehead Patterson, Deputy Commissioner of Disarmament, U.S.; Don K. Price, Vice-President, Russian Institute, Columbia University; David Rockefeller, Chairman of the Board, Chase National Bank; J. H. Van Roijen, Ambassador to U.S., Netherlands;

Dean Rusk, President, Rockefeller Foundation; Paul Rykans, Industrialist, Netherlands; J. L. S. Steele, Chairman, British International Chamber of Commerce, U.K.; Terkel M. Terkelson, Editor, Denmark; John M. Vorys, Member, Foreign Affairs Committee; Fraser B. Wilde, Comm. on Economic Development; Otto von Amerongen Wollf, Partner, Otto Wollf, Germany; W. T. Wren, Chairman Allied Iron Founders, U.K.; Paul van Zeeland, Financier, former Prime Minister of Belgium.

The Chairman was H.R.H. Prince Bernhard of the Netherlands. Strange, is it not, that the Prince should be the "front" for a powerful left-wing secret society?

Why were these people present? Who sent them? Who paid their fares? Who sponsored their meeting? What did they discuss? What did they decide? What orders were they given? Was there any common denominator of interest among them? Yes, they were all promoters of internationalism. Were they instructed in the next phase of the advance towards One World? The answer, beyond doubt, is Yes.

The *Sunday Times* reported during October 1957 that financiers and businessmen from Britain, the United States, Canada and thirteen other Western nations had begun private talks at Fiuggi, Italy, on the European free trade area and the Common Market projects. There were sixty delegates. Mr. Maudling, the Paymaster-General at that time and the Minister responsible for Britain's intended part in the proposed European free trade area, and Viscount Kilmuir, Lord Chancellor, attended. Lord Kilmuir said it was a point of honour that no immediate disclosure be made of the subjects under discussion. The whole point was that members should be able to discuss problems of interest on both sides of the Atlantic without committing their Governments. All the members were speaking as private individuals.

There is no difficulty in recognising in this secret gathering the mysterious Bilderberg Group, of which Prince Bernhard is the official sponsor. As the author surmised after the St. Simons Island meeting, the purpose was to speed up the cause of internationalism and it is interesting to have confirmed the fact that these agents of the Money Power were directly concerned with the European free trade area. Am I right in thinking that the work undertaken by the Bilderberg Group was once undertaken by such bodies as Chatham House? It may even be that the remorseless light I shed on Chatham House activities in the pages of the old *Truth* may have led to its manipulators seeking new facades behind which to work. As Lord Kilmuir maintained that all the Bilderberg Group's members spoke as private individuals would he also have known whether they paid their own expenses when attending these meetings in different parts of the world? If they did not, who did?

In September 1958 another meeting of the Bilderberg Group took place in Buxton, Derbyshire. With the exception of three very old residents, the Palace Hotel at Buxton was cleared of guests so as to accommodate these cloak and dagger boys, and not only that — the normal hotel staff was temporarily suspended during the invasion so that alien waiters and porters should have the exclusive duty of looking after the conspirators. It would be interesting to know how the foreign servants came to be collected for the job and just what international security tests they were called upon to pass.

The Mayor of Buxton, whose courteous function it was to welcome conferences to his town, was rudely ignored, as the Queen seems to have been, by Prince Bernhard of the Netherlands, whose presence on British soil one would have though necessitated a courtesy call on Her Majesty. Protocol goes by the board when esoteric international policies are to be discussed.

The security measures taken were prodigious. They made clear that if we had not the honour of entertaining the arch-conspirators in person, at least we had the doubtful distinction of being visited by their very highest agents. They came not in their official capacities but as private citizens. That fact was repeatedly stressed. Yet, according to rumour, there arrived for their use crates of official documents so secret that the crates had to be locked — together with a British officer as custodian — in a room at the Buxton police station. When asked about the authenticity of this rumour, the Conference's spokesman tried to laugh it off. However, after persistent enquiries the spokesman said: "Well, if General Schuyler (Chief of Staff of S.H.A.P.E.) brought along certain documents, that is his affair." I am not saying that General Schulyer did in fact bring along the papers; the above is merely a report of the conversation with the spokesman in front of many Press witnesses. Whatever the truth of the matter, the entire Buxton assemblage stank of its own furtiveness and concealed aims.

At least twenty-four of those who attended the Buxton meeting also attended that on St. Simons Island. Among these were John J. McCloy and David Rockefeller (both Chase Manhattan) and Paul Rykans, a Dutch banker and member of the Anglo-Dutch Trade Council and chairman of an "industrial development" organisation called MIDEC. One hundred and twenty European and six U.S. firms were in this organisation in 1960 for the purpose of "developing" the Middle East. One of the U.S. members of MIDEC was Rockefeller Centre Inc. Both David and Nelson Rockefeller have been and may still be members of the Council on Foreign Relations. James S. Rockefeller is or was the president of the First National City Bank of New York. Anybody who likes to get a Directory of Directors and a few dozen copies of the International Monetary Fund weekly will find plenty of evidence to indicate that a good deal of so-called "economic policy", whether in Washington or Indonesia, Australia or Sweden, emanates from a relatively small circle of interested parties.

The following is a list of the names of conspirators who attended the Buxton meeting. I use the word "conspirators" deliberately. Men pursuing purposes which will bear the light of day do not hold secret meetings in different parts of the world. The whole business could be treated as schoolboy silliness were it not for the fact that there emerged from such gatherings policies hostile to the traditional order of life. To deprive the public of using the Buxton hotel cocktail bar and other amenities so as not to intrude on the privacy of the plotters has about it something of the spirit of 1984 and would be better accepted by the cowed citizens of Moscow than it was by the wholesome burgesses of Buxton.

J. H. Retinger (Hon. Secretary); Jo. E. Johnson (Hon. Secretary in the U.S.); Herman J. Abs, Germany; Dean Acheson, United States; Giovanni Agnelli, Italy; Geo. W. Ball, U.S.; Walworth Barbour, U.S.; Wilfred Baumgartner, France; Sir Edward Beddington-Behrens, U.K.; Berthold Beitz, Germany; Fritz Berg, Germany; Muharrem Nuri Birgi, Turkey; P. A. Blaisse, Netherlands; Hans C. Boden, Germany; Erik Boheman, Sweden; Max Brauer, Germany; Randolph W. Burgess, U.S.; Louis Camu, Belgium; Guido Carli, Italy; Clifford P. Case, U.S.; Victor Cavendish-Bentinck, U.K.; Sir Ralph Cochrane, U.K.; Erich Dethleffsen, Germany; Fritz Erler, Germany; John Ferguson, U.S.; H. T. N. Gaitskell, U.K.; Walter L. Gordon, Canada;   Joseph Grimond, U.K.; Sir Colin Gubbins, U.K.; Walther Hallstein (Chairman, European Common Market Commission) ; Joseph C. Harsch, U.S.; Gabriel Hauge, U.S.; Denis Healey, U.K.; Michael A. Heilperin, U.S.; H. J. Heinz II, U.S.; Leif Hoegh, Norway; C. D. Jackson, U.S.; Viscount Kilmuir, U.K.; E. N. van Kleffens; Viscount Knollys, U.K.; Ole B. Kraft, Denmark; Thorkil Kristensen, Denmark; Giovanni F. Malagodi, Italy; John J. McCloy, U.S.; Geo. C. McGhee, U.S.; Philip E. Mosley, U.S.; Roger Motz, Belgium; Rudolf Mueller, Germany; Alfred C. Neal, U.S.; Geo. Nebolsine, U.S.; Paul H. Nitze, U.S.; David Ormsby-Gore, U.K.; P.F.S. Otten, Netherlands; P. N. Pipinelis, Greece, Alberto Pirelli, Italy; Pietro Quaroni, Italy; Sir Alfred Roberts, U.K.; David Rockefeller, U.S.; Michael Ross, U.S.; Jacques Rueff; Paul Rykans, Netherlands; Carlo Schmid, Germany; C. V. R. Schuyler; J. L. S. Steel, U.K.; Thomas Stone, Canada; Terkel M. Terkelsen, Denmark; Henry Tiarks, U.K.; Every A. Vermeer, Netherlands; Marc Wallenberg, Sweden ; Otto Von Amerongen, Germany ; Paul Van Zeeland, Belgium; J. D. Zellerbach, U.S.

In 1961 an article in the *Toronto Star* read as follows:

"The Tenth Bilderberg Conference attended by seventy delegates from Europe and North America wound up yesterday after three days of discussion of common problems. Participants, whose names were not disclosed, included leaders of the political, industrial, labour and professional fields of both continents, an official statement said. Chairman of the meeting was Prince Bernhard of the Netherlands, who left Quebec yesterday for home after making private visits to cities in Mexico, the U.S. and Canada. The statement said although the conference 'followed the original Bilderberg concept of not attempting to reach conclusions or to recommend policies, there was substantial agreement on the need to promote better understanding and more effective co-ordination among the Western nations. Points of particular concern included the role of the North Atlantic Treaty Organisation in world policy, the strengthening of both the nuclear and non-nuclear deterrent power of the alliance and the responsibility for control of atomic weapons inside Nato', the statement said. 'The implications for Western unity of the change in the relative economic strength of the U.S. and Western Europe also were discussed at some length.' "

To the unsuspecting all this may seem innocuous, perhaps even fatuous. For instance, there might not appear to be much danger in a body that does not attempt to reach conclusions or to recommend policies. However, there are other factors to be taken into account. Quite a lot of money is needed to fly seventy delegates from all over the world to an annual conference. Who finds that money and why? And who delegates the delegates? The author finds it hard to believe that the expense is incurred merely for the pleasure of staging discussions not aimed at any conclusion. Let there be no doubt about this business. When people like Frankfurter, Dean Acheson and Cyrus Eaton foregather it is not for the purpose of amiable chats and mutual back-scratching. If the Bilderberg conferences reach no conclusions and recommend no policies, it is because the conclusions have already been reached and the policies determined, so that the delegates assemble to be told what the form is. They do not need to be given their orders. Once the form is declared they know well enough what is expected of them, while for our part it can be affirmed with assurance that the Bilderberg "power-elite" would not discuss the nuclear power deterrence of the North Atlantic Treaty Alliance in any sense favourable to countries such as Great Britain retaining nuclear weapons under their own sovereign control.

Sir Edward Beddington-Behrens stated in *The Times* about June 1960, when writing an obituary of Joseph Retinger, that he, Retinger, "founded the Bilderberg Group, whose meetings under the chairmanship of Prince Bernhard of the Netherlands brought together the leading political and industrial personalities from the U.S. and Europe, to discuss ways of removing any source of conflict between the U.S. and her allies. The meetings, held without any kind of publicity in England, Holland, Turkey, Switzerland, or the United States, brought together leading statesmen who could discuss their problems in privacy and exchange points of view with men of equal eminence in other countries. It was Joseph Retinger who brought them together and knew them all personally."

The author finds it hard to believe that Retinger was anything other than an agent or promoter. Financiers rather than industrialists would be a more accurate description of the Group's inspirators. And no ordinary financiers. The men who find the funds are the international policy makers who seek to shape the world to their own particular specification. International financiers do not take orders from men like Joseph Retinger.

Retinger, I repeat, was an agent. The world is not run by stray idealists, although agents, of course, may be actuated by genuine idealism. That does not make their projects necessarily wholesome. I affirm that the influences behind the European movement which made use of Retinger's idealism are, from a national and Christian point of view, thoroughly unwholesome and indeed evil, in that what they seek is a monopoly of political and financial power. Evil, too, is the method. Nations are represented — at any rate according to a polite fiction — by their Governments. Who selects the "leading political and industrial personalities" who go cavorting around the globe to attend secret discussions upon world affairs? Is the Bilderberg Group a flying circus nominated by the Royal Institute of International Affairs and its dominating partner in America, the Council on Foreign Relations? Some kind of nexus seems certain. Both Chatham House and the Council fit the description of what has been called the Power Elite — "a group of men similar in interest and outlook, shaping events from invulnerable positions behind the scenes." And what is the Bilderberg Group if not precisely that?

We may be certain that the Group was not organised by Joseph Retinger as the principal. Who would the principal have been? Baruch? Frankfurter? The Kuhn, Loeb gang? And why the cloak and dagger stuff? Is the Bilderberg Group an apparatus of Grand Orient Masonry? Whatever the answer to that question the atmosphere of plotting in the dark which pervades it has a dank and very nasty smell. Sir Edward Beddington-Behrens would perform a service to the Western Nations if he would describe in more detail the work and background of Retinger, who was a very mysterious person indeed.

There are other points worth noting. It was possible for Dean Acheson, former U.S. Secretary of State, to slip in and out of Britain for the Buxton Conference without exciting any British newspaper comment. The Bilderberg Group had affirmed its desire to strengthen the Nato alliance, which was brought into being to contain Communism. Yet when two American juries found Alger Hiss guilty of perjury in denying that he was a Communist agent, Dean Acheson publicly reaffirmed his friendship with the traitor. Another Bilderberg enthusiast is Cyrus Eaton, the American millionaire who allowed his Pugwash home to be used for Bilderberg sponsored conferences. Yet Cyrus Eaton is notorious for his pro-Communist sympathies.

If it were possible to bring members of the Bilderberg Group before a Commission of Enquiry they would have these and many other matters to explain. They would also have to give a more satisfactory answer than any yet offered about the need for a secret society technique so stringent that not even the honest British waiters and waitresses at a Buxton hotel could be allowed within earshot of the conspirators. Until Prince Bernhard and his colleagues explain themselves, which is an improbable event, I propose to designate them as the chosen lackeys of the New York Money Power charged with the task of plotting to bring into being a One World tyranny.

My friend and colleague Austen Brooks drew the attention of readers of *Candour* to another exceedingly curious extra-governmental body working along lines which would suggest its affiliation with the Bilderburg group.
Early in 1962 a dozen "leading churchmen" (of whom, needless to say, one was Canon John Collins) published an "appeal to the British Government and people" urging that Britain should be prepared to renounce her independent nuclear deterrent. Commenting on this, the *Observer* wrote: "Behind the statement lies a strange and little-known relationship between Church leaders and some of Britain's best-known military pundits. The connection started back in 1955, when Richard Goold-Adams, foreign affairs commentator, Denis Healey, the Labour politician, Professor Blackett and Rear-Admiral Sir Anthony Buzzard, former head of Naval Intelligence and an active Churchman, were worried about the lack of serious thinking about strategy in Britain and, in particular, the undue reliance on the strategic H-bomb." (Note the nuclear surrender hand in the "strategic" glove.) This quartet, according to the *Observer*, "raised the problem" with the then Bishop of Chichester, the late Dr. Bell, who in turn "interested" the chairman and secretary of the Churches' Commission on International Affairs, Sir Kenneth Grubb and the Rev. Alan Booth, and in January, 1957, a conference — described by the *Observer* as "a strange assembly, eighty-strong, hard-headed military men, journalists and politicians surrounded by clerical cloth" — was held at the Bedford Hotel in

Brighton. A continuation committee was set up and the Brighton Conference Association came into being to work against "the undue reliance on the strategic H-bomb".

It was at this point of the story that the *Observer* opened the bag and let the cat out. "After a year or so," it wrote, "the money they had collected was beginning to run out. But just at that moment, Denis Healey managed to interest the Ford Foundation in this enterprise. He asked for only 10,000 dollars. They offered ten times as much, and with this the Brighton Conference Association wound itself up and the Institute for Strategic Studies came into existence."

The persuasive Mr. Healey, who "managed to interest" the Ford Foundation in the "enterprise" which was working to get rid of Britain's nuclear deterrent, was then the Labour Party's shadow Minister of Defence. He was also a leading member of the Fabian Society, a member of the Bilderberg group and, almost certainly, a member of the Royal Institute of International Affairs. Small wonder that the policy of the Institute for Strategic Studies, which the American Ford Foundation had brought into being, was soon adopted as the official policy of the Labour Party. In October, 1964, the Fabian Bilderberger Denis Healey became Minister of Defence, an appointment which was the signal for the almost immediate abandonment of a number of British military aircraft projects. Then, early in April, 1965, came what was for all practical purposes the renunciation of the British independent nuclear deterrent — the abandonment of the magnificent British aircraft TSR2. The announcement of this abandonment was made, curiously, not by Mr. Healey but by his colleague Mr. James Callaghan, the Chancellor of the Exchequer, in his Budget speech. What Mr. Callaghan did not announce was that only a couple of months earlier the Ford Foundation had made a further grant to Mr. Healey's Institute for Strategic Studies, a grant which made the 1958 sum of 100,000 dollars look parsimonious. This was a grant of 550,000 dollars over six years.

After the announcement that TSR2 was to be scrapped, the B.B.C. brought before the television cameras a strategic "expert" to reassure viewers that the decision was "quite right". The "expert" was Mr. Alistair Buchan, Director of the Institute for Strategic Studies. Strangely enough, the B.B.C. omitted to tell viewers of the part played by Mr. Healey and the Ford Foundation in providing Mr. Buchan with the job which "qualified" him to pronounce a benediction on the policy of Mr. Healey. If the Socialist Government wishes to economise, why does it not shut down the Ministry of Defence and transfer its powers outright to the headquarters of the Ford Foundation? That would seem to accord with the facts!

One final fact about the Bilderberg group. At its 1965 meeting it had a new recruit. His Royal Highness Prince Philip. In the present year of grace (1967), Prince Philip attended another secret Bilderberg meeting at St. John's College, Cambridge.

Chapter XXV

IS THE CONSPIRACY JEWISH?

MY purpose in writing this book will have miscarried if at this stage I have not convinced the reasonable reader of the existence of a conspiracy, or perhaps more accurately of a continuing policy enforced by a series of conspiracies that involve power groups which may often differ about methods but which direct their thoughts and acts to the attainment of the same broad objective. As Jewish influences are discernible at all levels, it may be asked how far is it a Jewish conspiracy. Gentiles, and Gentile bodies, including entire governments, have been so closely associated with what has occurred that it would be manifestly unfair to describe the plot, or series of plots, as the work of Jews and to leave it at that. But the driving force? That is a different matter.

The vast majority of Jews in the different countries are law-abiding citizens leading highly respectable lives, accepting the social customs of the peoples among whom they dwell and showing themselves to be well-disposed and kindly towards their neighbours. In business their codes are not invariably aligned with Gentile codes and their sense of solidarity, which is at once their strength and their weakness, gives them a distinct advantage over their Gentile competitors which is often resented and causes much bitterness. To visit upon the mass of Jews opprobrium, or worse, because of the actions of those we are about to discuss is not only unfair but infamous.

It is a fact that a minority of Jews, because of their greater intensity or whatever the reason may be, formed the hard core which promoted both the Menshevik and Bolshevik revolutions and have also been prominently identified with Communist movements in every other country. This support was not greatly diminished even after Stalin "liquidated" most of the Jews who founded the Soviet Union, not ostensibly because they were Jews but as alleged Trotskyists.

The attraction for a certain type of Jew of subversive activities cannot in honesty be gainsaid. Most defendants in the spy trials in Canada, following the revelations of Gouzenko, who defected from the Soviet Embassy, were Jews, and Gouzenko in his evidence affirmed that Moscow looked upon such people as being inherently suited for espionage work. The men charged with espionage relating to nuclear weapons in the subsequent United States trials were also mostly Jews. So were Jews the moving spirits in the espionage ring which sought out Admiralty secrets in Great Britain. Blake, for instance, despite the immaculately British name he adopted, was a Dutch Jew who had been given sanctuary in England when his family fled from the Nazi invasion of Holland. There is no evidence that he showed remorse at betraying the country which harboured him. Eighty per cent of the White defendants in the sabotage trials in South Africa were Jewish, although Jews form only about 10 per cent of the Republic's White population. Their strong sense of solidarity causes the law-abiding members of the Jewish community, whose outlook is often conservative, if not to defend the subversive elements, at any rate to embark upon rather slippery arguments that Jews are a religious and not a racial group, so that apostates are not to be looked upon as Jewish. Such arguments are specious and deceive only the simple.

Certainly no religious tests were applied to those participating in the trek to Palestine from every part of Europe in the immediate aftermath of the war. I doubt, moreover, whether either Begin, the head of Irgun Zwei Leumi, or the leader of the Stern Gang, both of which engaged in a murder campaign against the British and the Palestinian Arabs, was noted for his religious piety. It is true that racially the Jews derive from two main stocks — the Sephardim, who are true Semites, and the Ashkenazim, who come of Turco-Mongoloid stock and who embraced Judaism long after the birth of Christ. Such Sephardic claim to Palestine as there may have been had lapsed through the course of the centuries whereas the Ashkenazim had no claim whatever to a land they had never occupied. But when it came to the creation of the State of Israel no difference was recognized between the two stocks, and we have thus to regard World Jewry as one race, just as the British, with their Anglo-Saxon and Celtic components, are recognized as being one nation.

The creation of the State of Israel demonstrated the reality of Jewish power. In an effort to break the British attempt to hold the ring for the Arabs, every European Government was suborned to facilitate the illegal trek to Palestine of Jews from every part of the continent. The American Government, the American army in Europe and Jewish units in Europe serving under the British flag, and in British pay, were all used as agencies to defeat the policy of the British Government. When Chaim Weizmann, Zionist leader, went in some trepidation to see General Eisenhower, then Supreme Allied Commander in Europe, he was surprised at the welcome given to the scheme for defeating the British embargo on further immigration into Palestine — a welcome which took no account of the trust reposed in him by a loyal Ally. Weizmann's trepidations were groundless. Was not Eisenhower the protege of Bernard Baruch and had not Baruch assured Ben Hecht (who made a little holiday in his heart every time a British soldier was murdered) that he was ranged on the same side, albeit "a fighter in the long grass"?

It may be said that the Communist spies, agents and saboteurs arraigned in the various treason trials were only small fry and that the successful attempt to smash Britain's Palestinian policy had a limited objective — the establishment of the State of Israel. Both propositions are true. There is evidence, however, that Zionism has ambitions far beyond the creation of a Jewish State in the Levant. David Lilienthal, deviser of the Tennessee Valley project and of the Franco-German steel, iron and coal merger, and at one time chairman of the U.S. Atomic Energy Commission, wrote of the Jew that it was his destiny to lead mankind into universal brotherhood under a World Government. Here, I suggest, is the major Zionist objective — One World. It is a concept which appeals to the idealistic side of the Jewish mentality, but it appeals still more to that side of the Jewish mind which is preoccupied with the drive towards monopoly, above all a world monopoly of political power.

Had Israel been the main Zionist concern it is unlikely that when the cease-fire order was given to the British and French at the time of Suez the Israeli forces, within ten miles of the Canal, would have been required to evacuate the Sinai Peninsula. Israel has been given, either as compensation for that withdrawal or for other reasons, the opportunity to occupy key-positions in many of the territories which the Western nations have been forced to abandon. Ghana, for instance, after securing "independence" from Britain, placed the formation and training of its navy and air force in Israeli hands. Similar appointments, no less strange, were made in many other lands. The most mysterious development took place in Tanganyika. When part of the Tankanyika army mutinied the Nyerere Government packed off its British officers by plane in what they stood up in, all the way to Britain. Then another part of the Tanganyika army mutinied, this time placing Nyerere himself in jeopardy. The British Government, without requiring the reinstatement of the summarily dismissed officers, landed a Royal Marine commando to quell the mutiny and restore the situation. Was Nyerere grateful? Not in the least. Leaving Britain out of account, he placed the reorganization and training of the Tanganyika army in the hands of an Israeli military mission. Then there is Kenya. Some years ago the Israeli Consul in Nairobi made what at the time seemed an astonishing statement. He said that Kenya was essential to Israel as it stood on the main route between Johannesburg and Tel Aviv. Since then Israel has taken in hand the education of the notorious Mau Mau leader "General China". It has also promised the Kenyatta Government to make good whatever trade might be lost in a boycott of South Africa. Further developments may be expected. Israel has also made grants in aid to African countries, but as her own economy is dependent on grants from America and elsewhere it is perhaps a realistic appraisal of the situation to see Israel, not merely as an ideal with a strong emotional appeal to Jews, but perhaps even more as an advanced base for the largely Zionist take-over bid for Africa and the whole world.

The manipulation of the strands of economic and political power, it need scarcely be said, is done on a vastly wider scale than could be achieved through the medium of a small country in the Levant. When it be considered that Moscow and Peking are no more than branch headquarters of the conspiracy and that London, Tokyo, Bonn, Canberra and all the other capitals have been bulldozed into the almost complete acceptance of a satellite status, and that Washington itself is no more than the chief relay-station for the transmission of orders, then clearly Israel must be seen as no more than a midget in Wall Street's scheme of things. The mighty leviathan is New York. In New York is to be found the supreme headquarters for the overthrow of the West and the conspiracy to control the world. New York it is which has the underground nexus with the Soviet Union and Peking. It is from New York that the master-manipulators exercise direct power over Finance-Capitalism and indirect power over Communism. Are these master-manipulators and master-conspirators Jewish? Because of the power of the purse afforded by the control of credit and by preponderant participation in America's most powerful industries and commercial firms, and because of commercial preponderance in the economies of the so-called "free world", the answer is almost certainly "yes". Whether or not One World is the secret final objective of Zionism, World Jewry is the most powerful single force on earth and it follows that all the major policies which have been ruthlessly pursued through the last several decades must have had the stamp of Jewish approval. Indeed, common sense applied to such facts as have come to light must lead to the conclusion that the policies, directed against the most cherished Gentile values, were incubated by adroit Jewish brains and fulfilled, or carried to the verge of fulfilment, by the dynamism of the Jewish spirit. At the same time, so many Gentiles are associated with the conspiracy, both directly and through the formation of fronts, there are so many Gentile agents and agencies, and so many Gentile governments which have acquiesced in the conspiracy by falling into line with policies inimical to their own national interests, that it would be ludicrous to offload upon Jewish shoulders responsibility for the destruction, or near destruction, of Christendom and the Western world. Nevertheless it would be equally ludicrous to deny the Jewish part, especially where it is admitted. Early in 1962, for example, a *Jewish Chronicle* reporter interviewed the Rev. Saul Amias, a Rabbi who was co-chairman of the Jewish Group of the Campaign for Nuclear Disarmament. The interview was reported under the heading: "Role of Jews in C.N.D.", and included the statement that "there is hardly a single group of the Campaign for Nuclear Disarmament (except in areas where there is no Jewish community) which does not have a strong Jewish nucleus". The Rabbi was quoted as saying that about two-thirds of the London Committee of the C.N.D. were Jews, and there was a good Jewish representation in both London and the Provinces. Consider these facts in the light of the numbers of Jews in the Gentile world and their significance at once becomes apparent.

Had we of the Gentile nations stood firm in defence of our own traditions and values, instead of cravenly capitulating, the Jews would have remained what they ought to be — a small sect living contentedly and at peace with their neighbours, exercising neither national nor international power and entertaining no inordinate ambitions. That, as I wrote at the outset, is how most of them actually do live. That a minority of them has been able to mount such a stupendous drive for world power is not their fault but ours alone, and it is we who must put things to rights — or perish. The way to put things right is not to engage in "hate campaigns" (which in any event more often than play into Jewish hands) but to make a determined stand for our own legitimate and distinctive interests.

Chapter XXVI

THE SHODDY AIMS

I CLAIM, with submission, that what has been written in these pages proves the existence of a conspiracy for the destruction of the traditional Western world as the prelude to shepherding mankind into a sheeps'-pen run as a One World tyranny. Should legal minds aver that I have established no direct proof, my reply is that I have supplied an abundance of evidence, some circumstantial, some direct, and that where precisely the same policy can be traced and re-traced in one country after another, directed to precisely the same end, no reasonable person can argue that the chain of events has been adventitious and unplanned. If the idea of so large a conspiracy seems preposterous, it is not nearly so preposterous as the assumption that the post-war shaping of the world is innocent of design.

Admittedly part of what has happened can be attributed to factors inherent in the course of the historical development which immediately preceded our own times. When the Manchester School of thought had been left behind, and with it the individualism fostered by the *laissez-faire* philosophy, it followed that vested interests would elect to go forward in big battalions and that the battalions would merge to form, as it were, economic brigades, divisions, corps, armies and army-groups. Whatever the remnant of the Manchester School may think, the drive towards monopoly is the direct result of *laissez-faire*. Moreover, since the chief practitioners of High Finance and Big Business happen to be internationally dispersed, the formation of international trusts, combines and cartels has been a further logical development, and the idea of a centralized control over the whole range of the world's economic activity, so far from being the dream of a megalomaniac, has become something very much more than a practical possibility.

There is this further point to be considered. Beyond the satisfaction of a man's every physical need, vast accumulations of money have no value except to purchase power, and where the exercise of economic power does not automatically carry with it exercise of political power, as it very often does, it is only to be supposed that it will use every means, foul or fair, to dominate first the political life of the nation and then, through instruments devised for the purpose, the world of international political control in its every aspect, strategical as well as economic. We have no need to delve into Adlerian psychology to understand this lust for power. Evidence to prove its reality can be obtained as readily from observing the intrigues for the control of a local debating or dramatic society as from studying what goes on behind the scenes of the United Nations and its various agencies. Needless to say it is no part of my argument that political and economic power monopolies should be accepted: as their only logical end must be a Communist-dominated One World State we have to find some means first to curb them and then to smash them, that mankind may again live in freedom. But what I do mean is that up to this stage of the argument the drive for monopoly is explicable in historical and sociological terms.

However, in the world take-over bid and the conspiracy underlying it, there are certain overtones and undertones which cannot be thus explained. There is nothing natural in allowing the larger part of Africa to lapse into savagery, even though the disorder may be planned as the prelude to the imposition of a new order devised by the monopolists. There is nothing natural about the flooding of coloured immigrants into the British Isles. There is nothing natural in the universal cry for the "integration" of disparate races, the effect of which — as all experience teaches — is disastrous. And although national governments may be an obstacle to the exercise of international political power, there is nothing natural about the emotionally charged attack on national sovereignty and — with but one privileged exception (Israel) — the frenzied assault on patriotism. Admittedly, integration is no new thing. The North made an abortive attempt to impose it on the South after the American Civil War. It has been practised, with deleterious results, in the Cape, Brazil and elsewhere. Admittedly, the attack on national sovereignty began before the war. Admittedly, the besmirching of the concept of patriotism began in the 'twenties. Admittedly, these are all strands in the declared aims of Communism.

Nevertheless, to take Britain alone, Moscow would have no power to synchronise the voices of both Houses of Parliament, of the churches of all denominations, of the B.B.C. and I.T.V., of all the newspapers, of professors placed in key university positions and virtually every other medium of propaganda, all done apparently with the acquiescence of the Crown, so as to produce a concatenation of sounds indicative of approval of the policies pursued and of the trampling underfoot of the traditional patriotic values. The power to brainwash these institutions, that in turn they should brainwash the people, lay elsewhere. A pointer to it could well be that the technique, including the actual phrases, employed to still criticism of the coloured influx is identical with the technique used to still criticism of Jewry in the 'thirties. Here is my own explanation of the motives actuating the devisers of world policy.

When Hitler rebelled against the Money Power there arose an urgent necessity to smash him and his barter system. What must have appalled the manipulators of international finance was that a nation state, especially after the compliance of the corrupt Weimar Republic, should dare to control its own financial affairs. Mussolini had done much the same thing in Italy when he made speculation in the lira a criminal offence. In previous centuries a similar hostility was shown against monarchs because the money manipulators had been driven out of one country after another by royal decree. Hence the numbers of monarchies liquidated after each of the world wars. If nation states, even without benefit of monarchy, were to opt out of the international financial network, then there was an inherent danger in nation states as such, and after the liquidation of Hitler's Germany and Mussolini's Italy all remaining nations had to be softened up with a view to their absorption in federal bodies — such as the European Economic Community — and ultimately in a One World Federation. This could be done only by deriding the values of patriotism and nationhood and exalting in their place what are called internationalist ideals but which in reality are the slogans used by the power-addicts to make acceptable their supranational plans.

Then there is "race". Hitler's Germany had to some extent been founded on a concept of race — not a very clear concept in its positive aspect, but exceedingly clear in its negative aspect. It was anti-Jewish. If the Gentiles were not to be allowed to attach value to race, obviously all racial concepts had to be eradicated and — not only that — the races themselves had to become so inter-mixed, so "integrated", that no further pride in them would be possible. Hence the efforts of the Oppenheimer-backed Progressives in South Africa. Hence the extraordinary contortions in Australia to involve the aborigines in the White community and the relentless undermining of the White Australia policy. Hence the exhortation to New Zealanders "to embrace an Asian destiny". Hence the moves against "racial discrimination" in Great Britain. Hence the cry for integration everywhere on earth — except among the Jews. Tackled on this subject, Jewish spokesmen say, not very convincingly, that the Jew is neither a national nor a racial entity, but a religious entity. I believe, and have reason for my belief, that the Jews are the principal promoters of the idea of integrating peoples of disparate racial stocks. They have the mysterious power to mould public opinion, decide public attitudes and set intellectual fashions.

As for pressure on governments, that at the present time — so far as the Western world is concerned — is done by Washington on orders from New York. I am often asked by what means such pressures are brought to bear. The Suez *diktat* was one example. There is also the marginal grip on the economy of a country like Britain secured by an arrangement known as "off-shore procurement purchases". This means buying by the United States of, let us say, British fighter-planes for Belgium or perhaps of British frigates for Holland. Were this disguised "aid" to be dropped, there could be created almost overnight an appreciable rise in the British unemployment figures. Again, the recurring imbalance of payments crises place the British Government at the mercy of the International Monetary Fund, which in this and most other contexts is an euphemism for the United States Federal Reserve Board, a private company. British Governments, if they had the will and the courage, could wrest their country free of these suffocating foreign entanglements but in so doing they would have to risk incurring temporary displeasure at home and abroad, and the plain fact is that, to the best of my knowledge, since the war they have never once failed to fall into step with the requirements of the New York Money Power, because that happened to be the line of least resistance.

As long as such willingness to acquiesce remains a constant, so long is the will to impose likely to remain a constant, that being the nature of power. The examples are endless, but let me give just one more to underline this truth. There was a motion before the United Nations Assembly in 1963 — a motion directed against South Africa — which had the support of all member states except the United States, Great Britain and one or two other Western European nations. The delegates of these countries abstained. Next day, to the accompaniment of jeers from the so-called "Afro-Asian bloc", every one of the previously abstaining delegates arose to say that, after giving the matter further thought during the night, he had decided to vote for the resolution. It is most unlikely that any of the delegates, after intense midnight thinking, had decided upon a *volte face* — the coincidence would certainly have been remarkable. No, obviously Big Brother — a supranational authority — had issued peremptory orders to Washington, to London and other erring capitals, with the result that urgent telephone calls were put through to New York instructing their representatives to fall into line, which they did without a blush. Incidentally, the passing on of such an order must have been the last act of Douglas-Home as Foreign Secretary before he became Prime Minister.

What other reasonable explanation of the change of front fits the facts? And if mine is the correct explanation, does it not prove that there is indeed a supranational power which can, and does, dictate to governments? Nor should it be thought that only the larger metropolitan governments are subject to these pressures. Every member state composing the United Nations, whether well-established or parvenu, has accepted loans or aid under the patronage of the New York Money Power, expects further financial favours or is even being kept economically alive by subsidies. Any idea, therefore, that the United Nations represents the conscience of mankind is the most utter nonsense: the delegates are no more than the obedient spokesmen of puppet states in pawn.

As nature abhors a physical vacuum, so does it abhor a power vacuum. The world having become conditioned to accept the international exercise of power, it would be remarkable, indeed incredible, if that power were not exercised. What is more, as policy objectives and the means for their attainment are seldom, if ever, openly avowed, it follows that the planning is conspiratorial. Here and there may be hitches and setbacks in the fulfilment of any one plan or plans, but either they are overcome or alternative plans are put into operation.

Stated in other terms, and bearing in mind the constant urge towards power in the human psyche, all the factors which favour a conspiracy are present. Because the money and credit monopoly is controlled by a very few men, because all the other factors favouring a monopoly are provided by institutions created for that purpose, because time and again national governments have shown themselves submissive, one can only ask why, if there is no conspiracy, world policy ever since the war should have followed the same broad pattern. In brief, if there is no conspiracy, why is there no conspiracy? Why should nature abhor all power vacuums except this particular vacuum? If the means of controlling the lives and destinies of mankind exist, as undoubtedly they do exist, why should use of them go by default? It is not as though there was any shortage of unscrupulous manipulators. There would be no such power vacuum if nations held tenaciously to their sovereign independence, but, as we have seen, this independence has been bartered by venal politicians in return for the mere trappings of power and the opportunity to posture on the stage of public life.

I ask the reader to accept my thesis that the control is fully operative, and that, although Burns was right in saying that the best-laid plans of mice and men gang oft agley, given constancy of purpose the controllers are able to jettison plans which miscarry and substitute others which serve the same ends. In other words, I ask the reader to accept my assurance that a conspiracy of world-wide dimensions does exist and that unless we manage to defeat the conspirators, no matter how great the odds against us, we shall have nothing to pass on to our successors except the certainty of enslavement. In that event the grandchildren, and perhaps the children, of those now living will not be able to claim that they are citizens of no mean city, or subjects of no mean Realm or Republic, because the most they will be able to boast — and a sorry boast it will be — is that they are slaves of no mean production unit.

Chapter XXVII

HOW TO FIGHT BACK

WE have discovered in these pages much evidence about the existence of conspiracies. Men, selected by some unseen hand, gallivanting over the earth to hold sessions so secret that even hotel staffs have to be replaced for each such occasion, with strict security precautions and no admission of the Press, can only be called conspirators, whether or not the conclusions they reach are immediately embodied in governmental policies. Their "line" on any development can always be predicted, because the objective for which they work is known. But while evidence about the existence of conspiracies abounds, is there sufficient evidence to prove the existence of an overall conspiracy? The reader must reach his own conclusion from the facts and deductions I have placed before him. It may be helpful, however, if I draw his attention to certain significant features in the sequence of events in the post-war era.

The brief given to General Marshall for the Quebec Conference of 1943, that the biggest single obstacle to the expansion of American export-capitalism after the war would be not the Soviet Union but the British Empire, was obviously the basis upon which the United States was required to form its post-war foreign policy. Obviously, too, the same policy was adopted towards the other Western European Empires. The Dutch, almost at once, were expelled from their East Indian possessions; later the United States made the position of the French in Indo-China untenable and provided the spearhead of the drive to get the Belgians out of the Congo.

The British Empire, the greatest and most beneficent of all, was liquidated stage by stage, with relentless thoroughness and continuity of purpose. At every such stage the Soviet Union has obligingly made appropriate menacing noises while the United States has found the cash and exerted the economic pressure. Nor can it be said that this palpable conspiracy embraced as partners only the United States and Soviet Russia. We know that British officials themselves undertook the duty of letting the people of Singapore know that attachment to the British Crown had to be abandoned in favour of "Merdeka". We know that British officials, under orders from London, formed electoral teams to "educate" primitive peoples in every territory in the organization of elections that would lead to "self-government" and then to "independence". We know that British Governments freely acquiesced in the cutting of most of the painters and where they did not acquiesce they surrendered to economic *force majeure*. But we now know much else. Is it not of very great significance that, United States post-war policy having been decided upon as long ago as 1943 and probably many years before that date, the Royal Institute of International Affairs should have been given the facilities, while the war was still being waged, to bring to London from every part of the British world mysteriously selected persons who made proposals directed at furthering United States policy — proposals such as the abandonment of Imperial Preferences — Preferences which, although deeply resented by the U.S.A., had been of great benefit to the British Dominions and overseas territories, and the transference from the Colonial and Commonwealth Relations Offices of responsibility for liaison with the British Dominions, and for the governance of the territories, to the Foreign Office?

It matters not at all that the proposals were eventually jettisoned in favour of other plans based on longer-term programmes to achieve the same result. What does matter is that the Royal Institute of International Affairs was acting so much in cahoots with the American Council on Foreign Relations that the two organizations might have been one and the same body, as was the original intention. Superficially it could be said that those men in the British world working for the break-up of the British world-system were fifth columnists indoctrinated by the United States. In fact, it would be more realistic to describe them and their opposite numbers in the Council on Foreign Relations as functionaries, some idealistic, others more conscious of their roles, of the New York Money Power, the secret government of the United States and the *de facto* secret government of most of the rest of the world — the secret government which incessantly plots, through the United Nations, Nato, Seato and many other agencies, to become the open and acknowledged World Government which has so long been incubated.

The United States, as the more intelligent American patriots fully realise, is as much the victim and tool of this power elite as any other country, and theirs is the task of exposing and destroying it in their own land. Unfortunately the genuine Right-wing movement there is as fragmented as it is elsewhere — a situation which the common enemy encourages but does not need to create.
The factors creating the situation are attributable to those aspects of human nature which engender rivalry and jealousy between like-minded groups, which make minor differences in policy and approach appear much more important than the battle against the common enemy, and which develop in some men a leader-complex that results in schism and frustration. Only when an organization has gained sufficient strength and momentum to be able to exercise patronage is it possible to avert such splintering and not always even then.

For my part I am chiefly concerned with the sector of the battle-front which lies in Great Britain and the British nations overseas, as well as in countries such as

165

South Africa, which should be regarded as our natural allies and where the European community is under attack. As a result of my own writings and public addresses, as well as those of my trusted colleagues, we have built up a movement which, although small, is world-wide and in some countries exercises a certain amount of influence. This movement (which has counterparts elsewhere) is the answer to those many people who, surveying the scene as a whole and contemplating the tremendous odds against which the patriotic cause has to struggle, ask themselves, and us: "What can I do about it"? The implication more often than not is negative, conveying the belief that there is nothing to be done. But here at least is a standard round which they can rally and an organization which can make use of their talents in ways best suited to their own temperaments. We have activists who bravely carry the war into the enemy camp, rebutting lies and denouncing treason in high places. Others prefer to help in the dissemination of our literature or in public speaking or in lending a hand to get through the office work. All are able, in greater or less degree, to contribute to the funds without which no organization can remain in the line of battle. As long as resistance is offered to the conspirators, so long can it truthfully be said that the vital spark of the national spirit is being kept alive.

Among the many difficulties confronted by such a movement is the fact that its militancy and refusal to compromise leads to its being heavily smeared by the propagandists on the other side, and few people — especially in a time of decadence — relish the idea of being smeared by association or of being thought by others, who have been thoroughly brainwashed and conditioned to accept defeat, to hold unfashionable views, far less to be labelled cranks or fanatics. Moral courage has never been one of the most common of human virtues and today it is as precious as it is rare.

In stating our case we have approached all manner of men, and not a few have we convinced that our facts are correct and our deductions sound. But most of them, even after being convinced, find reasons for doing nothing about it and letting the conspirators have all their will of mankind. Some tell us that they propose to take up the fight as "lone wolves", which seems to us only a little less senseless than if a man had declared his intention to go into the battlefields of one or other of the Great Wars as a freelance. There are also men of some eminence, like the Marquess of Salisbury or Lord Milverton, who know the right thing to say, and if they say it half a dozen times a year in the House of Lords, or write half a dozen letters a year to *The Times*, imagine that they are doing all that can reasonably be expected of them. Their lack of continuity and drive ensures that they escape smearing, and therefore any suggestion that they should give countenance to an organization which has been smeared because it fights all the time makes them shudder.

There are also men and women who join our ranks, remain for some years, and then become discouraged because they find they are doing more than others, or else they lose heart because the conspirators win battle after battle and because decadence makes ever increasing inroads upon community life in the various British nations and especially the United Kingdom. They would be horrified to be told that their own morale has declined with the decline in the public morale, but is that not just what has happened? Some quit the battlefield abruptly or by perceptible degrees. Others rationalize their defection by embracing a cause on the remote periphery of the main cause, one which is more socially acceptable and will incur for them none of the odium attaching to those who remain in the thick of the battle. I have even heard men, in the process of quitting, put forward as an excuse their detestation of the depths into which the great mass of their fellow-countrymen have sunk, even though the mass knows nothing of the conspiracy, and of the brainwashing used to make it what it has become, whereas they themselves are very well informed about the planned creation of chaos, about whom the planners are, and about the supreme objective which the planners are determined to reach. Does not a very special responsibility reside in those who know, as distinct from those who do not know?

Every man and woman must be the judge of his or her own actions, just as every man and woman is entitled to his or her own opinions. My own opinion is that it is the crowning treason and the supreme cowardice of this or any time to have a glimpse of the conspiracy and its hideous visage, to know the truth, or some part of the truth about its aims and methods, and nevertheless to run full tilt from what is known. If, in the non-ecclesiastical sense, there is an unforgivable sin, it is surely this sin.

There are, thank Heaven, those who remain in the fight. Surmounting the bitterness of every defeat, undeterred by the defections of others, these men and women, of all age-groups, of all classes, of all denominations, standing fast in the defence of values and traditions elsewhere being trampled into the mire, are entitled above all others to be known as the choice and master spirits of our age. We who are privileged to lead them have refused to feed them on false encouragement. They know that we have approached in vain both Houses of Parliament, the Churches, the broadcasting systems, the national newspapers with urgent pleas for counter-action against the conspiracy to be taken. They know that we have proved petitions to the Crown to be an empty ritual. They may read with nothing more than a wry smile the news that Her Majesty's sister has been seen in public wearing stockings on which were designed symbols of the Liverpool "Beatles", and thereby lending the royal cachet to the prevailing mode of these fallen and unheroic times, but they do not smile, they take in deadly earnest, the machinations of the evil conspirators who work in a milieu far removed from the British Royal family and who plan the destruction of every crowned head as and when circumstances allow.

The dedication of the patriots who refuse to compromise will remain as long as they have life. It is for them a duty to carry the torch of a glorious past through an inglorious present and hand it over to what, if they can make it so, will be a glorious future. We who know the strength and insidiousness of the diabolical influences standing athwart their path can at least, in all humility, salute them and offer them all the support in our power. The captains and the kings have departed, the aristocracy has turned craven, the squirearchy has gone bad, but the true loyalists of every land still advance into battle with hearts unafraid and with intrepid souls.

CHAPTER XXVIII

LAST POST AND REVEILLE

SINCE this book was first published, in 1965, with a second and revised edition two years later, followed by the third in 1969, many attempts have been made from the Literary Supplement of *The Times* downwards (or upwards!) to discredit its theme. Only once, however, has a challenge of any of its facts succeeded and that is a minor matter in relation to the world picture as a whole. I stated that Greek Cypriots were in a minority until after the Turco-Greek war of 1922. Dr. Arnold Toynbee has been quoted as establishing that there was a substantial Greek majority when the island was ceded to Great Britain in 1880 and as I have no wish to mislead my readers I hasten to accept and publish the correction.

As this fourth edition goes to press, towards the end of 1972, all the policies directed to the destruction of Great Britain as a sovereign independent nation are about to be fulfilled: she has been bulldozed into the European Economic Community with a speed, an insensitivity, and a deceit beyond anything hitherto experienced in these islands. On January 1 1973 we become an integral part of a conglomerate colonial empire run by a cabal in Brussels, subservient to the power-masters of international finance in New York. When the electorate in 1970 returned a Conservative Government to Westminster it had the assurance of Edward Heath that he would not take the country into the Common Market without the full-hearted consent of the British Parliament and people. No definition of "full-hearted" was given, but even had it been the promise would not have stood in Heath's way: his determination—to wean his fellow-countrymen from their concept of Britain as an historical entity, and from their attachment to their kin overseas, was ruthless and totally devoid of conscience. When the European Economic Communities Bill was passing through the committee stage in the House of Commons, clauses destroying the ultimate powers of Parliament and the supremacy of the British courts were fiercely contested and on one occasion the Government scraped home with a derisory majority of five, which not even the most dim-witted supporters could claim to be evidence of full-hearted support. No matter. A majority of one would have served Heath's purpose.

It would be foolishly unrealistic to suppose that Edward Heath was more than a tool, albeit an effective one, in bringing upwards of a thousand years of our island history to so inglorious a close. As we have seen throughout this book the dominant political motif of the power-mongers all over the world (Israel only excepted) has been to eliminate nationhood and with it all sense of national allegiance, so as to bring mankind under the tyranny of a World Government dictatorship. The first steps were to weaken the European nations by robbing them of their overseas possessions and spheres of influence, which then passed under United States or Communist control—the control, that is, of the two empires relied upon to form the main pillars of the projected One World system. Every withdrawal of Western administration from African and Asian territory was notched up as a success for the supra-national cause, but the greatest triumph to date has been the capitulation of Great Britain and her incarceration within a Europe which henceforth will limit her control over her own destiny to a tithe—in other words, to nothingness.

By the time President de Gaulle died all the barriers to an acceptance of the British surrender had been removed. For practical purposes her overseas interests and spheres of influence had been filched from her, the latest being the withdrawal of the R.A.F. and supporting units from Bahrain and their replacement by an American garrison. Serving notice upon Great Britain that she could no longer act, or even think, as a world power, President Pompidou stated outright that on entering Europe she must change her identity—a statement, issued on the eve of Heath's visit to negotiate with him, which was received in this country without protest, let alone a cancellation of the Anglo-French meeting. At a later date Pompidou asserted that in future there were to be no European nations only the "European man". As no repudiation was forthcoming from Downing Street the clear assumption was that the British Government acquiesced in the down-grading of this country to provincial status.

The measures taken to destroy our national sovereignty amount to the biggest public relations campaign in all our annals, and the sheer force of the drive into Europe bespeaks the involvement of the dominant commercial and financial interests not only on both sides of the Channel but on both sides of the Atlantic. One of the chief arguments put forward by the Government is the alleged necessity to build a United Europe strong enough to attain parity of strength with the so-called "super-powers" and thereby successfully compete with them in the world market. As it is not in the nature of things for industry and business to welcome strong rivals, had this argument been soundly based the United States would have put every conceivable obstacle in the way of European integration. Instead, it has brought great pressure to bear, not only to push Britain into Europe but to insist that she subscribes to every clause of the Treaty of Rome, thereby surrendering her independence and power of self-defence.

During the many years that I have repeatedly issued warnings of the intentions of American finance-capitalism to destroy us as a national entity, I have been derided in the Press and B.B.C. as a man obsessed, seeing signs of a conspiracy where no conspiracy existed. Only when the fate of the E.E.C. Bill seemed to hang in the balance did the Transatlantic conspirators show their hand. A few months ago, shortly before his death, Dean Acheson, former Secretary of State and general factotum of New York's business interests, was brought to Britain for an hour-long interview broadcast by the B.B.C. His interviewer put to him the key question: "You have been quoted as saying that Britain has lost an empire and has yet to find a role. Is that still your opinion?" The Acheson reply was emphatic. "No," he said. "Britain has now found her role—to enter the Common Market and take the lead in Europe."

George W. Ball, former Assistant Secretary of State, member of the law firm deeply involved in the Congo take-over, now head of one of Wall-street's biggest inter-national lending-houses and (as was Acheson) a Bilderberger and member of the Council on Foreign Relations, also entered the arena to tell Britain where her future lies. He set forth his views in a long article in *The Times*. Here was his opening paragraph: "We Americans are watching Britain's agony over Europe with far more intensity than our silence would suggest. Though an habitually noisy nation we are being studiously discreet, since sensitive to the charge of outspokenness in the past, we are determined not to create any false issues that might this time impede an affirmative decision. Yet it would be a major error to assume that we regard the matter with indifference; on the contrary, this is a matter of fiscal hope and anxiety when, in the view of thoughtful Americans, the promise of a stable western system is being critically tested." If the intensity of America's interest is what Ball declares it to be, what would happen if it were not thus "discreetly" expressed? An ultimatum?

As the British Government has tried to play down the political aspects of the Treaty of Rome, boosting instead the alleged benefits which will accrue from our entry into the Common Market, it is significant that George Ball should write that Americans "tend to focus more on the political than on the purely *[sic]* economic implications of the Treaty of Rome". That was precisely, the line taken by President Kennedy and Dr. Hallstein ten years earlier. But of course the economics of the situation are not left entirely in the cold. Here is a further quotation from the Ball article:

"American business knows from its own experience that the Common Market has generated far more trade than it has deflected and taking account of the fact that United States' exports to the Six have increased seven fold since the Community first came into being they expect a further expansion of economic activity from British entry. Thus dozens of United States companies are waiting only for the final decision before regrouping their European operations under

head offices in London—the city that will, as we see it, emerge as not only the financial but the commercial capital of the new and larger Europe."
Therein lies the entire short term motivation of the conspiracy.Whatever high-flown language be used to describe London's role, she will at best serve as an advanced base for New York. One more quotation from Ball will show where he and his colleagues stand:

"For Britain to reject the brave chance now offered would be regarded in my country as a fatal sign of exhaustion and resignation one more proof that Europe can never be a serious partner, one more excuse for Americans to turn their backs on a continent that seems incapable of organising itself to meet the requirements of the modern age. I cannot believe that will happen."

As far as Britain is concerned that is the exact opposite of the truth.

Much more forthright was the statement of Harold Cleveland, president of the First City National Bank, when testifying to a Congressional Committee. One passage alone will serve to sum up his attitude and that of Wall-street as a whole. Here it is:

"If Britain baulks, it will be on grounds of narrow economic nationalism and little Englanders on one side of the House of Commons, with a dash of imperial nostalgia thrown in from the other side. The act would tend to confirm and strengthen the negative trends in British thinking. An inward-looking passive Britain would be unable to play the role in European economic and political affairs which U.S. interests require Britain to play."

The first part of this statement is nonsense, in that it is the little Englanders who are most determined to seek illusory refuge in a Continental hugger-mugger. The part about U.S. requirements is all too true, but it would be fascinating to learn what gave Cleveland the notion that Britain is obliged to dance to the Wall-street tune. I hope that all those politicians who over the last fourteen years insisted that only by adhering to the Common Market could Britain stand up to American competition have noted how much that alleged competition is desired by Wall-street banksterdom. Why has nobody in the House of Commons thought of asking Heath to explain the zeal with which Cleveland and his kind have been pushing us into Europe?

However, history is an ever-flowing stream and no federal or other political structure is necessarily permanent. Even in our own day we have seen the break-up of the Austro-Hungarian empire and a reorganisation of the Balkan territories following the two European wars. One of the latest examples of the resolving of *ersatz* nations into its component parts was the dismantling of the Central African Federation. Although the Treaty of Rome makes no provision for member states to opt out of the E.E.C. it would be possible at any time for Great Britain to withdraw from the cosmopolitan stews into which she has been pitch-forked. The problem would be—withdraw into what? As long ago as 1957 the Australasian nations, reading the writing on the wall, sent their trade missions all over the East to find alternative markets against the day—now dawning—when the British Government would leave them in the lurch. There are present indications that the traditional partnership between Australia and Great Britain is being replaced by a partnership between Australia and—of all people—Japan. Although special provision is being made for New Zealand, free entry of her goods into the British market is to be on a reduced scale and phased out of existence by the end of the decade. Preferences enjoyed by Canada, South Africa and (normally) Rhodesia are to go almost at once, so that the British economic world system, unless steps are taken in the very near future, is doomed. Great Britain will possess no complementary economy from which to draw for her raw materials and the balance of her food.

When the terms of the E.E.C. Bill were made known the Deputy Prime Minister of Australia and the Prime Ministers of that country's states came to London to protest, but in vain. Heath was hell-bent upon a course which had been laid down by the international money-masters, and all obligations of loyalty and gratitude to the Commonwealth were brutally disregarded. Canada, already alarmed by the huge extent of financial infiltration from her southern neighbour and sensing Great Britain's forthcoming betrayal, hastened to make her own trade pact with the Soviet Union. South Africa is seeking an outlet for her exports north of the Zambesi, where conditions everywhere are notoriously unstable, while Australia and New Zealand, having passed out of the sterling area into the world of the dollar, must soon become financial puppets of the United States and so commercially dependent on Asia for their markets that left to themselves they are certain to embrace what their traitors have claimed to be their Asian destiny—that is, become Asian countries in every sense of the word, not least ethnically.

All these disasters can to a large extent be averted if Great Britain manages in time to opt out of the E.E.C. That she will have every reason to do so cannot be doubted. Even today every Whitehall Ministry is a bottle-neck with vast accumulations of work with which to cope, and much the same applies to our law-courts. Civil cases awaiting trial by jury may have a further wait of two years before being heard. When the thousands of directives begin arriving from the Brussels Commission, many requiring elucidating by the courts and all adding a massive burden on our already over-stretched Civil Service, there could be a more or less complete break-down of our administrative and legal structures. Then would be the time to cut adrift from our deadly involvement in Europe, much to the benefit of Great Britain and our overseas kinsmen, and attempt to rebuild the British world system which has conferred such incalculable benefits upon mankind.

The problem in that event will be to find a Government clear-sighted and courageous enough to undertake so titanic a task. Despite their recent opposition to the E.E.C. Bill, Harold Wilson and almost all of his colleagues are strong pro-marketeers and took their stance against the Bill with no thought other than to bring down the Government, so that the entry into Europe might be stage-managed under their own auspices. Readers will remember Wilson's eulogy of the Common Market quoted in a previous chapter. Certainly it would be futile to expect Edward Heath and his henchmen to beat a retreat. The methods they used to secure Parliament's acceptance of the Bill showed their utter disregard for truth and fair dealing. They acted as men bespoke. Following Heath's promise to the electorate, which he had no intention of keeping, came his statement in the Commons that the E.E.C. Bill entailed no erosion of substantial sovereignty. "Substantial" was another word he omitted to define. To ensure the support of Conservative M.P.'s for marginal constituents and to keep in line those who believed that Ministerial posts were within their reach, Heath made known that in the event of the Bill not going through Parliament the Government would resign, which in the circumstances of the time would have meant a Labour victory. The Conservative Central Office went so far as to try to create disaffection in the constituencies of the Tory Anti-Marketeers. These shameful tactics paid off, in that if the same number of Conservative M.P.'s who voted against the E.E.C. at the outset had voted against the third reading the measure would have been thrown out and the independence of the British nations made secure. Instead, over half of them either abstained or even supported the Government. They are worthy examples for citation by those who hold that politicians are the lowest form of life.

The main thrust of the critics concerns the subordination of British law to E.E.C. law. When attempts by the Government to deny what is clearly explicit in the Treaty of Rome, failed, its spokesmen fell back on some very queer arguments. The quaintest (to be charitable) was the smug question put by the Solicitor-General about what would happen when the two legal systems clashed He wanted to know by what means the E.E.C. would be able to enforce Community law. No matter how much one loathes Great Britain's adherence to the Common Market, the idea that we would dishonour our obligations whenever convenient could only have risen in the squalid minds of Heath and his companions.

The fact that Heath was awarded a prize of £36,000 by the FVS Foundation of Hamburg, run by the allegedly anti-Communist Herr Toepfer (who happens to operate a flourishing corn trade with the Communist countries) and an additional sum of £4,000 from an American organisation, sheds some light on the importance attached to his work. Roy Jenkins also won monetary awards for his contribution, which was the simple one of abstaining when the voting took place. Let there be no mistake about the overwhelming importance that international capitalism has attached to the lowering of the flag of Britain's independence.

What is more the fifth column inside our own country is probably the most formidable that has ever been mobilized for any act of treachery. Some years ago I was shown a list of subscribers to Chatham House (the Royal Institute of International Affairs), which seemed to me to include every big financial, commercial and industrial complex in Britain. I had been criticizing some of its activities, whereupon the then Secretary-General took me to lunch to assure me that the Institute was debarred by Royal Charter from pursuing political objectives. My reply was that as the Institute had the power to appoint its Director of Studies (at that time Arnold Toynbee) and choose whatever lecturers and writers of papers it wished, the restriction was perhaps not altogether crippling. Secretary-General Macadam smiled what I could only take to be a smile of assent. Now, however, there would appear to be not even a pretence of impartiality. Chatham House has openly made common cause with Political and Economic Planning to build up support for Britain's entry into Europe. The essence of the P.E.P. gospel is rationalisation, which runs so closely parallel to nationalisation that P.E.P. and the Fabian Society are often found running in double-harness. It favours the giant complex as against the small company, and there is no coincidence in the fact that Government spokesmen on the Common Market assert that the international corporation has more to offer mankind than the nation state—a concept horrific enough to chill the blood.

The *Daily Telegraph*, always on the side of the big battalions, summed up the grand design in these words: "It is true that the multinational company, far from being a misfortune, is more in keeping with the needs of the present-day world than the national state. The political counter-point to the multinational company at present is the Common Market and at a later stage a free world economic order with a unified commercial law. The great mistake, as Professor Harry Johnson has forcefully observed, is to 'accept the rights of government to interfere with the operation of the corporation for its own frequently myopic and narrowly partisan purposes'.' All power to the Financial Capitalists!

As the world policy-makers have decreed the destruction of nationhood, so are they endeavouring by force of law to destroy all sense of racial disparity. By these means there has been implanted in Great Britain coloured communities of more than two million coloured immigrants who, whatever their personal characteristics, constitute alien bodies certain to create a major problem in times of economic or other crisis. Every post-war government must take a share of responsibility for this appalling situation. From earliest times these islands have received and absorbed peoples of other countries, but hitherto they have been of European stock, whereas today they are either negroid or asiatics with physical differences which no legislation can bridge. The newcomers have had no part in our island history and they simply do not fit into our island background. To walk or drive through the areas they inhabit, especially in London south of the Thames, gives the impression that one is in Jamaica or Sierra Leone, while a journey through Wolverhampton, Leicester or dozens of other places resembles an exploration of Bombay or Calcutta. That in the course of time there will be race-mixing must lead to the presence here of a half-caste population is scarcely open to doubt, and only those with a knowledge of the result of miscegenation in the Cape can have the faintest concept of the consequent misery and degeneration of the unfortunate victims. The very fact that Race Relations Acts are passed through Parliament shows how unnatural is the presence here of multi-coloured colonies.

One of the arguments used in an endeavour to bolster up the coloured cause is that massive repatriation would lead to a breakdown of many of our essential services. Why should that be? Continental countries, Germany in particular, manage very well without cluttering up their population with Asians and Africans. As we have over a million unemployed in Britain, we could manage very much better were we to be relieved of our immigration problem. In this connection it is significant that member states of the E.E.C., alarmed at the prospect of coloured people in Britain making use of the clause in the Treaty of Rome which permits the free passage of labour across national frontiers, have sought from Britain a clarification of the position and an assurance that the flood will not cross the Channel to create a similar problem on the Continent. Anxious to allay such fears, the British Government coined a new word "patrial" to define what was meant by the term "British national". Patrials were to be those able to claim some British European blood.

The sheer dishonesty of this device is seen in the argument used by the Government that the Act of 1947 bestowed British citizenship upon all inhabitants of the colonies, so that those with British passports were held to have the right under international law to enter the United Kingdom. Accordingly, when "independence" was granted to colonial territories British officials made passports available to all who sought them, with never a mention of "patrials". If they are indeed "British nationals", the fact that only a few of them can claim British lineage means that in relation to "patrials" they will rank as second-class citizens. The assertion by Heath, Douglas-Home and the egregious Hailsham that these are distinct issues is deliberately misleading and intellectually dishonest.

Owing to the antics of a former sergeant-major of the King's African Rifles—who attained the rank of general with supersonic speed—the British people appear at long last to have become aware of the genetical threat to the Anglo-Saxon and Celtic stock in their homeland. Amin's notice to quit served on Uganda's Asians led to the Heath administration's willingness to accept up to 50,000 of them in the British Isles and with it a sense of outrage by our country's indigenous inhabitants, who are how convinced that they are being ruled by men completely indifferent to the interests of the British people. As the conspiracy to place Great Britain under the control of a cabal in Brussels has taken shape, bodies in protest have been formed throughout the Kingdom and in the same way the crowning folly of treating Amin's rejects as British subjects (though not citizens of the E.E.C.) has resulted in a vast access of strength to organisations such as the National Front, which have been battling against the power of the Establishment in their efforts to preserve the British heritage.

Events in the world at large make the success of the British cause essential. Ever since 1917 the polarity of the United States and the Soviet Union has been fictional: under its cover the great capitalist countries of the West, those within the circle of patronage have built up the Russian economy in return for concessions to exploit the country's mineral and other wealth, but this process in 1972 has been taken much further and now amounts to something very much like a condominium. The genius who can claim credit for this sinister accord is a certain Henry Kissinger, described as Richard Nixon's adviser on defence. A German Jew by origin, Kissinger's expertise on defence has never been explained to the world, but as his functions seem to be all-embracing, such information may not be very important. It was this Winged Mercury who sped over the Himalayas to open negotiations with Chou-en Lai and there is every indication that China, in return for concessions, will also become the beneficiary of the benefits which international finance is able to bestow.

Only a resurgent British system would have the power and the wisdom to hold aloft the torch of civilisation in a world made dark by such unholy alliances. If the Last Post be sounded as Great Britain passes into the Common Market, let it be followed swiftly by the Reveille to indicate that we have awakened from our drugged sleep and regained the wisdom and the strength to lead the world back to sanity.

BIBLIOGRAPHY

Section A

The books in this section will prove useful to the reader who wishes to extend his study of the theme advanced in "The New Unhappy Lords". Those by the late A. N. Field are recommended without mental reservation. Where others diverge in any aspect (as, for instance, in Douglas Reed's curious views about Hitler) the present author is naturally prejudiced in favour of his own point of view, but nevertheless recommends them because of his substantial agreement with the rest of their arguments.

BEATY, John : *The Iron Curtain over America* (Wilkinson Publishing Co., Dallas, Texas)

BURDICK, Congressman Usher L. : *The Great Conspiracy* (Christian Nationalist Crusade, P.O. Box 27895, Los Angeles 27)

BROWN, S. E. D. : *The Anatomy of Liberalism* (South African Observer)

CHESTERTON, A. K. :
Britain's Graveyard (Candour Publishing Co.)
Naming the Enemy (Candour)
The Learned Elders and the B.B.C. (Britons Publishing Co.)
The Tragedy of Anti-Semitism (with Joseph Leftwich) (Robert Anscombe)
Royal United Service Institution *Journal*, August, 1951 to August, 1958.

DILLING, Elizabeth : *The Roosevelt Red Record and its Background.*

DOMVILE, Admiral Sir Barry, K.B.E., C.B., C.M.G. : *From Admiral to Cabin Boy* (Britons)

DOUGLAS, Major C. H. : *Brief for the Prosecution* (K.R.P.)

ELSOM, John P. : *Lightning over the Treasury Building* (Meador Publishing Co., Boston, Mass.)

EWELL, Mark : *Manacles for Mankind* (Britons)

FAHEY, The Rev. Denis: *The Rulers of Russia* (Regina Publications, Dublin)
The Mystical Body of Christ and the Reorganisation of Society (Regina)

FIELD, A. N. : *The Truth about the Slump* (Omni Publications, Hawthorne, California).
All These Things (Omni)

FLYNN, John T. : *While You Slept* (Devin-Adair, N.Y.)

FORD, Henry : *The International Jew* (Christian Nationalist Crusade)

GOSTICK, Ron : *The Architects behind the World Conspiracy* (Christian Nationalist Crusade)

GWYNN, Stephen (Ed.) : *The Letters and Friendships of Sir Cecil Spring-Rice* (Constable)

HUDDLESTONE, Sisley : *In My Time*

HUXLEY-BLYTHE, Peter: *The East Came West* (Caxton Printers, Caldwell, Ohio).

JORDAN, George Racey : *From Major Jordan's Diaries* (Harcourt, Brace & Co.)

KNUPFFER, George: *The Struggle for World Power* (Plain-Speaker Publishing Co.)

LEWIS, Wyndham:
Count Your Dead — They Are Alive (Hutchinson)
Left Wings Over Europe (Hutchinson)

McCARTHY, Sen. Joseph : *America's Retreat from Victory* (Devin-Adair)

O'GRADY, Olivia Marie : *The Beasts of the Apocalypse* (O'Grady Publications, Benicia, California)

REED, Douglas:
Far and Wide (Jonathan Cape)
From Smoke to Smother (Jonathan Cape)
Somewhere South of Suez (Jonathan Cape)

SOREF, Harold and GREIG, Ian: *The Puppeteers* (Tandem Books)

STORMER, John A.: *None Dare Call It Treason* (Liberty Bell Press, P.O. Box 32, Florissant, Mo.)

WEBSTER, Nesta:
The French Revolution (Constable)
Secret Societies and Subversive Movements (Britons)
World Revolution (Constable)

WELCH, Robert :
The Life of John Birch (American Opinion, Belmont, Mass.)
The Politician (American Opinion)

WITTMER, Felix : *The Yalta Betrayal* (Caxton Printers)

Section B

Here are listed books which are not unsympathetic to the general theme but which bear upon it only incidentally by their relation of facts.

CHAMBERLIN, W. H. : *America's Second Crusade* (Henry Regnery, Chicago)

CROCKER, George N. : *Roosevelt's Road to Russia* (Regnery)

ELIOT, T. S. and others : *The Dark Side of the Moon* (Faber & Faber)

FORRESTAL, James : *The Forrestal Diaries*

GEORGE, Professor W. : *Race, Heredity & Civilisation* (Britons)

GOUZENKO, Igor: *This Was My Choice* (Eyre & Spottiswoode)

GRENFELL, Capt. Russell, R.N. :
Main Fleet to Singapore
Unconditional Hatred (Devin-Adair)

HOLLIS, Christopher : *The Two Nations* (Routledge)

LASKY, Victor and DE TOLEDANO, Ralph : *Seeds of Treason* (Funk & Wagnalls, N.Y.)

MARTIN, David : *Ally Betrayed* (Prentice-Hall, Inc.)

MIKOLAJCZYK, Feodor: *The Pattern of Soviet Domination* (Sampson Low, Marston & Co.)

PUTNAM, Carleton: *Race & Reason* (Christian Nationalist Crusade)

SODDY, Professor Frederick : *Wealth, Virtual Wealth & Debt* (Omni)

STEED, Wickham : *Through 30 Years*

THEOBALD, Rear Admiral Robert, U.S.N. : *The Final Secret of Pearl Harbour* (Devin-Adair)

VENNARD, Wickliff B. : *The Federal Reserve Conspiracy* (Christian Nationalist Crusade)

Section C

The books in this section were written by authors either unaware of the implications of the policy-pattern described in "The New Unhappy Lords" or aware of the implications and approving of them. These books are also listed for the glimpses they afford of what goes on behind the scenes.

CLARK, General Mark : *Calculated Risk* (Harrap)

CORTI, Count Egon : *The Rise of the House of Rothschild* (Gollancz)

DENNY, Ludwell : *America Conquers Britain* (Alfred A. Knopf, N.Y.)

DISRAELI, Benjamin : *The Life of Lord George Bentinck*

EMDEN, Paul H. : *Money Powers of Europe* (Sampson Low, Marston & Co.)

HECHT, Ben : *A Child of the Century*

KIMCHE, Jon : *The Secret Roads* (Seeker & Warburg)

MORTON, Frederic: *The Rothschilds: A Family Portrait* (Seeker & Warburg)

ROOSEVELT, Elliott : *As He Saw It* (Duell, Sloan and Pearce, N.Y.)

ROTH, Cecil : *The Sassoon Dynasty* (Robert Hale)

SHERWOOD, Robert E. (ed.) : *The White House Papers of Harry Hopkins* (Eyre & Spottiswoode)

WILMOTT, Chester : *The Struggle for Europe* (Collins)

Previous editions of *The New Unhappy Lords* included a section for journals to assist readers in their understanding of the development of the policy-pattern outlined in this book. However, due to the passage of time almost all are now defunct and we have decided to omit this section from this fifth edition.

186

Nkomo, Joshua, 105
Nkrumah, Kwame, 70
None Dare Call it Treason, 123, 127
North Borneo, 66, 67
Northern News, 75
Nyerere, 156
Observer, 138, 142, 145, 151, 152
Ons Vaderland, 105
Oppenheimer, Harry, 79, 80, 85, 86, 105
Oppenheimer, J. Robert, 122, 135
Ormsby-Gore, D., 148
Overseas Consultants Inc., 52, 54
Pakistan, 43, 53, 54, 124
Palestine, 20, 49, 110, 155
Pearl Harbour, 29, 133
Pearson, Lester, 110, 112
Pegler, Westbrook, 144
P.E.P., 115, 116, 175
Perth, Lord, 59
Petain, Marshal, 118
Philby, Kim, 130
Philip, Prince, 74, 153
Philippines, 67
Poland, the British Government White Paper on the Defence of, 1943, 27
Pompidou, 119, 170
Princess Royal, 79
Progressive Party, South Africa, 79, 80
Quebec Conference, 1943, 30, 57, 107, 164
Race Relations Acts, 176
Radio Corporation of America, 135
Rahman, Abdul, 66
Razmara, General, 52, 54
Reading, Lord, 21
Renison, Sir Patrick, 73
Retinger, J. H., 145, 149, 150
Rhodes, Cecil, 79
Rhodesian republic, 173

Rhodesia Selection Trust, 79
Rhodesia (Southern), 80, 86, 93-100, 105, 173
Rhodesian Front, 94-97
Roberts, Sir Alfred, 148
Rockefeller Foundation, 134, 145-146
Rockefellers, the, David, James, John, Nelson, 83, 134-137, 143, 147
Roosevelt, Elliott, 55
Roosevelt, President F. D., 21, 26, 28-31, 33, 34, 35, 55, 62, 115, 128
Rothschild, Colonel, 36; the House of, 79, 85, 100, 103, 118; 129, 138 Lord, 80, 128; Evelyn, 79; Freres, 118, 119; Guy de, 118; N.M. & Sons, 79
Royal Institute of International Affairs (Chatham House), 132, 134, 137-140, 143-145, 150, 152, 165, 175
Rusk, Dean, 146
Russian Revolution, 20-22, 62, 154
Rutherford, 34
Sachs, Alexander, 135
Samuel, Herbert, 20
San, Aung, 44
Sarawak, 66
Sarnoff, David, 135
Saturday Evening Post, 135
Schiff, Jacob, 135; John M., 135
Schulyer, General, 147
Schumann Plan, 50
Schwartz, S. G., 89, 90, 92
Seato, 50, 165
Second World War, 22, 24, 28, 35, 36, 46, 57, 62, 136
Shah of Persia, 55, 56
Shaw, George Bernard, 44
Sieff, Israel Moses, 27, 115
Sikorski, General, 49
Singapore, 33, 65-67, 164

Tributes to "The New Unhappy Lords"

Here are some fine tributes to the book, among which must be reckoned the attack on it which appeared in The Times Literary Supplement.

"This is a book by one of the few top-level experts on the question of global subversion. A. K. Chesterton has behind him many years of important experience, allied with a brilliant mind. One may not always agree with every word he writes, but what he states must always be taken very seriously and, indeed, there can be no doubt that by far the greater part of this author's declarations and opinions are true. The New Unhappy Lords is a very valuable contribution to the study of the financial-communist take-over bid, which is now so close to world-wide success. . . . We see how the global subverters have gradually destroyed all those factors which could hinder their progress, and the vile work continues. Mr. Chesterton demonstrates convincingly the close connection between international high finance and communism and the singleness of purpose and organisation of the would-be enslavers, who already control so much of the globe."

Mr. George Knupffer in *The Plain Speaker*, Sept. 1965.

"Though Mr. Chesterton's postulates and tentative conclusions are often invalidated by this lack of court-room evidence—in many cases he explains why he cannot produce it—yet we must be grateful to him for marshalling actual, undisputed facts thus enabling us to draw our own conclusions, if we will. In formal logic there is something called the Fallacy of Division, which is when one persists in regarding, as separate and independent, sets of circumstances which one's nous or common sense tells us must be connected."

The Anglo-Portuguese News, 11-9-65.

"I would describe it without reservation as the most valuable contribution to historic literature since World War 1."

Mr. R. D. Molesworth.

"It is a brilliant piece of writing, and also a most courageous book."

Miss C. M. Savage.

"It is pathetic."

The Times Literary Supplement, 23-9-65.

"You did a superb job—neatly avoiding the pitfalls of over-statement, emotionalism, and potential libel. I think it is by far the best account of the current world situation that has been written. I just wish that every loyal American could read it."

Mrs. Bernadine Bailey, Chicago, Illinois, U.S.A.

"What a masterly analysis. I am amazed at your facility for condensation, though I can't help wishing that you had been able to be a little more expansive and had been able to include a few more dates. . . . It was kind of you to write that inscription and to send me this copy, which I shall treasure in memory of the bravest man I know."

Elizabeth, Lady Freeman.

"Your book is terrific, and the setting out in sequence of the steps one by one by which our downfall was achieved is particularly useful, as one tends to forget them also one by one. I shall try my best to make it known."

Air Commodore G. S. Oddie, D.F.C., A.F.C.

"A consummate epitome of the major world events of the last half-century and an expert analysis of their causes, or probable causes. Only the most obtuse reader could fail to have his mental processes stimulated. The book, from beginning to end, is a brilliant piece of writing, and undoubtedly is, whether or not it will ever be openly acknowledged as such, the most valuable contribution to political thought in this country in recent years."

Mr. D. S. Fraser-Harris.

"It is difficult to find words to express our joy and feelings of triumphant hope upon receipt of The New Unhappy Lords. You have made 1965 a year of profound significance for the cause of the Counter-Revolution and given us all what will long remain the classic indictment of the International Financiers. The cumulative effect of the case you build up so ably and so resonantly, chapter after chapter, is the most devastating possible."

Mark Ewell. Author of *Manacles for Mankind.*

"Your book is terrific. The New Unhappy Lords is badly needed, and your treatment of them is excellent."

M. Hilaire du Berrier, international political commentator.

"I have just read the book and wish I hadn't so that I could start all over again. It is marvellous. . . . It has a kind of cumulative effect when put together and written in such a masterful, quiet and obviously sincere manner. When I get home I will try and get the Public Library to buy some copies."

Mrs. I. Atherley.

"I was struck by the miracle of condensation; the scope and sweep of the movement all harmonised to render comprehensible to the average mind such a vast affair—is much more than a tour de force. I wonder what other man, if any, could have reduced to such simple terms so complex and involved a movement as that which threatens our civilisation: yet you bring it into compass and order and conviction so that the most ordinary minds can absorb and grasp its message."

Mr. Harold McCrone, Laxton.

"My first re-reading of your book proves if proof were needed—your mastery of the English language, your prodigious memory and that you have written the most important true detective work ever published. Restrained but biting to both the criminals and to those to whom 'the idea of so large a conspiracy seems preposterous' would not hearken to your writings in the past."

W. L. Taylor, Montevideo.

"I have been very pleased to learn of the success of your excellent book, The New Unhappy Lords, and to know that it has greatly pleased the various people in the academic world to whom I have introduced it."

Professor at University of Southern Mississippi, U.S.A. 17.12.1971

"You made a superb job of it. I can't think of another man in the patriot camp who, combining a sure and intimate knowledge of close-up and hidden detail with an easy mastery of the perspective on it all, could have put the pieces of the puzzle together so convincingly and compellingly as you have. In almost every letter I write I am urging people to read the book. And I hope to be able, presently, to order further copies of it."

Mr. W. G. Simpson, New York.

"This book is dangerous."

City Press, **London.**

"A living and truly momentous work. To me it sums up in words the whole sickening story of Britain's ignominious scuttle in face of the diabolical rulers of the West."

Mr. Kenneth Cousins.

"I am glad you sent me the 'New Unhappy Lords' for A. K. Chesterton has surpassed himself in what he calls 'an exposure of power politics' and though the subject is familiar to me, I found it fascinating to read, so easy to follow and with some extraordinary details of recent events that were new to me such as Prince Bernhard's secret society (chapter 23). I hope it gets a big circulation because it will do a lot of good. It is remarkable that—though A.K.C. makes no bones about expressing his disgust about the direction of power and its aims-- he pulls no punches, yet the book has a masterly restraint so that nobody can say that it is a work of hate cultivation. We all owe this man a debt for his courage, as well as for the rare ability he possesses as a writer, as embodied in this really magnificent piece of work. I shall commend it whenever and wherever I can."

Mr. George Hickling.

"The New Unhappy Lords is a masterpiece and makes magnetic reading. My hope is that it will enter the skulls of the general nit-wit public, from the top-heavy intellectuals down, I will do all I can to advertise it."

Dr. F. Endean, of Woolhampton, Berks.

"A.K.C. is without doubt the outstanding commentator and analyst on world events. . . . No man has linked more clearly, more analytically, the relation between Money Power and Red Non-Government and tyranny."

An American.

"This is a book which will shock and startle the reader . . . It cuts right through the elephant hide which is our outer skin and gets to the real sensitive flesh . . . the author, has been a student of world politics all his life and has uncovered information which has been kept as closely guarded secrets by international world financiers who, in the background. . . have plotted the destruction of the British Empire and of Britain herself . . . Worth every farthing since it throws light into what may prove to the dirtiest corner of European history."

Glasgow Illustrated.

"With typical English self-control and objectivity Mr. Chesterton traces the conspiracy through nearly six decades up to the present day. Historic events of world-shaking importance are related courageously and truthfully."

Lieut. General P. A. del Valle, U.S. Marines (Ret.)

"A.K. Chesterton is without doubt one of the greatest living commentators in the English language. His comments are eagerly read in South Africa and Rhodesia, as well as in Australia, New Zealand, Canada and the United States. What is the reason? A.K. Chesterton is the only living commentator who not only knows his history but has helped to make it. A thorough patriot, holder of the Military Cross for action as an officer, he fought in both World Wars in Africa and in Germany He saw in the events of these two wars and in the interim period the Great Design of the Money Power to destroy Britain after it had destroyed Germany. The New Unhappy Lords belongs with Spengler's *Hours of Decision* in the knapsack of every marching patriot."

Western Destiny, **10.1965**

"Recently I have received my copy of your intriguing book The New Unhappy Lords and have read it with close attention. Your ability to collect, collate, interpret and present in a most readable manner, facts and events of the last half century, aroused my admiration."

Philip de L. D. Pasey, Port Hope, Ontario, Canada. 8.10.1965

"We appreciate very much the copy of The New Unhappy Lords. Our President has already read it and is very much impressed with it. The importance of your thesis and story is growing more rapidly now than at any previous time. It should be widely read. Congratulations on a great piece of work."

Constance Dall Hart, Executive Vice-President, National Economic Council, Inc., New York, U.S.A. 18.10.1065

"Greeting to you from one of your many friends and admirers in the United States of America. I have carefully read and given away numerous copies of your very fine book, The New Unhappy Lords. One of these days I hope to have the pleasure of meeting you, in London or over here".

Col. Curtis B. Dall, Philadelphia, U.S.A. 28.1.1968

"I have recently finished your book, The Unhappy Lords, and I write to thank you for your truthfulness. It certainly must take a great deal of courage to write such a book. I thank God that we have such people as yourself who not only possess this courage but make good use of it."

Mr. and Mrs. M. J. S. Mich., U.S.A. 27.6.1970

"My sincere congratulations on your excellent interpretation of world affairs, and the masterly manner in which you are conducting your extremely important and difficult job, particularly at this crucial period"

A South African-born reader now living in Canada.

About A.K. Chesterton

Arthur Kenneth Chesterton was born at a gold mine where his father was an official in South Africa in 1899.

In 1915 unhappy at school in England A.K. returned to South Africa. There and without the knowledge of his parents, and having exaggerated his age by four years, he enlisted in the 5th South African Light Infantry.

Before his 17th birthday he had been in the thick of three battles in German East Africa. Later in the war he transferred as a commissioned officer to the Royal Fusiliers and served for the rest of the war on the Western Front being awarded the Military Cross in 1918 for conspicuous gallantry.

Between the wars A.K. first prospected for diamonds before becoming a journalist first in South Africa and then England. Alarmed at the economic chaos threatening Britain, he joined Sir Oswald Mosley in the B.U.F and became prominent in the movement. In 1938, he quarrelled with Mosley's policies and left the movement.

When the Second World War started he rejoined the army, volunteered for tropical service and went through all the hardships of the great push up from Kenya across the wilds of Jubaland through the desert of the Ogaden and into the remotest parts of Somalia. He was afterwards sent down the coast to join the Somaliland Camel Corps and intervene in the inter-tribal warfare among the Somalis.

In 1943 his health broke down and he was invalided out of the army with malaria and colitis, returning to journalism. In 1944, he became deputy editor and chief leader writer of *Truth*.

In the early 1950s A.K. established *Candour* and founded the League of Empire Loyalists which for some years made many colourful headlines in the press worldwide. He later took that organisation into The National Front, and served as its Chairman for a time.

A.K. Chesterton died in 1973.

About *The A.K. Chesterton Trust*

The A.K. Chesterton Trust was formed by Colin Todd and the late Miss. Rosine de Bounevialle in January 1996 to succeed and continue the work of the now defunct Candour Publishing Co.

The objects of the Trust are stated as follows:

"To promote and expound the principles of A.K. Chesterton which are defined as being to demonstrate the power of, and to combat the power of International Finance, and to promote the National Sovereignty of the British World."

Our aims include:

- *Maintaining and expanding the range of material relevant to A.K. Chesterton and his associates throughout his life.*

- *To preserve and keep in-print important works on British Nationalism in order to educate the current generation of our people.*

- *The maintenance and recovery of the sovereign independence of the British Peoples throughout the world.*

- *The strengthening of the spiritual and material bonds between the British Peoples throughout the world.*

- *The resurgence at home and abroad of the British spirit.*

We will raise funds by way of merchandising and donations.

We ask that our friends make provision for *The A.K. Chesterton Trust* in their will.

The A.K. Chesterton Trust has a **duty** to keep *Candour* in the ring and punching.

The A.K. Chesterton Trust Reprint Series

1. Creed of a Fascist Revolutionary & Why I Left Mosley - A.K. Chesterton.

2. The Menace of World Government & Britain's Graveyard - A.K. Chesterton.

3. What You Should Know About The United Nations - The League of Empire Loyalists.

4. The Menace of the Money-Power - A.K. Chesterton.

5. The Case for Economic Nationalism - John Tyndall.

6. Sound the Alarm! - A.K. Chesterton.

7. Six Principles of British Nationalism - John Tyndall.

8. B.B.C. - A National Menace - A.K. Chesterton

Other Titles from _The A.K. Chesterton Trust_

Leopard Valley - A.K. Chesterton

Juma The Great - A.K. Chesterton

32937812R00112

Printed in Great Britain
by Amazon